D1011528

LINCOLN ON LEADERSHIP FOR TODAY

LINCOLN ON LEADERSHIP FOR TODAY

★ ★ ★ ★ ★

Abraham Lincoln's Approach to
Twenty-First-Century Issues

DONALD T. PHILLIPS

Houghton Mifflin Harcourt
BOSTON   NEW YORK
2017

For information about permission to reproduce selections from this book, write
to trade.permissions@hmhco.com or to Permissions, Houghton Mifflin Harcourt
Publishing Company, 3 Park Avenue, 19th Floor, New York, New York 10016.

www.hmhco.com

Library of Congress Cataloging-in-Publication Data is available.

ISBN 978-0-544-81464-6

Printed in the United States of America

DOC 10 9 8 7 6 5 4 3 2 1

In memory
A.A.P.

Author's Note

★ ★ ★

THIS BOOK IS a journey. A journey through Abraham Lincoln's life from a leadership perspective. It's also one big story. A story about how a poor young boy, predestined to be a leader, became one of the most respected people in world history. In the main narrative, I write about what Lincoln said and did in his own day with regard to, ironically, many of the same issues that still confront us.

Over the years, when I've participated in speaking events or talked to the media, I've invariably been asked what Lincoln would do about the problems we have in our world today, or what his stance might be on specific issues. Although Lincoln is long gone, his legacy, his reputation for consistently doing the right thing, and his wisdom continue to serve generations of Americans as something of a moral compass. And so, inspired by the many people who have asked me to do so, at the end of each chapter I offer a page or two of my personal thoughts on how Lincoln might specifically handle some key issues of our day. I know it's a risky undertaking. And I certainly understand and respect that many people may disagree or, at the very least, be surprised by some of my conclusions. But these are honest and sincere opinions based on decades of study, and I accept full responsibility for what I have written. I also invite you to wrestle through what you think Lincoln might do in any given situation.

By studying Lincoln's life, along with his words and actions in the context of history, I believe we can glean meaning from the remarkably moral and ethical life he led. And the lessons learned just might become a model for more effective leadership in our own time. Abraham Lincoln's example represents the best of the America to which we may aspire. He showed us the kind of people we can be. Not an America that divides, but an America that pulls together. Not a shortsighted America, but an America that sees beyond and deeper. That is the Lincoln of this book. In the end, though, it's up to each of us individually to determine what part of Lincoln we might use in our own daily lives to help make this world a better place in which to live.

Donald T. Phillips

Contents

★ ★ ★

Prelude   1

1. A Just and Generous and Prosperous System   8

2. Nonintervention in Other Countries as a
   Sacred Principle of International Law   24

3. To Emancipate the Mind   40

4. Rising with the Occasion   52

5. The Eternal Struggle Between Right and Wrong   66

6. The Tendency of Prosperity to Breed Tyrants   81

7. The Better Angels of Our Nature   97

8. With Firmness in the Right   112

9. The Middle Ground   128

10. No Less Than National   141

11. The Fiery Trial   159

12. The Thunderbolt   176

13. A More Elevated Position   192

14. A Fair Chance in the Race of Life   209

15. This Terrible, Bloody War   226

16. With Malice Toward None   243

17. Peace with All Nations   262

     Finale   277

     Acknowledgments   281
     Notes   283
     Bibliography   305
     Index   309

LINCOLN ON LEADERSHIP FOR TODAY

He would sometimes mount a stump and begin giving a speech. Sure enough, all [work] would stop and [everybody] would gather around Abe to listen. Sometimes he gave political speeches to the boys.

— Dennis Hanks (Lincoln's cousin), recalling Abraham Lincoln's boyhood years

Prelude

★ ★ ★

BE GOOD to one another."

That was the last thing Nancy Hanks Lincoln said to her nine-year-old son, Abraham, and his older sister, Sarah. Spoken on her deathbed, they were not just words of hope and advice, they were words of faith.

By all accounts, Lincoln's mother was "a good Christian woman," very intelligent, and "naturally strong-minded." She read the Bible to her children, taught them both to read and write by using the scripture. And Nancy seemingly took literally the statement from Ephesians, *"Be kind to one another."* That's how people should be guided in life, she believed. *"Let all bitterness, and wrath, and anger, and clamor, and evil speaking, be put away from you, with all malice."*

When Abraham Lincoln was born in a one-room log cabin in the Kentucky backwoods on February 12, 1809, Thomas Jefferson was still president of the United States, Kentucky was officially part of Virginia (a slave state), and Illinois had just become a new territory. Although dirt-poor, Nancy Lincoln and her illiterate husband, Thomas, had a strong sense of morality. They were members of the Separate Baptist Church, a mostly anti-slavery denomination whose influence may have contributed to the family moving to a 300-acre farm in the new free state of Indiana. It was there that Nancy Hanks Lincoln died (in 1818), and by the next year, Thomas had married Sarah Bush Johnston, a widow with three children of her own. Now a member of a larger family, young Abe and his new stepmother quickly bonded. Some contemporaries believed she even favored him over her own children. "He never told me a lie," she said of her stepson. "He never evaded, never equivocated, never dodged, nor turned a corner to avoid any chastisement or other responsibility."

By all accounts, as a boy Lincoln was amiable, good-natured, unusually bright, and very gentle, especially with animals. Although he grew up in a community where hunting was a way of life, Abe didn't take to it. He had, of course, accompanied his father hunting, but when, at the age of eight, young Lincoln shot and killed a turkey himself, it upset him to the point that, as he said years later, "[I have] never since pulled a trigger on any larger game." The boy was so tenderhearted toward animals of any kind that he once chastised a group of 10-year-old pals for putting hot coals on the backs of some turtles, and later lectured his stepsister on an ant's right to life.

Young Lincoln was also an especially curious boy who loved to learn — a trait that was both recognized and encouraged by his stepmother. It was not uncommon for him to walk a mile or more to borrow and return books. He read while lying on the dirt floor of their cabin, his legs propped up against a wall. He read while doing chores, while walking, and while helping his father plow a field. "He [had to] understand everything, even to the smallest thing, minutely and exactly," Sarah Lincoln remembered. "He would then repeat it over to himself again and again, and when it was fixed in his mind, he never lost that fact or his understanding of it." Even Lincoln, himself, recalled that it bothered him *not* to understand something. It "disturbed my temper," he said, to the point where he would spend "no small part of the night walking up and down" trying to sort something out or "hunt down an idea."

As the years passed, young Lincoln's knowledge accumulated exponentially, and it became obvious to Sarah that her stepson possessed an extraordinarily good memory. "He would hear a sermon preached on Sunday," she said, and then come home, "take the children outside, get on a stump or log and repeat it almost word for word." Lincoln's cousin Dennis Hanks noted that Abe developed a skill for telling stories, which he would often do at gatherings such as house-raisings. "He would sometimes mount a stump and begin giving a speech," Hanks recalled. "Sure enough, all [work] would stop and [everybody] would gather around Abe to listen." Sometimes he gave political speeches "to the boys," and sometimes he told jokes, which left them "bursting their sides with laughter."

It wasn't long before the teenage Lincoln was regarded as the natural leader in his age group. He rarely "quarreled or fought, and always was the peacemaker," his friends remembered. "If there was any fighting about to commence, he would try to stop [it]" by telling a joke or a story. And often, "he was the one chosen to adjust difficulties between boys of his age and size," and usually "his decision was an end of the trouble."

By his mid-teens, Abe Lincoln had shot up to over six feet in height (he would eventually reach six feet four inches). But with his height came long arms, a homely complexion, coarse black hair, and a gawky awkwardness, which made him self-conscious, especially around members of the opposite sex. "He didn't go much with the girls," recalled Dennis Hanks, largely because he was shy and unsure of himself when around them.

Lincoln also grew to be immensely strong, with an ability to carry "a load of six hundred pounds" on his back. Yet despite his awkwardness, he was a good athlete — an excellent wrestler, for example, who rarely lost a match. His strength was developed by learning the value of hard work in the fields with his father. "I was raised to farm work," Lincoln wrote in 1859. Along with the normal "plowing and harvesting seasons," such work included clearing Indiana's "unbroken wilderness" and "fighting with trees and logs and grubs," as he put it. He also said he "had an axe put into his hands" at a very young age, and was almost constantly handling "that most useful instrument" until he was 23 years old. "[Abe Lincoln] could sink an axe deeper into wood than any man I ever saw," said one contemporary. Other friends sometimes saw him perform a trick that demonstrated his upper body strength. He would take a full-size axe, hold it at the tip of the handle with only his thumb and forefinger, and then extend it at arm's length for several minutes. All the other young men around tried, but no one could ever duplicate the feat — and Lincoln sometimes performed it with two axes and both arms extended.

Abe Lincoln continued to learn all during his youth. He read law books and then put his knowledge to work by preparing legal documents for his friends and neighbors. He read the history of the American Revolution, studied the founding of the nation, and pored over biographies of heroes like George Washington. Lincoln also took time to read the U.S. Constitution, the Bill of Rights, and, his favorite, the Declaration of Independence. Some say he could quote verbatim from all three documents the same way he could pull up a quote from just about anywhere in the Bible and use it to enhance one of his stories or to illustrate a point.

One story Lincoln was fond of telling in later years was about his first trip on a flatboat down the Mississippi River to New Orleans. He was 18 years old at the time and had properly asked his parents' permission to make the journey with two of his buddies. "I belonged to what they call down South, the 'scrubs' — people who do not own slaves are nobody there," he said. "We had succeeded in raising, chiefly by my labor, sufficient produce to justify taking it down the river to sell." Lincoln went on to explain how, on the way, he had earned his first dollar when two men asked him to take them and their luggage out to a steamer coming down the river. He did so, and each tossed him a silver half-dollar for his efforts. "I could scarcely [believe] that I, a poor boy, had earned a dollar [by honest work] in less than a day," he recalled. "The world seemed wider and fairer before me. I was a more hopeful and confident being from that time."

Lincoln's elation at having earned his first dollar, however, was tempered by his experience in New Orleans. While there, he and his friends happened upon a slave auction. A black woman was being sold, and the sellers "pinched her flesh and made her trot up and down like a horse" so the "bidders might satisfy themselves." Lincoln apparently became both upset and angry at the scene. One of his pals later claimed that "slavery ran the iron into him then and there." And Lincoln, himself, is reported to have said, "Let's get away from this. If I ever get a chance to hit that thing (slavery), I'll hit it hard."

Fourteen years later, Lincoln witnessed a similar scene while traveling on the Mississippi River and, afterward, sat down and wrote about it to a friend. He described 12 black slaves who had been purchased in Kentucky and were being taken to a Southern plantation. "They were chained six and six together," he wrote. "A small iron clevis was around the left wrist of each, and this fastened to the main chain by a shorter one . . . so that [they] were strung together precisely like so many fish upon a trot-line." Then Lincoln stated his deeper sense of what was happening to those 12 individuals. "They were being separated forever from the scenes of their childhood, their friends, their fathers and mothers, and brothers and sisters, and many of them, from their wives and children — and going into perpetual slavery where the lash of the master is . . . ruthless and unrelenting."

Clearly, Abraham Lincoln was emotionally impacted at the sight of people in human bondage. He related these incidents to many friends over the course of his life, so he must have thought deeply about the institution of slavery in those early years. One can imagine him coming up with an appropriate quote from the Bible, such as the slaveholders deserving punishment, because *they sold the righteous for silver, and the poor for a pair of sandals*" [Amos 2:6]. Or perhaps he "reckoned" that they would have to answer on Judgment Day when *"all the nations will be assembled before Him" [Matthew 25:32]*. Whatever Lincoln may have thought in those moments, it is abundantly clear that he believed slavery was a great moral wrong and it conflicted with the principles upon which the United States of America was founded. "There is no reason in the world," he said in 1858, why a black person "is not entitled to all the natural rights enumerated in the Declaration of Independence — the right to life, liberty, and the pursuit of happiness." Even toward the end of his life, he pointed out that he was "naturally anti-slavery," and could not "remember when I did not so think and feel."

To Lincoln, the values in the Declaration of Independence and the Bible were linked together — just as the slaves he saw were linked together on that chain. To him, life, liberty, equality, righteousness, and justice were all part of the book of human rights. And while the links on the slaves' chain could be broken, those between the Declaration and the Bible could not. Young Abraham Lincoln read the history of the United States himself. The Bible was first read to him by Nancy Hanks Lincoln. "All that I am or hope ever to be I get from my mother," he once said to a friend, "God bless her."

As he began his adult journey in life, Abraham Lincoln carried his mother's last words in his heart:

"Be good to one another."

All the nations will be assembled before Him. And He will separate them one from another. . . .

Then [He] will say to those on His right . . . "Come, you who are blessed by my father. Inherit the kingdom prepared for you from the foundation of the world. For I was hungry and you gave me food, I was thirsty and you gave me drink, a stranger and you welcomed me, naked and you clothed me, ill and you cared for me, in prison and you visited me."

Then the righteous will answer Him and say, "Lord, when did

*we see you hungry and feed you, or thirsty and give you drink, . . .
a stranger and welcome you . . . naked and clothe you . . . ill or in
prison and visit you?"*

*"Whatever you did for one of these least brothers of mine, you
did for me."*

*Then He will say to those on the left . . . "Depart from me . . .
into the eternal fire prepared for the devil and his angels. For I
was hungry and you gave me no food, thirsty and you gave me
no drink, a stranger and you gave me no welcome, naked and
you gave me no clothing, ill and in prison and you did not care
for me."*

*Then they will answer and say, "Lord, when did we see you
hungry or thirsty or a stranger or naked or ill or in prison, and not
minister to your needs?"*

*"What you did not do for one of these least ones, you did not
do for me."*

*And these will go off to eternal punishment, but the righteous
to eternal life.*

The Judgment of the Nations
[Matthew 25:32–46]

It does not increase the tax upon the *"many poor"* but upon the *"wealthy few"* by taxing the land in proportion to its value. . . . If the wealthy should [complain], it is still to be remembered that *they* are not sufficiently numerous to carry the elections.

— Lincoln, defending a new Illinois revenue law
March 2, 1839

ISSUES
Economic Development
Handling a Recession
Protective Tariffs / Free Trade
Education

1

A Just and Generous and Prosperous System

★ ★ ★

I AM HUMBLE ABRAHAM LINCOLN," he said. "I have been [asked] by many friends to become a candidate for the legislature. I have no wealthy or popular relations to recommend me. I have no other [ambition than] that of being truly esteemed of my fellow men — by rendering myself worthy of their esteem. If elected, I shall be thankful. If not, it will be all the same."

That's what Abraham Lincoln said, in part, when first introducing himself to the people. It was March 1832. He was 23 years old.

The next month, Lincoln enlisted in the frontier militia organized to push Chief Black Hawk of the Sauk Native American tribe back across the Mississippi River into Iowa. Young Lincoln was promptly elected captain of his company — a success, he said in later years, "which gave me more pleasure than any I have had since." When an elderly Indian wandered into camp one night with a safe-conduct pass, some of the men feared he was a spy and threatened to kill him. Lincoln quickly pushed the others away and stepped in front of the old man. "If anyone wants to hurt this fella, he's going to have to come through me!" he essentially said. "And if any one of you doubt it, let him try!" One contemporary remembered that the "Lincoln Company was the hardest set of men he ever saw and that they would fight to the death for [their leader]." Lincoln and most of his men mustered out of the service not long before the Battle of Bad Axe ended the short-lived Black Hawk War. They took part in no real military action, and Lincoln used to joke that the only bloody battles he had were with mosquitoes. The men of the Lincoln Company were reported to have walked all the way home from the Wisconsin Territory.

By mid-July, our "military hero" was attending a political rally in the small town of Pappsville, Illinois. It was only a few weeks before the general election, and Lincoln, who had not planned to speak, was encouraged to say a few words. As he mounted the platform, a fight broke out in the crowd. Seeing one of his friends attacked, Lincoln jumped down and, as a witness described it, grabbed the attacker by the scruff of his neck and the seat of his trousers and threw him 12 feet away. Then he calmly walked back up to the stage and made his speech. "My politics are short and sweet, like the old woman's dance," he said. "I am in favor of a national bank . . . , the internal improvement system . . . , and a high protective tariff."

Abraham Lincoln lost that election. He finished 8th out of 13 candidates. *[Only the top 4 were elected.]* As he would say later, it was the only time he "was ever beaten by a direct vote of the people."

Over the next couple of years, Lincoln was appointed postmaster of New Salem, Illinois, and worked as a deputy for the

Sangamon County surveyor. Then, in 1834, he tried again for the state legislature. This time he won, finishing second in the field of candidates.

When Abraham Lincoln was first elected to the Illinois House of Representatives, the United States of America was still very young. George Washington had taken office as the first president only 45 years earlier. Thomas Jefferson and John Adams had died 8 years before (in 1826, both on the 50th anniversary of the signing of the Declaration of Independence). John Marshall was still chief justice of the Supreme Court, Illinois had only been a state for 16 years, and Chicago had a population of barely 3,000 and had not yet been incorporated as a city.

There were two major political parties on the national scene back then — the Democrats and Whigs. Illinois was dominated by the Democrats, who were led by Andrew Jackson (one year into his second term as president). Jackson's supporters were made up mostly of farmers and uneducated city laborers, reflecting America's largely agricultural society. The Democrats were the conservative party back then. They believed in non–government intervention for almost everything, were against establishing a public education system, and, although somewhat divided on the big issue of the day, were mostly pro-slavery. On the other side, the fledgling Whig Party, having been founded by Kentucky senator Henry Clay less than two years earlier, was in the minority nearly everywhere. Whigs were liberal and progressive. Their supporters included businessmen, bankers, intellectuals, and artists. They favored government involvement to promote economic growth and expansion, supported public education, and were mostly anti-slavery.

The striking contrast between today's Democratic Party and the Democratic Party of Lincoln's day is interesting for its almost 180-degree turn in political positions. However, Abraham Lincoln, himself, once noted that such change was not new but, rather, typically American. After once hearing a comment that the two leading political parties so frequently reversed their platforms that they began sounding like their rivals, Lincoln responded with an anecdote:

> I remember once being much amused at seeing two partially intoxicated men engage in a fight ... which ... after a long, and rather harmless contest, ended in each having fought himself *out* of his own coat, and *into* that of the other. If the two leading parties of this day are really identical with the two in the days of Jefferson and Adams, they have performed about the same feat as the two drunken men.

Abraham Lincoln did not hunt, fish, smoke, swear, or drink. His leisure time was spent reading books and newspapers. In New Salem, Illinois, he was surrounded by farmers, family, and friends who were passionate Democrats and ardent supporters of Andrew Jackson. Lincoln went against the grain and joined the Whig Party.

★ ★ ★

Abe Lincoln spent four 2-year terms in the Illinois House of Representatives. During those years, he served on 14 committees (including the powerful House Finance Committee), was elected Whig floor leader, and was defeated twice for Speaker of the House (mainly because the Whigs were always in the minority). Nearly his entire career in the state legislature was devoted to championing economic development. In 1834, there was no real transportation infrastructure in Illinois that could help foster commerce and trade. In fact, there was not a single railroad anywhere in the state. Lincoln's position was simple: Build an infrastructure that will aid commerce, and the associated businesses will follow. Essentially, it was an *"If you build it, they will come"* strategy.

Early on, Lincoln threw his support toward funding construction of a nearly 100-mile-long canal that would connect the Great Lakes with the Mississippi River (from the shores of Lake Michigan near Chicago via the Illinois River). And during his second term, he both co-sponsored and vigorously lobbied for passage of a $10 million bill to fund a wide range of internal improvements, including the construction of a 1,300-mile network of railroads across Illinois. A young state representative from the Springfield area led the Democrats in support of the new legislation. His name was Stephen A. Douglas.

Before passage of the bill, Lincoln noted that such a system would be "very desirable," because the railroad was "a never-failing source of communication between places of business remotely situated from each other." He also justified his support to the voters by noting that with such a transportation system, they would be able to "export" their farm products and "import" goods from abroad. Of course, the young state legislator understood well that people would be concerned about such a large amount of state government money being allocated to projects that would take years before any visible signs of progress would be realized. In point of fact, the interest payments on the loans that had to be taken out to pay for the legislation exceeded the entire amount of revenue brought in by the state in 1837. But everybody was optimistic, perhaps overly so, because Illinois's general economy was quite good for a western state. And after all, similar projects had been successful in the eastern United States. So why wouldn't they work in Illinois?

"However high our imaginations may be heated at thoughts of . . . a railroad through our country, there is always a shock accompanying [the] cost," the pragmatic Abraham Lincoln noted. "There cannot justly be any objection to having railroads and canals, any more than to other good things, provided they cost nothing. The only objection is to paying for them — and the objection to paying arises from the want of ability to pay."

Sure enough, nearly everybody tried to find fault with Lincoln's improvement plans. Anti-business people complained that private companies would reap all the rewards and leave nothing for anybody else. Opposing legislators expressed fear that the plan would create inordinately high taxes, debts, and deficits. And businessmen grumbled that profits would come too far in the future. To the anti-business groups, Lincoln pointed out that everything would be "lost and go to ruin if the principle be adopted that no one shall have anything for fear that all shall not have some." To counter one negative legislator, Lincoln told the following story:

> Mr. Speaker, this gentleman reminds me of a grizzled frontiersman with shaggy overhanging eyebrows who always saw big bugaboos in everything. One morning, he thought he saw a squirrel in a tree, so he took down his gun and fired at it, but missed. He fired a dozen shots or more and became more and more frustrated at each failure. Finally, he threw down the gun and claimed that there was something wrong with it.
>
> "The rifle's all right," said his son, who had been watching. "But where is your squirrel?"
>
> "Don't you see him?" thundered the old man, pointing to the exact spot.
>
> "No, I don't," said the son.
>
> Then, turning and staring into his father's face, the boy smiled. "Father, now I see your squirrel. There's nothing there in the tree! You've been firing at a bug on your eyebrow!"

For businessmen who didn't want to wait years for potential profits, Lincoln worked with his colleagues in the legislature to persuade the businessmen to get involved — and Illinois was able to raise several million dollars in financial support. It was an early attempt at government and business working together in a common endeavor. Illinois also created its own corporation with stock in an effort to help fund the improvements program.

Overall, Lincoln and his colleagues intended to pay for the internal improvements program mostly through bonds and loans secured with the help of the new Illinois State Bank, which had been created in 1835. The bill was so controversial that it passed in the House by only one vote. *[Lincoln voted in favor.]* His support was based on a belief that the bank would not only be a safe place to keep public funds, but would also generate credit and interest from the paper money it printed. His commitment to government-regulated banking was recorded in an 1839 detailed speech he made in support of a national bank. Among other things, he said: "No duty is more imperative on [the United States] Government than the duty it owes the people of furnishing them a sound and uniform currency."

Abraham Lincoln and his colleagues were feeling pretty good about the vast internal improvements program that they believed was sure to launch Illinois on the road to economic expansion and prosperity. But then something happened they had not counted on — a national recession.

There's still debate about what actually caused the Financial Panic of 1837. Among the contributing factors, however, were high inflation, a large foreign trade deficit, the bursting of a land and housing bubble, and the fact that President Jackson had vetoed a bill that would have renewed the charter of the Bank of the United States. The ultra-conservative Jackson didn't like paper money (which banks were allowed to print on their own), so he issued an executive order that all public land had to be paid for in gold and silver coinage. That, in turn, caused paper money to lose its value. Then the banking system across the United States began to collapse. Businesses failed. Companies went bankrupt. Unemployment soared. Farmers lost their land. Average people lost their homes. The Financial Panic of 1837 became the worst economic crisis the young nation had yet experienced — and it lasted five long years.

As revenues in Illinois plummeted and the State Bank struggled, supporters for continuing the internal improvements plan became scarce. There was even talk of abandoning the plan entirely. But Abraham Lincoln stubbornly fought to save the project, which had made a good start, especially in building a railroad system. "[We] are now so advanced in a general system of internal improvements, we cannot retreat from it without disgrace and great loss," he argued. "Though not *legally* bound, [we are] *morally* bound to adhere to [this system] through all time to come!"

Lincoln took the lead in offering a series of proposals that would increase revenue to salvage the program. While he supported a variety of austerity measures introduced by others (including cutting the pay of state workers), Lincoln was more creative and bold in the legislation he introduced. First, he submitted a plan to borrow $5 million to buy all the federally owned public land in the state and then sell it for a profit. In essence, Lincoln was proposing that the state go into business for itself by using federal assets to help reverse the recession and stimulate the economy. He also advocated that the federal government take unilateral steps to help deal with the recession, which both Andrew Jackson and his successor, Martin Van Buren, refused to do. Lincoln pointed out that action on a national scale would help the states. "No commercial object of government patronage can be so exclusively *general,* as to not be of some [specific] *local* advantage," he noted. "But on the other hand, nothing is so *local* as to not be of some *general* advantage."

Unfortunately, Lincoln's land purchase plan was defeated in the House and, as the recession worsened, our "pragmatic" state legislator believed that "expenditures must be met," so he turned to a political taboo that existed even back then — raising taxes. *[Lincoln wasn't alone in this thought, as most of the struggling state governments began revising their tax laws in order to cope with the struggling economy.]* In the 1838–1839 session of the Illinois legislature, Lincoln joined a group that introduced a bill which proposed generating revenue through higher property taxes (then being assessed on a flat percentage rate for everybody). The proposal was for a graduated system in which the more land a person owned, the more taxes he would pay. Average or poor Illinoisans would pay about the same or less. But wealthy citizens were going to have to shoulder a higher burden.

After the bill was passed and signed into law, the resulting public blowback was enormous. Illinois already had a strong anti-tax bias, but this increase was viewed as both a betrayal by state government officials and an unconstitutional act against the people. Wealthy land barons screamed bloody murder, as did their employees, who feared losing their jobs as a result of the higher taxes. Protest rallies sprang up around the state, and several legislators were threatened with bodily harm. Lincoln, however, stood firm and convinced his colleagues to call a public hearing so they could explain why they had sponsored and voted for the legislation. "The passage of a Revenue law is *right* within itself, and I never despair of sustaining myself before the people upon any measure that will stand a full investigation," he wrote to a friend. Then, on April 5, 1839, he and the others sent out a notice for the public hearing. "We invite every man in the County who opposes the Revenue Law to come armed with all arguments against it that he can," read the notice, "and we confidently believe we will be able to show that none of them are well-founded."

Privately, Lincoln stated that the new law would be sustained, because it was equitable, fair, and constitutionally justified. Besides, he said, "it does not increase the tax upon the *'many poor'* but upon the *'wealthy few'* by taxing the land in proportion to its value. . . . If the wealthy should [complain], it is still to be remembered that *they* are not sufficiently numerous to carry the elections."

Unfortunately, none of the revenue-raising measures could save Illinois from financial collapse, although, had some of Lincoln's suggestions been implemented, the damage might have been lessened. The state eventually defaulted on the interest payments associated with its internal improvement loans. Within a few years, the State Bank had closed and no one would accept its now worthless paper money. Illinois went bankrupt, although in that national crisis, the state was not alone. Others suffered similar fates, including Georgia, Indiana, Maryland, Michigan, Missouri, New York, North Carolina, Pennsylvania, South Carolina, and Virginia.

Lincoln did not seek reelection after the 1840–1841 legislative session, and he left office knowing he had failed to implement his internal improvements plan. To the end, he tried to "save something from the general wreck," as he put it. In fact, his last vote as a state legislator was to authorize completion of the Illinois and Michigan Canal. *[The canal was eventually finished in 1848, operated until 1933, and made Chicago one of the main transportation hubs in the United States.]*

It was a measure of Abraham Lincoln's character that he did everything he could to save what he believed to be a program that would guarantee a prosperous future for the people of his state. His deep-seated refusal to give up was perhaps best illustrated by his remarks at a debate the day after Christmas in 1839, when things looked exceedingly bleak. In his part of the debate (the Democrats were led by Stephen A. Douglas), Lincoln spoke out in favor of a strong national bank. He decried "the evil spirit" of "political corruption" that "reigned" in Washington, and he further blasted the Jackson administration by correctly predicting that its policies would bring "distress, ruin, bankruptcy, and beggary" on the country.

Yet even when all others had given up hope, Lincoln remained defiant. "I cannot deny that all may be swept away," he said. "Broken by it, I may be. Bow to it, I never will. . . . The *probability* that we may fall in the struggle *ought not* to deter us from the support of a cause we believe to be just. It *shall not* deter me."

Lincoln vowed to "stand up boldly and alone" to fight for what he believed to be right. "I swear eternal fidelity to the just cause . . . of the land of my life, my liberty, and my love," he pledged. "If we fail, be it so. [But even then], we shall have the proud consolation of saying to our consciences . . . that we never faltered in defending [our nation]."

★ ★ ★

The system Abraham Lincoln was trying to help create in Illinois was typically American. He believed that economic development anchored in a vibrant transportation network would generate high employment through newly created business, industry, commerce, and trade. And once the industries were created, he wanted to shield them from outside forces. So he advocated *for* a protective tariff and *against* free international trade.

A tax on imported goods to raise the competition's prices and make them less attractive to consumers would benefit American industry and serve the average worker. Lincoln even used an example of cotton harvested in South Carolina and sent to Manchester, England, to make his point. "Raw cotton . . . is carried by water to England where it is then [made into cloth and] carried back [to America]," he wrote. The revenue paid to England for making the cloth with American cotton does not go to American businesses, he noted. So Lincoln's conclusion was obvious: "Why should it not be spun, wove & [sold] in the very neighborhood where it both grows and is consumed?" Obviously, the extra money paid to industrialists in England would then stay in the United States, which, in turn, could be used to create more jobs or pay existing workers a higher wage.

"Give us a protective tariff and we will have the greatest country on earth!" said Lincoln. But to do without it and allow unrestricted free international trade would, he argued, cause American industry to produce a blighted landscape where "all is cold and still as death [and where] no smoke rises, no furnace roars, no anvil rings." Lincoln may have been overly dramatic with this metaphor, but his point was clear. He did not want to send goods and potential revenue overseas when they could be used to help Americans at home. "We must look [toward] having constant employment," said Lincoln. And if it meant that the wealthy few would have to take lower profits, then so be it. "By this system, the burden of revenue falls almost entirely on the wealthy and luxurious few," said Lincoln, "rather than on the laboring many." And that was okay with him.

Lincoln's position of having the wealthy pay a higher share of "the burden," as he liked to phrase it, sounds a bit socialistic in its tenor. However, he made it clear that he was not in favor of handouts or free rides. As a matter of fact, Lincoln took this position with his own stepbrother, John D. Johnston, who wrote to request a loan of $80, because he was "broke." Rather than granting the loan outright, Lincoln first scolded Johnston and then offered him a rather generous proposition. "You are not *lazy*, [but] you *are* an *idler*," Lincoln wrote. "I doubt whether you have done a good day's work [since I last saw you]." Then Lincoln urged him to "go to work for the best wages you can get. To secure you a fair reward for your labor, I promise you that for every dollar you [earn over the next four months], I will give you one other dollar. [So] if you hire yourself at ten dollars a month, you will get ten more from me, making twenty dollars a month." Lincoln concluded the letter by stating: "You have always been [kind] to me, and I do not mean to be unkind to you." But he implored Johnston to follow his advice and accept the offer.

We can conjecture that Lincoln felt it was "kinder" to offer to pay Johnston for work performed rather than simply giving him a handout. And that might have been true. But he also felt strongly that if a person was willing to work for a living, he should be paid. To that end, in a later speech Lincoln urged people to get a good education and go to work. But he also acknowledged that not everyone could succeed all the time. "Some will be successful . . . , others will be disappointed," he said. "Don't take it too much to heart," he counseled. "Adopt the maxim, 'better luck next time,' and then, by renewed exertion, make that better luck for [yourself]."

Abraham Lincoln's entire economic philosophy was rooted in creating a system that would help the little guy rise and be successful. Essentially, he was telling average people to take it upon themselves to get a good education. The government would provide a just and fair system to help put that education to use. It was up to them to do the rest.

The prudent, penniless beginner in the world labors for wages awhile, saves a surplus with which to buy tools or land for himself, then labors on his own account another while, and at length hires another new beginner to help him.

This is free labor — the just and generous, and prosperous system, which opens the way for all — gives hope to all, and energy, and progress, and improvement of condition to all.

Abraham Lincoln
September 30, 1859

LINCOLN ON LEADERSHIP FOR TODAY

Economic Development

During Lincoln's time, the nation was just opening up to economic development. Vast areas were completely undeveloped. As we saw with Lincoln's strong support for the building of canals and expansion of the railroad, he clearly understood the importance of long-range economic growth. As a state representative, he advocated building a transportation network (railroads) in order to foster development across Illinois. And 30 years later, as president, Lincoln fully supported the construction of the transcontinental railroad to do the same for the western half of the United States.

Today, most areas of the nation are well developed and, in fact, some are overdeveloped. This reality has led to controversy and competing interests when it comes to economic development of land and resources. Pro-development advocates point to job creation, a higher standard of living, and boosting the overall economy. Anti-development activists cite environmental degradation, loss of traditional cultures, and a fostering of greed.

If Lincoln were alive today, in my humble opinion, he would advocate a balanced policy of *"If you build it, they will come,"* with a sensitivity to the individual rights of existing property owners. He would be a champion of economic development as a tool for achieving constant employment. He would involve local citizens in making decisions about what should or should not be developed. He would also be vigilant in monitoring and mitigating greed as a prime motivation in pushing new business. And he would promote laws to protect the environment from overzealous developers.

Handling a Recession

Abraham Lincoln experienced two major recessions during his political career — the Financial Panic of 1837 and the Financial Panic of 1857. The actions he proposed as a state representative to deal with the first recession were not enacted because he did not have enough power or support. But as president, the actions he took to counter the next recession (which were essentially the same as those he had previously proposed) not only worked, but helped to garner victory for the North during the Civil War.

Periodic recessions are a normal part of the modern business cycle, having occurred at an average of one every seven years since World War II. Most recently, the Great Recession of 2007–2009 (the worst economic crisis since the Great Depression of 1929–1933) resulted in unprecedented levels of unemployment, mortgage foreclosures, and global banking credit crises. Its impact was eventually relieved by extraordinary and intense federal government intervention. Major controversy erupted about whether or not to enact forceful new laws to prevent the unscrupulous actions that precipitated the Great Recession, and whether or not to prosecute those who had been involved.

Judging from his views on recessions during his time, I believe Lincoln would have approved of using the power of the federal government to take actions such as saving the automobile industry, bailing out "too big to fail" corporations, and implementing the Troubled Asset Relief Program (TARP). But he would have deplored the unregulated, greedy, and dishonest practices (such as the subprime mortgage crisis) that helped precipitate the Great Recession in the first place. My sense is that he would propose to Congress and push for tough legislation to prevent such abuses in the future. And Lincoln would prosecute those responsible and advocate harsh prison sentences to send a message so that such abuses should never happen again.

Protective Tariffs and Free Trade

In Lincoln's day, the U.S. economy was largely agriculture-based and the modern Industrial Revolution was in its infancy. But times have changed. The Industrial Revolution is over, and we are now in the Global Information Age. Seventy-five percent of the U.S. economy is service-based, and less than a quarter is manufacturing-based.

Today, there is major controversy over open markets and protectionist policies. Are free trade agreements really lucrative open markets for the production and sales of manufactured goods — or open invitations to domestic industries to move their factories to other countries that employ cheaper labor? Are protective tariffs barriers to free trade — or valuable tools to protect domestic manufacturers? Are consumers better or worse off? Are jobs gained or lost?

A prudent Lincoln of today would survey both the domestic and global economic landscape and recognize (as all great leaders do) that success rests in an ability to change with the times. To implement major protective tariffs on U.S. manufactured goods would likely result in retaliatory actions by nations from which goods are imported. That, in turn, would cause prices to rise on non–U.S. manufactured goods and harm the economy. On a grand scale, free trade agreements aid in forging a vibrant and robust economy. But they most definitely result in a net loss in domestic manufacturing jobs. I believe Lincoln would support international free trade agreements. But he would also create major incentives for American manufacturers (including lower taxes for both large and small businesses) in order to keep, expand, and promote domestic manufacturing operations.

Education

In his first political statement on March 9, 1832, Abraham Lincoln said that education was "the most important subject which we as a people can be engaged in." It's still true.

My feeling is that if Lincoln were around today, he would be enthusiastically pro-education. He would be in favor of high national education standards. He would encourage the implementation of new technologies in schools as quickly as possible, including online education initiatives. Lincoln would support and expand the Department of Education. He would take federal action (and encourage state action) to support teachers and improve public schools so that every person can receive a high school diploma. He would use the resources of the federal government to make a quality college education affordable for every American citizen who wants one.

Allow the President to invade a neighboring nation, whenever *he* shall deem it necessary to repel an invasion, and you allow him to . . . make war at pleasure.

— Lincoln, justifying his stand against President
James K. Polk's invasion of Mexico
February 15, 1848

ISSUES
Starting a War with a Militarily Weak Country
Military Intervention in Other Countries
Term Limits
Accepting Lucrative Jobs After Service in Congress

2

Nonintervention in Other Countries as a Sacred Principle of International Law

★ ★ ★

RATHER PREFER THAT your paper let it 'stink and die' unnoticed."

That's what Abraham Lincoln wrote to Benjamin F. James, editor of the *Tazewell Whig,* on February 9, 1846. Lincoln was trying to secure the Whig Party's nomination for U.S. Congress from his district. But as part of a smear campaign, supporters of former congressman John J. Hardin had released a flyer that Lincoln said was "an attempt to injure me." So he appealed to James, who ran the leading Whig newspaper in the largest county in Illinois. "I wish you would let nothing appear in your paper which may operate against me," he wrote. "You understand."

Benjamin F. James did, indeed, understand, because Illinois Whigs had previously agreed to rotate candidates for national office, effectively endorsing term limits. The incumbent congressman Edward Baker's term was up, and Hardin had already served a stint. Lincoln felt he was now in line, and, as he said, "turn about is fair play." As a matter of fact, two years earlier, he had endorsed Baker with the understanding that Baker would support him the next time around. So, as indicated by Lincoln's constant letter writing to key Whig officials and newspapers in Illinois, he was going to do all he could to influence public opinion in order to secure his chance to be a United States congressman.

Lincoln eventually did receive the *Tazewell Whig*'s endorsement for the party's nomination, which he won handily. Then, running on his "bread-and-butter" platform of economic development through internal improvements, Lincoln defeated Methodist preacher Peter Cartwright in the August 3, 1846, general election. However, due to the way things worked back then, he would not take his seat in Washington until December 6, 1847, a full year and four months later. During the interim, the United States went to war with Mexico.

When fighting broke out near the U.S.-Mexico border (not far from present-day Brownsville, Texas), President James K. Polk quickly sent a message to Congress declaring that, in spite of his sincere attempts to negotiate a purchase of new territories, "Mexico invaded our territory and shed American blood of our fellow citizens on our soil." Two days later (on May 13, 1846), Congress declared war on Mexico, even though many Whigs were suspicious of both Polk's motives and his version of events.

The actual causes of the Mexican-American War have been debated by historians for years. Polk had run for president on a platform to expand American territory to the Pacific Ocean, including the prized Mexican possession of California. And his pro-slavery stance implied that the institution should be allowed in any new territories acquired. This was all part of Manifest Destiny, a term coined in 1845 (the first year of Polk's presidency) by John L. O'Sullivan, editor of the *Democratic Review* newspaper, who wrote that it was America's "manifest destiny to overspread the continent allotted by Providence for the free development of our yearly multiplying millions."

The Polk administration had been trying to buy California and New Mexico for $25 million, but the government of Mexico steadfastly refused to sell or even negotiate terms. So in an effort to intimidate and force Mexico to the table, Polk sent several hundred troops under General Zachary Taylor down to a disputed area between the Nueces River and the Rio Grande that both countries had unofficially recognized as part of the Mexican state of Coahuila. Polk claimed that it was unquestionably U.S. territory, but Mexico said it was definitely theirs. *[Most historians would later take the middle ground and say it was "disputed" land.]* In April 1846, General Taylor sent some of his forces across the Rio Grande to occupy the small town of Matamoros. Mexican troops retaliated by crossing the river themselves and attacking an American regiment. Within a couple of weeks, two more significant battles had been fought (Palo Alto and Resaca de la Palma), both of which were won by the Americans with moderate casualties. It was at this point, on May 11, 1846, that President Polk asked Congress to declare war on Mexico. The United States then sent full-scale invasion forces into California, New Mexico, and the heart of Mexico, itself. This was America's first major foreign war, and one that many people, especially members of the Whig Party, believed was instigated against a militarily weak neighbor in order to grab vast expanses of new land.

Before Congressman-elect Lincoln jumped to such a conclusion, however, he drew back and "carefully examined the President's messages to ascertain what he himself had said and proved." Lincoln was a deliberate man when it came to taking a position on any important issue. But as many of his friends and colleagues learned, once he arrived at a decision, he rarely retreated from it.

And Lincoln's final position on this issue was that Polk had pro-voked an unnecessary war and was morally in the wrong. "It is a fact," said Lincoln, "that the United States Army, in marching to the Rio Grande, marched into a peaceful Mexican settlement, and frightened its inhabitants away from their homes and their growing crops. . . . That soil was not ours," and Congress never did "annex or attempt to annex it." Lincoln decided to hold his tongue until he actually became a U.S. congressman, however, believing that "all those who, because of knowing too *little*, or be-cause of knowing too *much*, could not conscientiously approve of the conduct of the President" should "as good citizens and patri-ots remain silent . . . at least till the war [was] ended."

★ ★ ★

When Abraham Lincoln, his wife of five years, Mary Todd Lin-coln, and their two sons, Robert (age four) and Eddie (not quite two), arrived in Washington, D.C., the nation's capital was a bus-tling city of around 40,000 people. Unable to afford upscale housing, they rented a room at a boardinghouse near the Capi-tol Building. John Quincy Adams (sixth president of the United States) was a member of the House of Representatives at the time, and the Washington Monument was still in the planning stages. *[When Adams died in February 1848 at age 80, Lincoln was a member of his congressional burial escort. Lincoln also took part in the ceremony for the laying of the cornerstone of the Washington Monument (on July 4, 1848).]*

Abraham Lincoln was sworn in on December 6, 1847, and took his seat in the 30th United States Congress. Because of his ex-perience as a postmaster, he was assigned to the Committee on Post Office and Post Roads. He also served on the Committee on Expenditures in the War Department. Lincoln was the only congressman from the state of Illinois who was a member of the Whig Party, and he wasted no time in becoming a leading spokesman against President Polk's conduct regarding the start of the Mexican-American War. *[At that point, there was still a lot of fighting taking place, although it had lessened since September, when General Winfield Scott's forces captured Mexico City.]*

First, Lincoln submitted legislation on December 22, 1847, requesting that Polk clarify facts concerning the exact spot where the war began. Specifically, Lincoln wanted to know:

> Whether the *spot* of soil on which the blood of our citizens was shed . . . was, or was not, within the territories of Spain, at least from the treaty of 1819 until the Mexican revolution.
>
> Whether that *spot* is, or is not, within the territory which was wrested from Spain, by the Mexican revolution.
>
> Whether that *spot* is, or is not, within a settlement of people, which had existed ever since long before the Texas revolution. [Italics added.]

Lincoln's so-called spot resolutions were ignored by President Polk and virtually everybody else. Undeterred, he voted for a larger House resolution, which stated that "the war with Mexico was unnecessarily and unconstitutionally commenced by the President." Then, on January 12, 1848, Lincoln took to the floor of the House of Representatives to deliver a blistering 45-minute attack on Polk's conduct of the war. Basically, Lincoln accused him of lying to the American people. "The President falls far short of proving his justification [for the war]," he said, "and he would have gone farther with his proof, if it had not been for the small matter that the *truth* would not permit him." Lincoln reasoned that the entire issue was, "from beginning to end, the sheerest deception," and that Polk provoked the war hoping "to escape scrutiny by fixing the public gaze upon the exceeding brightness of glory." And Lincoln stated straightforwardly that "it is a singular fact that . . . the President sent the army into a settlement of Mexican people who had never submitted to the authority of Texas or the United States."

Even though he knew it was a dangerous thing to do politically, Lincoln had this speech printed in pamphlet form for distribution back in his home district. He was willing to face the fire, and sure enough, opposition newspapers and political opponents blasted him. The *Illinois State Register* called Lincoln's remarks "unpatriotic" and "treasonable," and labeled him the "Benedict Arnold of our district." And most Democrats began mocking him by using the derisive term "Spotty Lincoln."

Lincoln's law partner William Herndon later recalled, "I earnestly desired to prevent him from committing what I believed to be political suicide." And Herndon argued that "if it shall become necessary to repel invasion, the President may, without violation of the Constitution, cross the line, and invade the territory of another country."

But Lincoln did not back down. "If you had been in my place you would have voted just as I did," he told Herndon. "[Polk was] clearly proved to be false [just as] you can prove that your house is not mine. Allow the President to invade a neighboring nation, whenever *he* shall deem it necessary to repel an invasion, and you allow him to . . . make war at pleasure. This our [Founders] understood to be the most oppressive of all Kingly oppressions — and they resolved to so frame the Constitution that no one man should hold the power of bringing this oppression upon us."

Herndon also suggested that to denounce the war was to denounce the soldiers fighting in it. To this, Lincoln responded that veterans in Washington did "not hesitate to denounce as unjust the President's conduct in the beginning of the war," and he later pointed out that the government "constantly had [his] votes for all the necessary supplies." Lincoln further stated that Polk had not "even an imaginary conception" as to "when the war might end."

But for all Lincoln's detailed analysis of what he believed President Polk had done wrong, he invariably suggested that both Manifest Destiny and starting a war with a militarily weak neighbor was morally wrong. "I honestly believe that all those who wish to keep up the character of [our nation], do not believe in enlarging our field, but in keeping our fences where they are," he said in September 1848. "Would you venture to consider those acts [too small for notice] had they been committed by any nation on earth against the humblest of *our* people?" [Italics added.] "Then I ask, is the [Golden Rule] obsolete? — of no force? — of no application?"

Lincoln continually applied his reasoning not only to the United States, but to all nations everywhere. A few years later, for instance, in commenting on the "People's Spring" revolutions in Europe, specifically "the interference of Russia in the 1848 Hungarian struggle," Lincoln stated, "It is the duty of our government to neither foment, nor assist such revolutions in other governments" or "legally or warrantably interfere abroad to aid . . . such revolutions." Rather, Lincoln advocated that "we should at once announce to the world our determination to insist upon . . . nonintervention as a sacred principle of international law."

[The Mexican-American War officially ended when, on March 10, 1848, Congress ratified the Treaty of Guadalupe Hidalgo. As a result, the United States gained more than half a million square miles of new territory, including what is now California, Nevada, Utah, Arizona, and parts of New Mexico, Colorado, and Wyoming. The United States military suffered 17,000 casualties (13,000 killed, 4,000 wounded) during the war. It is estimated that there were between 16,000 and 25,000 Mexican casualties.]

★ ★ ★

During Abraham Lincoln's two years as a United States congressman, he had a 97 percent attendance record (missing only 13 roll call votes). He was an active and loyal member of the Whig Party who campaigned for his colleagues in their home states. He was known as a member of a small group of Whig congressmen who called themselves the Young Indians, which included Alexander Stephens of Georgia (who would later become vice president of the Confederate States of America). Lincoln also reached across the aisle to the Democrats, forging alliances, enacting legislation, and making many friends in the process. Much of the freshman congressman's work was to continue his fight to secure federal government aid for state internal improvements. When President Polk threatened to veto any such national aid based on his idealistic belief that the states should pay for such projects themselves, Lincoln stood up in the House and ridiculed Polk's reasoning. "An honest laborer digs coal at about seventy cents a day, while the president digs abstractions at about seventy dollars a day," he said. "The *coal* is clearly worth more than the *abstractions*." On a more serious note, Lincoln criticized the Democratic platform, which claimed that federally paid internal improvements would be too costly, would create inequality in shared benefits, and would be unconstitutional.

"The sum of these [objections is to say]," noted Lincoln, "'Do nothing at all, lest you do something wrong.'" And then Lincoln offered a solution: "Let the nation take hold of the larger works, and the states the smaller ones. . . . What is made unequal in one place may be equalized in another, extravagance avoided, and the whole country put on that career of prosperity, which shall correspond with its extent of territory, its natural resources, and the intelligence and enterprise of its people."

Also while in Congress, Lincoln made his first significant move toward what would become a lifelong dream — the elimination of slavery. In addition to voting for every piece of legislation that would prohibit slavery in territories acquired from Mexico, he proposed a resolution to ban slavery in the nation's capital. Lincoln knew that there were upwards of 2,000 slaves in Washington, D.C., and that one of the nation's largest slave trading companies, Franklin & Armfield, had a facility not far from the Capitol Building where their "merchandise" was collected, sold, and shipped south. So on January 10, 1849, he floated his idea to halt the practice in D.C. by offering a gradual change in which owners would be compensated with federal dollars for the loss of their "property."

In order to garner support for his idea, Lincoln spent quite a bit of time negotiating and offering compromises. But most members of Congress were hardened in their positions regarding the most divisive issue confronting the nation. Many Southerners refused to even consider the idea because they believed it would be the first step toward abolishing slavery in the entire country. Lincoln's moderate and reasonable approach failed, however, and he never formally introduced the bill. "Finding that I was abandoned by my former backers and having little personal influence," he said later, "I dropped the matter knowing it was useless to [move forward]."

★ ★ ★

Abraham Lincoln would serve only one 2-year term in the United States Congress. When William Herndon encouraged his law partner to run again, Lincoln referred to the previous agreement about rotation in office. "I made the declaration that I would not be a candidate again," he replied. "My word and honor forbid [me] to enter myself as a competitor." John J. Hardin and Edward Baker had their turns and now Lincoln's former law partner Stephen T. Logan wanted to run for Congress. "Turn about is fair play," Lincoln said. Regarding term limits, Lincoln would later state that under "the frame of government [the people] have wisely given their public servants little power for mischief, and have with equal wisdom provided for [their] return . . . at very short intervals."

Many contemporaries believed that Lincoln's passionate opposition to the Mexican-American War cost the Whig Party its long-held Seventh Illinois District seat in Congress, because Logan was defeated by the Democratic candidate in the next election. Lincoln, himself, was well aware of the controversy, and when asked whether he would take a similar stand against the war if he had to do it all over again, he jokingly referred to Justin Butterfield, a prominent Illinois Whig who had once paid a political price for opposing the War of 1812:

Butterfield was asked at the beginning of the Mexican War if he was opposed to it. He replied, "No, I opposed one war. That was enough for me. I am now in favor of war, pestilence, and famine!"

While waiting for his term to expire, Lincoln, now a lame-duck congressman, was offered a number of jobs that came with both money and prestige. Lincoln turned down the position of commissioner of the U.S. General Land Office, a prestigious Chicago law firm's lucrative offer, and an appointment to be governor of the Oregon Territory.

"Well, what are you going to do now?" Lincoln was asked.

"I will go home and resume my law practice, at which I can make a living," he said. "And perhaps some day the people will have use for me."

LINCOLN ON LEADERSHIP FOR TODAY

Starting a War with a Militarily Weak Country

As a one-term U.S. congressman, Lincoln spoke out forcefully against the 1846 U.S. invasion of Mexico, particularly blasting the Polk administration as having done so under false pretenses. That military action, of course, led to the one-sided Mexican-American War, which resulted in the United States acquiring vast quantities of land in the West.

In 2003, the United States invaded Iraq for the stated reasons of (1) disarming Iraq of weapons of mass destruction (nuclear and biological), (2) ending dictator Saddam Hussein's support for terrorism related to the 9/11 attacks on the United States, and (3) freeing the Iraqi people. The war itself lasted eight years, cost $845 billion in U.S. taxpayer dollars, and resulted in 4,486 American lives lost and more than 32,000 Americans wounded. Iraqi casualty estimates vary widely but are generally agreed to have been in the hundreds of thousands. Saddam Hussein was overthrown, captured, and later executed. The invasion of Iraq destabilized the Middle East and resulted in expanded and ongoing terrorist actions against the United States.

At the time of the invasion, many critics questioned the George W. Bush administration's evidence for Iraq possessing weapons of mass destruction and for Saddam Hussein having any ties to Osama bin Laden or al-Qaeda. Subsequent investigations determined that Saddam was not allied with any terrorist group responsible for the attacks — nor were any weapons of mass destruction ever discovered by American troops during the Iraq War. Many Americans believe that the invasion of Iraq was instigated under false pretenses for financial gain.

Had Lincoln been in Congress during this time, the evidence seems to strongly suggest that he would have carefully studied the issue and, in my opinion, would have been a leading spokesman against the actions of the Bush administration. Had Lincoln been president at the time, the United States *would not* have invaded Iraq. Provoking a war with a militarily weak country is morally wrong. It becomes an even worse offense when leaders apparently lie to the people they represent to justify such actions. Neither money generated from waging an unnecessary war nor land acquired from an inevitable victory is worth the toll in human lives and suffering.

Military Intervention in Other Countries

While in a leadership position, Abraham Lincoln witnessed revolutions in other countries. In 1848, for instance, while he was in the U.S. Congress, a series of political revolutions took place across Europe (sometimes referred to as the People's Spring). Citizens in more than 50 countries (including Hungary, France, Germany, Austria, and Italy) rose up to press for democratic reform. Nearly all of the revolutionaries were beaten back, sometimes at the cost of tens of thousands of lives. During Hungary's quest for independence from the Austrian Empire, Russia sent in a quarter of a million troops to effectively smash the rebellion and, thereby, end the Hungarian quest for democracy over despotism. And beginning in December 1861 (and lasting throughout the Civil War), *President* Lincoln was faced with the fact that Emperor Napoleon III of France had instigated a military invention and set up a puppet regime in Mexico.

Such things still occur today all over the world. From 2010 to 2012, for example, protests in Tunisia set off a wave of political protests in more than a dozen nations throughout North Africa and the Middle East. This movement came to be known as the Arab Spring. One resulting conflict was a disastrous civil war in Syria pitting Bashar al-Assad's government against local rebels and, eventually, members of the terrorist group ISIS (or ISIL). Tens of thousands (perhaps hundreds of thousands) of Syrians were killed or wounded. In October 2015, Russia became involved militarily to support Assad. Although pressure mounted on the United States to become involved in the conflict, the Obama administration preferred to stay out and concentrate military efforts on containing and defeating ISIS.

As seen in this chapter, Abraham Lincoln was very clear on his position about U.S. involvement in foreign military conflicts. "It is the duty of our government to neither foment, nor assist such revolutions in other governments," he said, or "legally or warrantably interfere abroad to aid such . . . revolutions." Nonintervention, he further said, should be "a sacred principle of international law." As president during the Civil War, Lincoln also strategically stayed out of France's attempt to control Mexico, due to his pragmatic "One War at a Time" policy.

Lincoln today would realize that the United States cannot be the military policeman for the entire world. There is too much unsettling activity around the globe to be everywhere at all times. The cost would simply be too high, in terms of both U.S. military casualties and taxpayer dollars. However, I believe Lincoln would carefully evaluate each situation separately for its potential impact on the United States and for possible atrocities such as genocide or any unusually negative impacts on human rights. In such cases where intervention was deemed appropriate, he would likely leverage resources and work with the United Nations in forming a coalition to end the violence. And Lincoln would most certainly not hesitate to deploy American forces for the protection of nations with which the U.S. is allied via treaties (such as NATO).

Term Limits

Abraham Lincoln served only one term in the U.S. House of Representatives. He did not run for a second term, largely because it was the custom of Illinois members of the Whig Party back then to rotate candidates for office. However, Lincoln's unpopular stance against the Mexican-American War may have prevented him from being reelected even if he had decided to run again because, as it turned out, his party actually lost that House seat in the next election. Back then, there were no limitations on how many terms a congressman, senator, or president could serve. Today, congressmen and senators may serve an unlimited number of terms, but presidents of the United States are limited to two terms. The presidential restriction is due to ratification of the 22nd Amendment to the Constitution in 1951, largely as a reaction to Franklin D. Roosevelt having been elected to four consecutive terms.

Whether or not to impose term limits on members of Congress is a perennial and controversial issue. Generally, the American people realize that there are too many career politicians in Congress who vote largely in their own self-interest to get reelected. And 85 to 90 percent of those who seek reelection are successful. In effect, then, it is only when a vacancy is announced due to retirement that somebody new has a decent chance of being elected. Those who support term limits have three main arguments: (1) they would help eliminate career politicians; (2) representatives and senators would be more likely to vote to do the right thing rather than protect their own self-interests; and (3) term limits are supported by a majority of citizens, which is indicated by the many states that impose them on their own representatives. Those against term limits state that (1) they will cause states to lose the seniority and experience of longer-serving members, (2) a high turnover in Congress would lead to an inefficient federal government, and (3) term limits are unconstitutional.

Because Lincoln was not concerned about trying to get reelected, he was free to follow his conscience and both speak out and vote against the Mexican-American War. Had he been worried about committing political suicide, he might have been more soft-spoken. I believe his position today would be that term limits would prevent members of Congress from becoming career politicians, would bring new faces and fresh ideas to government, and would keep things energetic and dynamic. The argument that people lose experience and seniority when a good public servant leaves office is a deceptive excuse.

I believe Lincoln today would sponsor and support a constitutional amendment requiring term limits for U.S. congressmen and senators. Even as president, Lincoln's first thought was *not* for his own self-interest or staying in office. His first thought was always to do what was best for the country. As we will see in a later chapter,

Abraham Lincoln was willing to risk losing an election if that was the price he had to pay for doing the right thing.

Accepting Lucrative Job Offers After Service in Congress

When Abraham Lincoln left Washington, D.C., after his one term in Congress, he was offered a number of prestigious positions, including the governorship of the Oregon Territory, commissioner of the U.S. General Land Office, and a lucrative job with a major Chicago law firm. He turned them all down and went back to Springfield, Illinois, to practice law. And it is clear that he intended to do the same thing after serving a second term as president of the United States. "Let it [the Lincoln and Herndon shingle] hang there undisturbed," he said to his law partner William Herndon in 1861 upon leaving for Washington. "If I live I'm coming back . . . and we'll go right on practicing law as if nothing had ever happened."

Today, the few members of Congress who do find themselves out of a job every couple of years are courted by special interest groups to either work for them directly or become independent lobbyists on their behalf. A good number accept such positions and get rich, or should I say richer, because most members of Congress are already multimillionaires. It's no secret that congressmen and senators are beholden to special interest groups, corporations, and individuals who contribute massive amounts of money to get them elected and keep them in office. This system is so widespread today that nearly everybody accepts it as a fact of life in American politics. In some extreme cases, our national representatives are nothing more than agents for some industries and corporations, doing their bidding on the floor of the House or Senate. Allowing former legislators to move into high-paid lobbyist positions merely perpetuates a revolving-door system that sees them walking right back into the Capitol to use their contacts and knowledge of the legislative process to represent special interest groups rather than the people at large.

In my view, Abraham Lincoln would be outraged that our system of government has evolved into such a state. With regard to public servants leveraging their former positions to enrich themselves after they leave office, I believe Lincoln would actively sponsor and support legislation to halt the practice. He would advise former legislators to go back to their districts and try to secure a position in which they can earn a respectable living. And then, if they are truly esteemed, the people may have use for them.

Of all the forces of nature, I should think the wind contains the largest amount of power to move things. . . . And yet it has not, so far in the world's history, become [proportionately] valuable as a motive power.

— Lincoln, on discoveries and inventions
April 6, 1858

ISSUES
Science and Climate Change
Technology and Access to Information
Lawyers and the Legal Profession

3

To Emancipate the Mind

★ ★ ★

In fording streams, Lincoln was frequently sent forward as a scout or pioneer. His extremely long legs enabled him to test the depth of the stream, find the most shallow water, and thus pilot the party through the current.

We would stop at a farm house for dinner. While there, Lincoln would hunt up some farming implement, machine, or tool and he would carefully examine it all over — first generally and then [in detail]. He would "sight" it to determine if it was straight or warped. If he could make a practical test of it, he would do that. He would turn it over or around and stoop down, or lie down, if necessary, to look under it. He would shake it, lift it, roll it about,

up-end it — and thus ascertain every quality and utility [it had].
Then he would stand off and examine it at a distance.

Those are just two of the hundreds of anecdotes recalled about Abraham Lincoln when he rode the Eighth Judicial Circuit in Illinois with judges and other lawyers. It was a 400-mile round trip, twice a year (in the spring and fall), and usually lasted about 10 weeks, depending, of course, on the number of cases tried. Lincoln rode one of his horses, "Old Tom" or "Old Buck," and is reported to have been the only lawyer who always covered the entire circuit, staying to the end of every court proceeding. After traveling through the backwoods and reaching the next town, the group would ordinarily spend the night in a local tavern. Sometimes they would have to sleep two to a bed or even on a dirt floor. While most of the men grumbled about the conditions, Lincoln rarely complained. In the winter, if more wood was needed for the potbellied stove, he would scare up an axe, take off his coat, and split logs himself. Then everybody would sit around the fire telling jokes and stories. Sometimes they had contests as to who could spin the best yarn, and Lincoln often won. When he told or heard a joke that was particularly funny, he would erupt in high-pitched laughter and his body would shake all over. On those chilly nights, Lincoln often wore over his shoulders an old gray shawl fastened with a large safety pin. Some of the men thought Lincoln had very poor taste in clothes or just didn't care much about them. "I used to wonder why he did not appear to be dressed up," recalled one colleague. "But [when] I looked at him a second time, I would see that he was as well dressed as the average lawyer, wearing a plain broadcloth suit, a high hat, and fine boots. But his angularity and [awkwardness] were so pronounced that the clothes seemed to lose their character."

"From 1849 to 1854," Lincoln wrote, "[I] practiced the law more assiduously than ever before." He did so, in part, because his stand against the Mexican-American War had proved so unpopular in Illinois as to seriously hamper a future in politics. But after a brief period of despair, Lincoln recovered and decided to make good use of his time on the circuit. "I hold the value of life is to improve one's condition," he once wrote. And in Lincoln's mind, one of the best ways of improving himself was to learn as much as he could on all subjects. And learn Lincoln did.

He almost always had a book or two in his coat pocket — Shakespeare's plays, the poetry of Robert Burns and Lord Byron, or perhaps the stories of Edgar Allan Poe. He once noted that during these years, he had "studied and nearly mastered the Six Books of Euclid" (the ancient Greek mathematician and philosopher). From these books, Lincoln learned the principles of geometry and trigonometry (with their propositions, theorems, proofs, etc.), along with the basic rules of logic and reason. One contemporary recalled that Lincoln "wanted something solid to rest upon and hence [had a] bias for mathematics and the physical sciences." So it is not surprising that Lincoln acquired and read some of the most important science books of the 19th century, including Charles Lyell's *Principles of Geology* (1830), Robert Chambers's *Vestiges of the Natural History of Creation* (1844), and, when it came out in 1859, Charles Darwin's *On the Origin of Species.*

Lincoln's law partner William Herndon reported that Darwin's work "interested him greatly," that "he was deeply impressed with the notion of evolution," and that he "seemed to grow into a warm advocate of the new doctrine." It is pretty clear that Abraham Lincoln was interested in, and believed strongly in, science. "There are no accidents in my philosophy," he once said. "Every effect must have its cause. The past is the cause of the present, and the present will be the cause of the future. All these are links in the endless chain stretching from the finite to the infinite."

Lincoln's interest in science continued to the end of his life. As president, he often visited the Smithsonian Institution and, on the way to his retreat at the Soldiers' Home, would sometimes stop by the U.S. Naval Observatory to look at the heavens through a newly installed telescope. Lincoln also spent hours in conversation with eminent scientists, such as the noted Swiss geologist Louis Agassiz. Furthermore, it was during the Lincoln administration that the National Academy of Sciences (NAS) was established (on March 3, 1863). The president, himself, supported and signed the bill not only because of his interest in science, but for the more practical reason that the NAS could test many new inventions being received at the patent office. More than 16,000 patents were filed during the Civil War, and the legal charter for the NAS was, in part, "to investigate, examine, experiment, and report upon any subject of science or art" that might be requested by government officials. This meant that President Lincoln could now ask that one of the NAS's 50 charter members scientifically study the viability of any new weapon or device that might aid the war effort.

Abraham Lincoln was fascinated with engineering and new technology of all kinds. He is, for instance, the only U.S. president to have secured (on May 22, 1849) his own patent (No. 6469). It was for a well-thought-through method of making grounded boats more buoyant in order to lift them over shoals. *[The device was never manufactured, and Lincoln made no money from it.]* Additionally, Lincoln was very interested in the telegraph, which was patented in 1840 by Samuel Morse. It took decades before the new invention was established widely (largely because the infrastructure had to be built). But when the telegraph became common in cities and towns, Abraham Lincoln was right there to see how it worked. One day in 1857, he walked into Western Union's office in the small town of Pekin, Illinois, and met Charles A. Tinker, who later recalled the moment:

> One afternoon, [Mr. Lincoln] came to my office in the corner of the room, and, looking over the tall railing, said: "Mr. Operator, I have always had a curiosity to see the telegraph work. You don't seem to be very busy, and as I have a half-hour or so to wait for dinner, I wonder if you would explain it to me."

"Certainly, sir, I should be pleased to do so," [I said,] and inviting him inside the gate, I proceeded to show [Mr. Lincoln] the "working of the telegraph," explained the battery and its connection to the instruments, and the wires leading thence out of the window and away to the world without.

I was encouraged by the readiness with which he comprehended it all. [Lincoln] seemed to grasp its intricacies, and remarked: "How simple it is when you know it all!"

The invention of the telegraph revolutionized communications around the world. By transmitting electrical signals over wires to other connected stations, people were, for the first time, able to get in touch with each other over long distances almost instantly. Four years later, when Abraham Lincoln became president of the United States, there were no telegraph lines at the War Department. So he immediately had a new telegraph office built there and, in so doing, virtually changed the nature of communications for the executive branch of government. Now the president would not have to rely on sending couriers to his generals and then sometimes wait days for a response.

Abraham Lincoln was not only *interested* in new technology, he embraced it and *applied* it as fast as he could. Why? Because he knew that in leadership, communication is key. The more quickly leaders can communicate with people in their organizations, the better. In Lincoln's case, he made many treks to the War Department's telegraph office to communicate with troops in the field. Most historians agree that his quick application of this important new technology helped win the Civil War.

It wasn't an accident that Lincoln applied the telegraph to the Union's advantage. He thought a lot about inventions, because he wanted to find things that might make a difference in society. As a matter of fact, Lincoln thought so much about the subject that between 1858 and 1859, he gave a long lecture titled "Discoveries and Inventions" in a number of Illinois towns. Many people attended these speeches and heard him talk about the first invention mentioned in the Bible — Adam's fig leaf, and the spinning and weaving of Abraham's "thread" (Genesis 14:23) — and the first mention of an "instrument of iron" (Numbers 35:16), which Lincoln thought must have been an axe. He also spoke about the history of transportation, from the wheel to water navigation, and the history of power generation from the sun, water, steam, and wind. He further speculated on where additional methods of power might be derived. "Of all the forces of nature, I should think the wind contains the largest amount of power to move things," he said. "And yet it has not, so far in the world's history, become [proportionately] valuable as a motive power. All the power exerted by all the men and beasts and running water . . . [would not] equal one-hundredth of what is exerted by the blowing of the wind over and upon the same space."

The whole idea behind Lincoln's lecture was, as he said, to "emancipate the mind" for "the great mass of [people]" so that "their minds were capable of improvement." He was essentially saying that the freedom to think and to learn made all the difference in the world when it came to human progress. According to Lincoln, the creative process began with an "observation [by] a single individual." Then an "idea, once being conceived," would be "reflected upon" and "extended to others" for collaboration and collective thought. Finally, the new invention would be perfected and patented. And the patent was an important final step, because "it secured to the inventor, for a limited time, the exclusive use of his invention and thereby added the fuel of interest to the fire of genius, in the discovery of new and useful things."

★ ★ ★

During those years riding the circuit and practicing law from his Springfield office, Abraham Lincoln became one of Illinois's most capable and best-known lawyers despite the fact that he never attended law school. His success was a result of hard work and applying what he had learned. He took a significant amount of time to research and prepare his cases, for instance, often working long hours at home. Taking nothing for granted, he once told his law partner that he dared not trust a case "on presumptions that [the] court knows all things." Rather, he argued a case "on the presumption that the court did not know anything." Lincoln also frequently employed Euclid's lessons of reason and logic in order to solve a problem, arrive at a conclusion, or decide his stance on an important issue. A good example is contained in some written notes he jotted down about slavery on April 1, 1854, which read something like a mathematical proof:

> If A can prove, however conclusively, that he may, of right, en-slave B — why may not B snatch the same argument, and prove equally, that he may enslave A?
>
> You say A is white, and B is black. It is color, then — the lighter, having the right to enslave the darker? Take care. By this rule, you are to be slave to the first man you meet, with a fairer skin than your own.
>
> You do not mean color exactly? You mean the whites are in-tellectually the superiors of the blacks, and, therefore have the right to enslave them? Take care again. By this rule, you are to be slave to the first man you meet, with an intellect superior to your own.
>
> But, say you, it is a question of interest; and if you can make it your interest, you have the right to enslave another. Very well. And if he can make it his interest, he has the right to enslave you.

Over Lincoln's 25-year law career, he had three law partners (John T. Stuart, Stephen T. Logan, and William Herndon), and, together, they handled more than 5,000 cases. One of Lincoln's most famous was that of Nance Legins-Costley, a black woman who had been sold as a slave to David Bailey. But the seller, a man named Cromwell, died before receiving the agreed $400 price, so the Cromwell estate sued Bailey for payment. Meanwhile, Nance Legins-Costley declared that she was owned by no one and went to court to fight for her freedom. She lost four times but kept appealing. One of those verdicts reads: "A servant is a possession and *can be* sold." Finally, she hired Lincoln, who took the case to the Illinois Supreme Court in 1841. In *Bailey v. Cromwell*, he argued simply that a woman could not be bought and sold in the state of Illinois because it was a free state and slavery was illegal (by virtue of its constitution). Lincoln prevailed, the court reversed the original judgment, and Nance Legins-Costley was freed.

Far and wide, Lincoln gained a reputation as a fair man. He was referred to as "Honest Old Abe," and was approached by people from all walks of life, from all around the state. He would listen carefully to those who wanted to retain him. If he thought their claims had merit, he would say, "You are in the right," and then proceed to represent them. If not, he would often simply respond: "Do not bring a suit. You are in the wrong." And Lincoln's fees were usually modest, especially if his clients were without means.

With time, younger lawyers sought his advice, and Lincoln had plenty to say. "Never stir up litigation," he wrote in 1850. "A worse man can scarcely be found than one who does this. Who can be more nearly a fiend than he who habitually overhauls the register of deeds in search of defects in titles, whereupon to stir up strife, and put money in his pocket?" Lincoln also wrote that "there is a vague popular belief that lawyers are necessarily dishonest." But then he made a stern statement directed to any young attorney. "Resolve to be honest at all events," he said. "If in your own judgment, you cannot be an honest lawyer, resolve to be honest without being a lawyer. Choose some other occupation."

* * *

Although Lincoln and his wife, Mary, suffered through the loss of their four-year-old son, Eddie, in 1850, they were generally happy and contented in the five years after moving back to

Springfield from Washington, D.C. *[Eddie Lincoln's death was officially recorded as "chronic consumption" (tuberculosis).]* Lincoln had forged a successful career and was making a comfortable living, he had developed many lifelong friendships, and Mary had given birth to two more sons, William Wallace (Willie) Lincoln (on December 21, 1850) and Thomas (Tad) Lincoln III (on April 4, 1853).

In 1854, Abraham Lincoln was only 45 years old, although his appearance was far more weathered. "I was losing interest in politics," he wrote. But when, in January of that year, his old friend Illinois senator Stephen A. Douglas introduced legislation to allow the spread of slavery to Kansas and Nebraska, Lincoln stood up and took notice.

I sold milk in Springfield for years. Most mornings, Lincoln would walk over to my place with a small bucket in one of his hands for the milk he was going to buy. He was usually barefoot and had one of his boys sitting on his shoulders, chirping like a bird.

Lincoln's old milkman

LINCOLN ON LEADERSHIP FOR TODAY

Science and Climate Change

Abraham Lincoln was interested in, and believed strongly in, science. He studied geology and read Charles Darwin's work on the theory of evolution when it first came out in 1859. And while Lincoln was president, the National Academy of Sciences was founded, with his enthusiastic support. Science, he understood, is the pursuit and application of knowledge and understanding of our physical and natural world. That's what it was in Lincoln's day, and that's what it is now.

Today, there is overwhelming scientific evidence that the earth's climate is changing due to human activity. The polar ice caps and the Greenland ice sheet are melting. Glaciers are receding or gone. Ocean temperatures are warming. Sea levels are rising. Global air temperatures are increasing. Nearly all reputable climate scientists agree that climate warming trends over the past century are very likely due to human activities (mostly adding CO_2 and greenhouse gases to the atmosphere). But many conservative activists are skeptical of science and do not believe either in climate change or that human activity is causing it. Major carbon-producing industries and corporations deny that their products' emissions are warming the earth. This issue is one of the most significant of the 21st century — perhaps *the most significant.* The projected sea level rise alone will pose risks to infrastructure, disrupt commerce and the economy, cause mass migrations, and seriously affect human health.

I firmly believe that if Abraham Lincoln were here today, he would say that science is real and must be trusted. He would recognize that evolution is no longer a theory but a fact. And he would tell us that when the overwhelming majority of scientists show that their data indicates climate change is occurring and is caused by human activity, we must believe them.

Abraham Lincoln would not mess around on this issue. My sense is that he would both propose and support forceful long-term action to eliminate greenhouse gas emissions and to reverse the global warming trend. He would lead an effort to bring other nations of the world into the fold and create a joint effort to combat climate change. And he would do so with hope and inspiration, because he would understand that the earth has a remarkable power to heal itself. Lincoln would also take a firm stand in lowering carbon emissions and supporting a worldwide switch to renewable green energy, such as wind and solar. He would realize that, in doing so, new industries, new jobs, and new opportunities would energize us all. And he might say, "We shall nobly save, or meanly lose, the last, best hope of humankind — the planet Earth."

Technology and Access to Information

Abraham Lincoln was a technology geek. He was fascinated with all kinds of new gadgets and equipment. As a lawyer traveling the circuit in Illinois, he examined new farming machinery to see how it worked. As president, he screened all kinds of new weaponry to see if it might give the Union army an edge. When he recognized that the telegraph could revolutionize communications, he quickly had it installed in the War Department — and the telegraph office became one of his favorite hangouts. Now, in the 21st century, new technology is changing the world faster than ever before. Communications are instant. News happens live via video streaming. Social media allows everyone to have a voice and be heard. We now have the ability to store and transmit vast amounts of information.

But technology's rapid advance presents a myriad of new questions. Should access to public information be controlled? What about government information — federal, state, and local? Many surreptitiously released federal documents have exposed wrongdoing, untruths, controversial facts, and so on. Should we rethink what the government lists as "classified"? Should access to the Internet be free? Or should the government allow access and regulate pricing?

Lincoln today, I believe, would say that new discoveries, inventions, and technology should be embraced and applied as fast as possible in order to help improve society. He would also agree that the freedom to think and learn is a God-given right that must be supported by a free government. Therefore, access to information is paramount in our ability to arrive at proper conclusions and decisions — not only for the moment but for the future. No citizen or organization should suffer discrimination over the fair right of access to information.

Were he here today, Abraham Lincoln would encourage open access to all government and public information. He would limit what federal government information can be designated "classified" or in other ways not open to the public. In theory, making key information less secret would lead to more honesty and integrity among our government officials in the performance of their duties. He would support laws that mandate effective online security for both the public and private sectors and prosecute individuals who illegally hack into and release classified government information. And I suspect Lincoln would support legislation that encourages affordable or free access to information worldwide, including an open Internet based on net neutrality.

Lawyers and the Legal Profession

In his own time, Abraham Lincoln noted that "there is a vague popular belief that lawyers are necessarily dishonest." Today, more than a century and a half later, the same universal feeling still holds true. Only now, it's worse, because there is far more money involved. To a very large degree, there has been a degradation and cheapening of the legal profession, much of which is designed to benefit those with massive fortunes. In essence, the system is stacked against the little guy. But it doesn't have to be that way.

If Lincoln were here today, I believe he would advise individual attorneys to start building reputations as honest lawyers and to take more steps to demonstrate to the public that they often do good things to help people. He would urge them to do more pro bono work and to charge more modest fees, especially for those without means. I believe that Lincoln would also encourage attorneys to police their profession more by, for example, renewing ethics standards in local bar associations and perhaps requiring mandatory pro bono work. A decent wage can still be earned and a comfortable life lived.

I have no prejudice against the Southern people. They are just what we would be in their situation. If slavery did not now exist amongst them, they would not introduce it. If it did now exist amongst us, we should not instantly give it up.

— Abraham Lincoln, from a speech
on the repeal of the Missouri Compromise
Peoria, Illinois
October 16, 1854

The occasion is piled high with difficulty, and we must rise with the occasion.

— Abraham Lincoln
December 1, 1862

ISSUES
Unpopular Supreme Court Decisions
Health Care

4

Rising with the Occasion

★ ★ ★

NEW LIGHT BREAKS upon us," said Abraham Lincoln. "Now congress declares [the policy of prohibiting slavery in new territory] ought never to have been and . . . must never be again. The sacred right of self-government is grossly violated by it! . . . Oh, how difficult it is to treat with respect such assaults upon all we have ever really held sacred."

With these words, Lincoln blasted passage of the Kansas-Nebraska Act, which may have been the single most important event leading up to the American Civil War. The new bill had been sponsored and ramrodded through Congress from January to May 1854 by Illinois senator Stephen A. Douglas — then quickly signed by President Franklin Pierce. Its effect was to split the country right down the middle, politically speaking. All Northern Whigs and most Northern Democrats voted against it. All Southern Democrats and Southern Whigs supported it. Douglas, himself, predicted it would "raise a hell of a storm." And Lincoln, particularly, was "thunderstruck and stunned." He viewed it "not as a *law,* but as *violence*" personified. "It was conceived in violence, passed in violence, is maintained in violence, and is being executed in violence," he wrote to a friend. So why was Abraham Lincoln so upset? What exactly did the Kansas-Nebraska Act do?

Back in 1820, Congress had passed a compromise law allowing Missouri to enter the Union as a slave state, but restricting the spread of slavery in the western territories north of the 36° 30' parallel (essentially the present-day border between Arkansas and Missouri extended west to the Pacific). After 34 years, the Kansas-Nebraska Act effectively repealed the Missouri Compromise. Slavery could now spread unchecked across the entire western United States if the people in those territories and states voted for it. Ostensibly, the purpose of the new law was to both secure a route for a transcontinental railroad and spur growth for the economic development that would follow. Its passage was engineered by the two major special interest groups of the day: (1) the railroad industry and (2) slavery, itself, which was *the* most profitable financial enterprise in the country at the time. With passage of the Kansas-Nebraska Act, slave labor could now be used to build the railroads, construct cities and towns, and develop farmland. Blacks would continue to be held as property and be forced to do all the work for free. Rich whites could sit back and reap the extensive profits gained by not having to employ paid laborers. The Southern plantation way of life would be extended far and wide — and perhaps, eventually, to the Northern states, too.

Well, Abraham Lincoln was having none of this. But his objections were not economic-, material-, or secular-based. His interpretation was that this new law "assumes there can be . . . moral right" in the enslaving of one man by another. But the United States had never formally assumed such a stance. And when Lincoln said that "the sacred right of self government is grossly violated by it," he was referring to the fact that black individuals had no choice in the matter of their own freedom. In essence, he was saying that if liberty, equality, and self-government don't work for some people, they don't work for all people. So as far as Abraham Lincoln was concerned, the repeal of the Missouri Compromise raised the issue of slavery to an entirely new moral level — and it was time for him to "rise with the occasion" and fight back.

But how was he going to do it? He had been out of politics for five long years. What could an ex-congressman, now just a private citizen, do that might make a difference? How could he possibly take on the entrenched institution of slavery and all the special interests that came with it? After all, the amount of money invested in the slave industry was more than that invested in railroads, banks, and businesses combined. *[Remember, this was before the Industrial Revolution.]* Slavery was a major economic engine of the United States, tied to other industries (cotton, sugar, tobacco, etc.) and other countries through foreign trade. More daunting was the fact that it was the foundation of a social order and way of life for half the nation. Slavery was ingrained, entrenched, and enormously powerful. Most people were firmly convinced that *nothing* could damage it and, certainly, total abolition was out of the question. Lincoln, of course, knew what he was up against. Here are just a few of the statements he made in sizing up the situation:

Look at the magnitude of the subject! About one sixth of the whole population of the United States are slaves! Owners . . . consider them property!

The people of the South have an immediate palpable and immensely great pecuniary interest; while, with the people of the North, it is merely an abstract question of moral right, with only slight, and remote pecuniary interest added.

The slaves of the South, at a moderate estimate, are worth a thousand millions of dollars [a billion dollars]. Let it be permanently settled that this property may extend to new territory, without restraint, and it greatly enhances, perhaps quite doubles, its value at once.

The ever-pragmatic Lincoln knew he could not call for a permanent end to slavery (although abolitionists all across the Northern states were doing just that). Such a position was too extreme at this stage, and simply had no chance of success. Rather, Lincoln decided to take the middle position and support containment. If slavery was not allowed to spread, it would lead toward "ultimate extinction" and die a natural death, which is the course Lincoln believed it to be on before the Missouri Compromise was repealed.

Even after making this decision about *what* to do, Lincoln still had to come up with a strategy about *how* to move the needle in the other direction. First and foremost, he was going to have to think long term. He knew that little could be achieved in the short term, because the train was already out of the station. Slavery had to be settled "on some philosophical basis," he said. "No policy that does not rest on some philosophical public opinion can be permanently maintained." Therefore, Lincoln set his sights on changing the nation's majority position on the institution of slavery, which, of course, would take time. Second, in his speeches Lincoln decided to stick with one issue. He would no longer talk about internal improvements, protective tariffs, state banks — or anything else, for that matter. He would speak about slavery and slavery alone.

Lincoln chose to begin his quest by going on a speaking tour during September and October of 1854, during which he gave seven major public addresses around the state. His exhaustively prepared three-hour Peoria speech, in particular, was later printed in segments over the course of a week by the *Illinois State Journal.* "I wish to *make* and to *keep* the distinction between the *existing* institution [of slavery] and the *extension* of it so broad, and so clear," he said, "that no honest man can misunderstand me, and no dishonest one [can] successfully misrepresent me." Lincoln's clarity and eloquence seemed to have their effect, as newspaper reporter Horace White attested. "[His] eloquence was of the higher type, which produced conviction in others, because of the conviction of the speaker himself," wrote White. "[Mr. Lincoln's] speaking went to the heart, because it came from the heart."

Because Lincoln realized that he had to change the thinking of large groups of people with monetary self-interest, he made a conscious decision not to personally attack those involved with slavery. "The slaveholder does not like to be considered a mean fellow," he noted, "and hence he has to struggle within . . . and sets about arguing himself into the belief that slavery is right." Lincoln had studied human nature and believed that slavery was "founded in the selfishness of man's nature," and that the "immense pecuniary interest [had] its influence upon their minds." So in his speeches, Lincoln revealed empathy regarding those who thought differently than himself. "I have no prejudice against the Southern people. They are just what we would be in their situation," he said. "If slavery did not now exist amongst them, they would not introduce it. If it did now exist amongst us, we should not instantly give it up. . . . When it is said that the institution exists and that it is very difficult to get rid of it in any satisfactory way, I can understand and appreciate the saying. I surely will not blame them for not doing what I [do] not know how to do myself."

In order to have any chance of getting through to his audience, Lincoln strategically chose to argue the case on moral grounds. "We have before us this whole matter of the right or wrong of slavery in this Union," he said. "Nearly eighty years ago, we began by declaring that all men are created equal but now ... we have run down to the other declaration that for *some* men to enslave others is a 'sacred right of self-government.'" According to Lincoln, these two "declarations" were inconsistent and contradictory. "They can not stand together," he warned. "Repeal the Missouri compromise ..., repeal all past history," he said, "you can not repeal human nature."

With soaring rhetoric, exceptional preparation, and extraordinary eloquence, Abraham Lincoln soon became the leading national spokesman against the spread of slavery in the United States. His words were heard far and wide, and, certainly, discussed all over the state of Illinois. Of course, by taking the middle (or moderate) position, Lincoln angered both extremes — slaveholders and abolitionists alike. But members of the Whig Party were so impressed that they asked him to become a late candidate for election to the U.S. Senate.

In those days, senators were elected in the state legislatures after the November general elections. Lincoln was committed to reinstating the Missouri Compromise, so on November 10, 1854, he let it be known that he would allow his name to be placed in nomination. And when the legislature convened on February 8, 1855, he came up only four votes shy of winning on the first ballot. But after it became clear that he could not secure the needed 51 votes for victory, and that there was a very real danger of a pro-slavery Democrat winning, Lincoln released his supporters and asked them to vote for Lyman Trumbull (an anti–Kansas-Nebraska Democrat who had received only five votes on the first ballot). When asked to stay in the race, Lincoln demurred, saying that if he did, "you will lose both Trumbull and myself and I think the cause is to be preferred [over the] men." So it was Lyman Trumbull who became the next United States senator from Illinois. Although Lincoln was discouraged that he had not won, he was "not too disappointed to congratulate my friend Trumbull," which he did personally at the victory party. People were deeply impressed by this simple gesture. In defeat, Lincoln gained many new friends, because they now realized he stood for something more important than winning an election.

★ ★ ★

The month after Abraham Lincoln was defeated in his bid for the Senate nomination, a group of anti-slavery Whigs and Democrats in Wisconsin founded the Republican Party. The Grand Old Party (GOP), as it eventually came to be known, was created primarily to organize opposition to the Kansas-Nebraska Act, which was not being done effectively by either the Whig Party or the Northern Democrats. Within two years, the Republicans were solidly organized in more than 20 states of the Northeast and Midwest. Apart from Missouri, there was little if any support for the new political party in slave states or the South.

Ever the loyal Whig, Lincoln delayed joining the Republicans until it became obvious that, among anti-slavery forces nationwide, only they had a chance to win the next presidential election. "I am *in!*" he wrote to Senator Lyman Trumbull, who had also joined up. So by early 1856, Lincoln was helping shape the Republican Party in Illinois and would quickly become one of its acknowledged leaders. Moreover, he had become so well known for his oratory that the awkward-looking lawyer from Illinois was seriously considered for the vice presidential slot at the first Republican National Convention (held in Philadelphia that summer). Lincoln lost out to William L. Dayton of New York, while the top of the ticket went to former California senator John C.

Frémont. Unfortunately for the Republicans, the Frémont-Dayton combination lost to Pennsylvania's Southern-leaning Democrat James Buchanan and his running mate, John C. Breckinridge, of Kentucky.

Two days after Buchanan took the oath as president on March 6, 1857, the United States Supreme Court issued the *Dred Scott* decision — which held that neither the slave Dred Scott (who was suing for his freedom) nor *any other black person* (free or slave) could be a citizen of the United States. Blacks were viewed by the Court, rather, as "beings of an inferior order ... [who] had no rights which the white man was bound to respect." The 7–2 split decision further declared that the 1820 Missouri Compromise was unconstitutional (and therefore an invalid law), because Congress did not have the power to prohibit slavery in any territory.

With the decision coming so soon after the president's inauguration, Republicans suspected collusion by the pro-slavery Democratic leadership. First, Stephen A. Douglas had introduced the Kansas-Nebraska bill, which was supported and signed by President Franklin Pierce. Then James Buchanan, while president-elect, had cajoled members of the Supreme Court to vote his way on the *Dred Scott* case. Finally, 76-year-old Chief Justice Roger B. Taney (a former slaveholder appointed to the Court by Andrew Jackson) pushed through the decision and wrote the majority opinion.

Abraham Lincoln, outraged by the Court's action, held his tongue for several months, in part so he could cool down and prepare an appropriate response. When he finally did take the stage in Springfield, Illinois (on June 26, 1857), he provided something of a future guide for citizens who honestly disagree with a Supreme Court decision.

First, Lincoln let it be known that he acceded to the Supreme Court. "We believe in ... respect for the judicial department of government," he said. "We think its decisions ... should control

. . . the general policy of the country, subject to be disturbed only by amendments of the Constitution. . . . More than this would be revolution."

Second, he pointedly stated, "We [the Republicans] think the Dred Scott decision is erroneous." Then Lincoln noted that the Court was not "unanimous," that there was "apparent partisan bias" involved, and that the ruling was "based on assumed historical facts which are not really true."

Third, Lincoln cited and agreed with the dissenting opinion of the two justices in the minority, and pointed out that the majority judges disagreed with one another in their reasons for coming to their decision. Fourth, he specifically exposed errors in the Court's opinion. For example, Lincoln pointed out the precedent that blacks had already been viewed as citizens by several states. They had voted in 5 of the original 13 states, and "in the last three or four years" 2 of those 5 states (New Jersey and North Carolina) had given free blacks "the right of voting." Lincoln also took issue with the statement made in Taney's opinion that "the right of property in a slave is distinctly and expressly affirmed in the Constitution." In fact, Lincoln noted, there is no mention of slaves or slavery in the Constitution at all.

Fifth, Lincoln addressed the moral problem created by the *Dred Scott* decision, stating that when the Founders wrote "all men are created equal," they were not limiting it to only white people. "I think the authors of that notable instrument, [the Declaration of Independence] . . . , did consider all men created equal in 'certain inalienable rights, among which are life, liberty, and the pursuit of happiness,'" he stated. "This they said, and this they meant. . . . [They placed it] in the Declaration . . . for future use [as] a stumbling block," he continued, "to those who . . . might seek to turn a free people back into the hateful paths of despotism [that] would find left for them at least one hard nut to crack."

Sixth, and finally, Lincoln stated that it was "not disrespectful to treat [the Supreme Court's decision] as not having yet quite established a settled doctrine for the country." Rather, he said, "we know the court that made it has often overruled its own decisions, and we shall do what we can to have it overrule this." In other words, Lincoln was saying that the same issue was bound to be raised again, and when that happened, the decision could be reversed.

★ ★ ★

After the *Dred Scott* decision, Lincoln did a lot of hard thinking about what was happening in the country. One side of him was seriously pessimistic about the chances of reversing the course set by the Democrats. He had already written to a friend that "there is no peaceful extinction of slavery in prospect for us" and that "the condition of the slave in America . . . is now fixed and hopeless of change for the better." Another side of Lincoln, however, was optimistic—and his plan to continue fighting was a mark of great leadership.

Abraham Lincoln understood that major change is more evolution than revolution. It takes time. And the more difficult the change, the longer it takes to achieve. An entrenched institution like slavery had to be approached gradually, step by step, over a long period of time. Containment was only Lincoln's first stated objective, but he would simultaneously appeal to the "natural sense of justice" in all Americans by continuing to insist that slavery was a moral wrong.

Lincoln also recognized that to have a major impact, he was going to have to get even more politically involved. Stephen A. Douglas, as one of the national leaders for slavery's expansion, needed to be challenged more often and more aggressively than ever before. In 1858, Douglas was coming up for reelection to the Senate, and Republicans believed he would be vulnerable. Here was another opportunity for Lincoln to "rise with the occasion." But it would take a lot of courage to run for Congress again. Everybody knew a big fight was brewing and not a single spot in the nation would be free from violence — including the U.S. Senate, itself.

On May 22, 1856, South Carolina congressman Preston Brooks, accompanied by two other Southern congressmen (Laurence Keitt of South Carolina and Henry A. Edmundson of Virginia), calmly walked into the Senate chamber, approached Massachusetts senator Charles Sumner at his desk, and savagely beat him with a heavy cane. After receiving repeated blows to the head, face, and shoulders, a bloodied Sumner staggered into the aisle, where Brooks continued to beat him until the cane broke into pieces. Sumner ultimately collapsed, unconscious, beaten to within an inch of his life. It would be three years before he would recover and return to the Senate.

LINCOLN ON LEADERSHIP FOR TODAY

Unpopular Supreme Court Decisions

Abraham Lincoln was outraged by the Supreme Court's *Dred Scott* decision (March 6, 1857), which ruled that no black person could be a citizen of the United States. After cooling down, Lincoln reaffirmed his respect for the Court, but spoke out forcefully against the decision, saying that it was "erroneous" and involved "partisan bias." He further exposed errors in the Court's reasoning, addressed the inherent moral problem with the decision, urged that it be overturned, and, finally, stated that it was "not disrespectful" to disagree with such a ruling. A major blow against the *Dred Scott* decision occurred with ratification of the 13th Amendment to the Constitution outlawing slavery (December 6, 1865), and it was finally rendered moot by the 14th Amendment, which granted citizenship to "all persons born or naturalized in the United States" (July 9, 1868).

Such controversial rulings are less frequent but still happen today. In 2010 and 2012, for example, two very controversial Supreme Court decisions were issued (one related to campaign finance and the other regarding the Affordable Care Act).

In *Citizens United v. Federal Election Commission* (January 21, 2010; 5–4), the Supreme Court held that the government may not prevent corporations from spending unlimited amounts of money to support or denounce election candidates. The Court based this ruling on the First Amendment's guarantee of free speech, essentially ruling that corporations are, in effect, human beings, which, according to the dissenting justices, they definitely are not. There are three significant impacts of this case: (1) wealthy citizens are allowed to control elections; (2) special interest groups, many of which represent the pecuniary interests of major industries and corporations, are also allowed to have undue influence on elections; and (3) the costs of election campaigns are effectively increased significantly, and average American citizens without the right political connections are prevented from being elected to important positions.

In *National Federation of Independent Business v. Sebelius* (June 28, 2012; 5–4), the Supreme Court upheld the individual mandate to purchase health insurance as being valid under the Constitution through the power of Congress to tax its citizens. A singular problem with this ruling was that even though the mandate was not sold to the American public as a tax, the Supreme Court treated it as one. In fact, government representatives repeatedly and explicitly stated that the federal mandate to acquire health insurance was *not* a tax. This ruling set a dangerous precedent in that it requires citizens to purchase something they may not want.

My sense is that if Lincoln were here today, he would be just as outraged with these two Supreme Court rulings as he was with the *Dred Scott* decision. He would advise American citizens to (1) advocate respect for the Supreme Court, (2) formally state their disagreement with the Court's rulings, (3) cite and express support for dissenting opinions, (4) specifically expose errors in the Court's majority opinion, (5) point out the moral objections to the ruling, and (6) work to get the issue back before the Supreme Court so the decision can be reversed. Additionally, as president of the United States, Lincoln would strive for balance on the Supreme Court by appointing more moderate justices and avoiding extremists.

Health Care

Back in Lincoln's day, *the* entrenched institution with *major* pecuniary interests at stake was slavery. Today in the United States, it is health care. More than half of all bankruptcies are health care related, because costs are enormous. Thousands of people die unnecessarily every year because they cannot get access to affordable and quality health care. The growing gap between the haves and have-nots is most obvious when it comes to people receiving adequate medical services.

An increasing number of progressives would like to see a new U.S. system modeled after those in European nations. But many conservatives object and describe such systems as socialist in nature. Nearly every developed nation in Europe has universal health care, although the plans are implemented in varying ways. They may be funded by the government or the private sector, but taxes for the European systems are definitely higher. Medical, physician, and prescription drug costs are more reasonable and better kept in check. In Washington, D.C., the health care industry spends many millions of dollars to lobby members of Congress to keep control of the American health care system in the hands of major corporations.

Abraham Lincoln's reputation as a humanitarian is well known, and I believe his position would be that every American citizen should have access to reasonably priced and quality health care. A person's ability to purchase medical services *must not* be treated like a commodity with an option to be purchased in varying sizes and qualities. Lincoln would also say that it is morally wrong to make obscene profits off people's health. Neither should citizens face bankruptcy if they come down with a life-threatening disease.

So how would Lincoln change things? First of all, he would realize that the flawed national health care system cannot be changed overnight. Leaders who wish to heal such a system must develop a long-term plan and try to achieve change in small increments. Lincoln would avoid taking an extreme position and work to expose moral problems with the current system. He would urge people to get more involved politically and to support representatives who will serve the vast majority of citizens rather than special interests. If he were president now, I believe Lincoln would advocate for a single-payer, or "Medicare for all," government-sponsored system. He would also encourage and support a constitutional amendment that would guarantee affordable health care for every American citizen as a basic human right.

[Stephen A. Douglas] is blowing out the moral lights around us. . . . He is penetrating . . . the human soul and eradicating the light of reason and the love of liberty. . . . He is in every possible way preparing the public mind, by his vast influence, for making the institution of slavery perpetual and national.

— Abraham Lincoln
Galesburg, Illinois
October 7, 1858

This government of ours is founded on the white basis. It was made by the white man, for the benefit of the white man, to be administered by the white man.

— Stephen A. Douglas
Chicago, Illinois
July 9, 1858

ISSUES
The 24-Hour News Cycle
Campaign Finance Reform
Alcohol and the Legalization of Marijuana

5

The Eternal Struggle Between Right and Wrong

★ ★ ★

I T WAS A SPECTACLE, an entertainment extravaganza. Twelve thousand people showed up, more than twice the number of eligible voters in that political district. Both candidates were escorted into town by mile-long parades replete with horse-drawn carriages, brass bands, pretty "young ladies," grand marshals, and dozens of individual riders serving as escorts. People, buckboards, and buggies lined the crowded streets. Party stalwarts waved political banners. Hotels and private houses were so full that thousands had to camp out in the surrounding countryside. And that was just the first debate on August 21, 1858, in Ottawa, Illinois (about 90 miles west-southwest of Chicago). There would be six more over a two-month span at various locations across the state. Each would draw thousands. All would attract an unprecedented amount of media coverage. And the entire country would take notice.

The Ottawa open-air debate took place at two o'clock in the afternoon on a simple wooden platform. The mayor was there. Local leaders from both the Republican and Democratic Parties took their places. Then the two candidates mounted the stage. And what a contrast they presented. Stephen A. Douglas was five feet four inches tall and impeccably dressed in a plantation-style blue suit, a white ruffled shirt, and a dapper gray felt hat. Abraham Lincoln, at six feet four inches, was a foot taller. He wore an all-black, ill-fitting, wrinkled suit, a plain linen shirt, and a large stovepipe hat. Douglas looked like a puppet. Lincoln resembled a scarecrow. Douglas had a deep, booming voice and, in private, often used profanity. Lincoln had a high-pitched voice that, at times, became quite shrill—but he never cursed. Douglas was the incumbent United States senator running for reelection. Lincoln, the challenger, was merely a private citizen. Douglas believed that the extension of slavery should be allowed. Lincoln fought it.

One would assume that these two very different political adversaries would have little to do with each other. But, in fact, they were good friends who had known each other for years. Both had practiced law in Springfield in the 1830s and had served together in the Illinois legislature. They had a mutual respect, even an admiration, for one another. Douglas called Lincoln "my friend," and "a very able, very honest man." When some people commented offhandedly that his opponent would be easy to dispose of in the debates, Douglas corrected them. "[Lincoln] is the strong man of his party, full of wit, facts, and dates," he said, "and the best stump speaker, with his droll ways and dry jokes, in the West. . . . If I beat him my victory will be hardly won." Likewise, Lincoln admired Douglas, also called him "my friend," and said, approvingly, that the "politicians of his party have been looking upon him to be the President of the United States." William Herndon noted that Lincoln believed Douglas to be "fair," "generous and honest," and that "it was only in politics" they had major differences.

The truth is that the two men had spent many a long winter's night debating state and national issues with other lawyers and judges around potbellied stoves in the old days. In 1839, they had even joined forces to move the capital of the state from Vandalia to Springfield. Lincoln and Douglas also frequently saw each other at social gatherings, and as young bachelors, both had been rivals for the hand of Mary Todd.

On one occasion, Lincoln was offered a drink and politely declined. "Mr. Lincoln, won't you take something?" asked Douglas.

"No, I think not."

"What? Are you a member of a temperance group?"

"No, not a member of any temperance society," replied Lincoln. "But I am temperate *in this*. I don't drink."

By all historical accounts, Abraham Lincoln did not consume alcohol, but in his position regarding others partaking, he was both tolerant and liberal. In the 1838–1839 Illinois House of Representatives, he voted against a prohibition measure that went down to defeat. He also spoke out on the issue a number of times, once saying the "position that all habitual drunkards [are] utterly incorrigible and therefore must be turned adrift and damned without remedy" is "repugnant" and "uncharitable." Lincoln further stated that "we non-drunks do not deserve any particular credit" and that "drinkers just may be our superiors," because there is a "proneness in the brilliant to fall into this vice." Alcohol, he said, often seems to drain "the blood of genius and generosity."

Lincoln never did change his position against the prohibition of alcohol, much to the chagrin of temperance workers who visited him in the White House after he became president. One group gave him a long sermon that too much drinking by Union generals was the cause of military defeats, to which Lincoln replied: "I can't quite see it, because the rebels drink more and worse whiskey than we do!" He is also reported to have shocked other temperance people who complained about General Ulysses S. Grant being drunk on whiskey at the Battle of Shiloh by saying: "Maybe we should send a bottle of that whiskey to all our generals!" Even Secretary of State William Seward took note of Lincoln as a teetotaler. "I have always wondered how any man could ever get to be President of the United States with so few vices," said Seward good-naturedly. "The President, you know, I regret to say, neither drinks nor smokes." Lincoln, who was standing nearby and overheard the remark, stepped up. "Now, that is a doubtful compliment," he said. "I recollect once being outside a stagecoach in Illinois, and a man sitting nearby offered me a cigar. I told him I had no vices. He said nothing, but smoked for some time, and then grunted out: 'It's been my experience that folks who have no vices generally have very few virtues.'"

Stephen A. Douglas made no secret of the fact that he enjoyed a cocktail at social gatherings. And as a politician fighting for his seat in the Senate, he did not hesitate to use alcohol to try to make Lincoln look bad in the eyes of the public. In their first debate in Ottawa, for instance, Douglas noted that he and his opponent went way back together. "I was a school teacher in the town of Winchester, and he was a grocery keeper in the town of Salem," said Douglas. *[In those days, "grocery" was another word for saloon. So Douglas was insinuating that Lincoln sold liquor.]* In his response, Lincoln stated that Douglas was "woefully at fault," that he had "never kept a grocery anywhere in the world," but that "I don't know as it would be a great sin if I had."

★ ★ ★

Abraham Lincoln kicked off his campaign for the United States Senate on June 16, 1858, with a carefully prepared speech at the Illinois State Capitol in Springfield. Prior to its delivery, he showed a draft to some friends and asked for comments. William Herndon, especially, objected to the content as being too radical for the occasion. "The proposition is indisputably true, and I will deliver it as written," Lincoln responded. And then he said that he wanted to "use some universally known" expression "in simple language" so that it may "strike home to the minds of men in order to rouse them to the peril of the times." The "expression" to which Lincoln was referring came from the New Testament, specifically the Gospels of Mark (3:25) and Matthew (12:25). The most important passage read as follows:

> A house divided against itself cannot stand. I believe this government cannot endure, permanently, half slave and half free. I do not expect the Union to be dissolved — I do not expect the house to fall — but I do expect it will cease to be divided. It will become all one thing or all the other. Either the opponents of slavery will arrest the further spread of it, and place it where the public mind shall rest in the belief that it is in the course of ultimate extinction; or its advocates will push it forward, till it shall become lawful in all the States, old as well as new — North as well as South.

From there, Lincoln took on both the Kansas-Nebraska Act and the *Dred Scott* decision as posing major dangers to the nation. It was a bold, morally courageous speech to make at the time, because many people were thinking and whispering the same sentiments but were afraid to speak out. Lincoln, however, felt that the path on which the country was headed needed to be both confronted and discussed openly. He further audaciously suggested that "the power of the present political dynasty" had to be "met and overthrown." "That is what we have to do," said Lincoln, and if America did not act, and act soon, he continued, "we shall lie down pleasantly dreaming that the people of Missouri are on the verge of making their state free — and we shall awake to the reality, instead, that the Supreme Court has made Illinois a slave state."

Lincoln would continue the strong moral tone of his "House Divided" speech throughout the Senate campaign, and certainly in his debates with Stephen A. Douglas. As a matter of fact, Lincoln frequently raised the stakes to be nothing less than the difference between right and wrong. "When Judge Douglas says that whoever, or whatever community wants slaves, [and] they have a right to have them, he is perfectly logical if there is nothing wrong in the institution," said Lincoln at the Quincy debate. "But if you admit that [slavery] is wrong, he cannot logically say that anybody has a right to do wrong." Furthermore, Lincoln went on to remark that their entire "difference of opinion, reduced to its lowest terms, is [nothing] other than the difference between the men who think slavery a wrong and those who do not think it a wrong."

Douglas responded to his opponent's moral reasoning by attacking him. "Mr. Lincoln has not character enough for integrity and truth," he said. Douglas also deliberately and relentlessly played the race card. Lincoln, he said, was one of the "Black Republicans" in favor of "Negro equality." "I do not regard the negro as my equal," he said. "This government of ours is founded on the white basis. It was made by the white man, for the benefit of the white man, to be administered by white men." To cheers from his supporters in the crowd, Douglas also said, "I am in favor of preserving . . . the purity of the blood, . . . the purity of government from any mixture or amalgamation with inferior races."

Such racist comments put Abraham Lincoln on the spot, not

to mention the defensive. He was dealing mostly with a white supremacist electorate (all men and all white) who did not like his anti-slavery comments. Lincoln had to be careful not to alienate them too much, so he often made statements he may not have meant. But he almost always followed up with a moral clarification. For example, in the Ottawa debate, Lincoln said: "I agree with Judge Douglas [the black man] is not my equal in many respects — certainly not in color, perhaps not in moral or intellectual endowment. But in the right to eat the bread, which his own hand earns, he is my equal and the equal of every living man." Here was Lincoln, the politician, skirting the boundaries of propriety so as not to offend too many voters. And he did it more than once. However, when compared with his more frequent remarks about the moral cause for which he stood, there was little doubt what he would do once he obtained a powerful enough position.

Douglas also strategically attacked Lincoln's time in the United States Congress: "He distinguished himself by his opposition to the Mexican War, taking the side of the common enemy against his own country," he charged. He further accused Lincoln of voting against the appropriation bill that sent supplies to soldiers in the field. That allegation was particularly upsetting to Lincoln, who, according to one witness, grabbed O. B. Ficklin by the coat collar "and in no gentle manner lifted him from his seat as if he had been a kitten, shook him until his teeth chattered, and screeched: '[Ficklin] was a member of Congress at the time and he personally knows it to be a lie!'" Ficklin then stood up and corroborated Lincoln's statement. *[After the debate, Ficklin came up to his old friend and said, "Lincoln, you nearly shook all the Democracy out of me today!"]*

Lincoln was often perplexed at how to respond to the litany of false charges Douglas leveled against him. "I don't want to quarrel with him [or] call him a liar," he said on one occasion, "but when I come square up to him, I don't know what else to [say] if

I must tell the truth." Another time, the frustrated Lincoln joked, "I have really come to the conclusion (for I can reconcile it no other way) that [Judge Douglas] is crazy!" Once in a great while, Lincoln would also blast his opponent for repeated demagoguery. "He is blowing out the moral lights around us," said Lincoln at the Galesburg debate. "He is penetrating . . . the human soul and eradicating the light of reason and the love of liberty. . . . He is in every possible way preparing the public mind, by his vast influence, for making the institution of slavery perpetual and national."

★ ★ ★

Lincoln felt he had to refute Douglas's false claims as quickly as possible, because if he did not, they might be printed as fact the next day. And back then, if something made it into print, most people took it as gospel. Newspapers were the mass media of the day. People all over the country read them everywhere — at home, on trains, in hotels, and on the streets. Every city and most small towns in America had at least one newspaper that provided a daily stream of news and information. They were enormously influential on public opinion and, with time, became increasingly partisan. There were Democratic and Republican newspapers, conservative and progressive newspapers, Northern and Southern newspapers. Some tried to remain independent. But all not only reported the news, they frequently told their readers how they should think and feel about any political issue or event.

Certainly, the Lincoln-Douglas debates were big news in the state of Illinois. Chicago and Peoria newspapers sent reporters to transcribe every word the candidates uttered and then printed full texts in the next day's issue. Minor story lines were exploited — where Douglas dined, what train Lincoln rode on, when they arrived, whom they met, when they left. And it wasn't long before the rest of the country became interested. The *New York Times* labeled Illinois "the most interesting political battle ground in the Union," and its editor, Henry J. Raymond, sent his own reporter to the field for exclusive coverage.

Through most of his political career, Abraham Lincoln took special care to cultivate and maintain good relationships with reporters. "He never overlooked a newspaper man who had it in his power to say a good or bad thing of him," said William Herndon. And indeed, Lincoln frequently dropped in on local newspaper offices during his travels around the state. In West Urbana, for example, he met a young editor named William O. Stoddard of the *Central Illinois Gazette,* who promptly reported in the next issue that "the Hon. Abraham Lincoln" had visited. "Few men can make an hour pass away more agreeably," Stoddard wrote. *[William O. Stoddard would later become an assistant to President Abraham Lincoln in the White House.]*

Lincoln was also extraordinarily careful about what he communicated to members of the press. "Write no letters which can possibly be distorted . . . ," he once advised Senator Lyman Trumbull. "There are men on the constant watch for such things." And although he treated reporters "with extreme courtesy," Lincoln was not averse to correcting them when they made errors. To the editor of the *Missouri Republican,* Lincoln once wrote: "Please pardon me for suggesting that if the papers, like yours, which heretofore have persistently garbled and misrepresented what I have said, will only fully and fairly place it before their readers, there can be no further misunderstanding."

★ ★ ★

The final Lincoln-Douglas debate took place in Alton, Illinois, on October 15, 1858, only two weeks before the general election. Between the seven debates, Lincoln had been barnstorming the state, usually traveling by train, staying in local taverns and hotels, and eating at local restaurants. By the end of the campaign, Lincoln was running out of money, because he bore most of the travel costs himself. "I have been on expenses so long without earning anything, that I am absolutely without money now for even household purposes," he wrote to a friend. "[Adding that] to my loss of time and business, bears pretty heavily upon one no better off in this [world] than I."

Political campaigns back then were financed primarily by the local political parties and the candidates, themselves. In addition to paying his own personal expenses, Lincoln contributed $500 to the statewide effort, but by the end of the campaign, the Republican state committee had run up a debt of more than $65,000. To make up the difference, party leaders sent out $300 assessments to its members across the state — including the candidate, himself. And after the election, Lincoln studiously helped collect the assessments and pay off the debt.

Funding political campaigns had always been a tricky business for a candidate who really didn't think much about money, except to worry that he didn't have enough. During the presidential election year of 1860, Lincoln initially balked at running for president at all, because he couldn't afford it. "I cannot enter the ring on the money basis — first, because it is wrong — and secondly [because] I have not, and cannot get the money," he wrote to a friend. "But for certain [things] in a political contest, the use of some [money] is both right and indispensable."

★ ★ ★

On November 2, 1858, Illinois voters turned out in record numbers for the general election. The Republicans won a majority of the popular vote, but they did not garner enough seats to gain control of the state legislature, which remained in Democratic hands. Had U.S. senators been elected by a direct vote of the people back then, Abraham Lincoln probably would have won the election. As it stood, however, Lincoln was defeated on a straight party-line vote (54–46) when the new legislators convened on January 5, 1859.

Lincoln had lost again. Privately, he was depressed. Publicly, he remained upbeat. To one friend, he said, "Douglas has taken this trick, but the game is not played out yet." To another, he wrote, "The fight must go on. Let no one falter. The *question* is not half settled."

"I am glad I made the late race," Lincoln also wrote to a supporter. "It gave me a hearing on the great and durable question of the age. . . . And although I now sink out of view and shall be forgotten, I believe I have made some marks which will tell for the cause of civil liberty long after I am gone."

On August 21, 1858, at the end of the first debate in Ottawa, "an immense crowd, numbering at least five thousand persons, lifted [Abraham Lincoln] upon the shoulders of two stout men" and carried him along the street, followed by a brass band and people shouting "Hurrah for Lincoln."

Two months later, on October 15, 1858, Lincoln ended the last debate in Alton with these words:

"That is the real issue. That is the issue that will continue in this country when these poor tongues of Judge Douglas and myself shall be silent. It is the eternal struggle between these two principles — right and wrong — throughout the world. They are the two principles that have stood face to face from the beginning of time, and will ever continue to struggle. The one is the common right of humanity and the other the divine right of kings. It is the same principle in whatever shape it develops itself. It is the same spirit that says, 'You work and toil and earn bread, and I'll eat it.' No matter in what shape it comes, whether from the mouth of a king who seeks to bestride the people of his own nation and live by the fruit of their labor, or from one race of men as an apology for enslaving another race, it is the same tyrannical principle."

LINCOLN ON LEADERSHIP FOR TODAY

The 24-Hour News Cycle

Back in Lincoln's day, candidates were celebrities, and national and statewide elections were partly entertainment. Although there was no 24-hour news cycle as we now know it, newspapers competed for breaking news, which was released as fast as possible. In fact, like television today, newspapers were the mass media of the day. People read them everywhere, they grew to be increasingly partisan, and, as a result, they became enormously influential on public opinion.

Today, most newspapers are available online. Cable television and radio news channels are on all day and all night. It's called the "24-hour news cycle," but it should really be termed the "24-hour news *business*" due to intense competition among media organizations for audience share. The truth is that the 24-hour news cycle has become more of a race for ratings and advertisers than a forum dedicated to reporting relevant news and information. Demands by media corporations for increased profits have led to a decline in professional journalistic standards and neutrality. Statements and opinions made by the media are often not grounded in reality or fact. Real news is often nothing more than tabloid journalism, and what is referred to as "analysis" sometimes more resembles gossip. The real issue, just as it was in Lincoln's day, is that many people simply believe what they see and hear, whether it is true or not.

If Lincoln were here today, I believe he would remind us that media organizations, even though most claim to be unbiased, naturally divide into partisan factions. So masking opinion as news is nothing new. He would also counsel us that the 24-hour news cycle is not going away. It really can't be changed all that much, and it is certainly not going to be eliminated in a nation where freedom of speech is a guaranteed right under the Constitution. So if it cannot be ignored, then it must be dealt with in some form or fashion.

My bet is that Abraham Lincoln would advise us to participate in the process whenever and wherever we can. He'd say we should use new media, such as blogs, podcasts, Internet chats, online videos, and social media. If he were president, he'd strive for more direct access to the people, so he could tell them the truth himself. He'd hold town hall meetings in Louisville, Kentucky, or Hannibal, Missouri. He'd convene cabinet meetings on the West Coast or in New Orleans or Chicago. He'd make sure the press was there so that people all across the country could watch. Most important, I think, is that Lincoln would advise today's leaders and candidates not to use sound bites so much. Make time for dialogue, discussion, and debate. And *listen, listen, listen* to what the people have to say. Only if you know their wants and needs, their desires and expectations, and their hopes and dreams can you ever hope to lead them effectively.

Campaign Finance Reform

When Abraham Lincoln was a politician, campaigns were financed primarily by the local political parties and the candidates themselves. Lincoln, for instance, paid nearly all of his own personal and travel expenses. He could get his message out back then because the newspapers constantly competed for campaign substance and information.

Today, political candidates have to pay to get their messages out — on radio, on television, in newspaper advertisements, and so forth. In fact, getting elected to national office has turned into a multimillion-dollar industry unto itself — where the candidates with the biggest war chests are the most likely to get elected. In turn, fewer and fewer average people are accorded fair and adequate representation in our government. And those who *are* elected tend to be beholden to special interest groups with major financial assets. It has reached the point where congressmen and senators spend more than half of their working days at call centers asking for donations so they can get reelected.

Many people believe that because of the high costs of national campaigns, the government in Washington, D.C., has become a faceless and soulless private club, which nobody but the rich and famous or the well-connected can join. So what would Abraham

Lincoln say about all this? I think he'd say that this exclusive "club" needs to be eliminated immediately, as it has lost sight of what our representatives are elected to do.

More important, what would Lincoln actually do to fix this problem? I believe he'd lead an effort in the highest levels of the federal government, including the legislative and judicial branches, to take corrective action. And if they refused to act, then "We the People" must organize and take action on our own initiative. We must create a system where our public representatives spend most of their time helping the people of their districts or states, rather than begging for money. We must go back to the Supreme Court and reverse *Citizens United*. We must propose and support new campaign finance laws that have severe penalties for violations — and then *enforce those laws*. Some possible solutions include (1) limiting the amount of money that can be spent on campaigns, (2) prohibiting special interest groups and major corporations from having undue influence on the outcome of elections (possibly by limiting or even eliminating their contributions altogether), and (3) banning all so-called soft money from American politics.

This one issue is destroying our democratic system of government. It is becoming a government of the *rich* people, by the *rich* people, and for the *rich* people. And that has to change.

Alcohol and the Legalization of Marijuana

In Abraham Lincoln's day, there were people who drank robustly, there were people who preached the evils of alcohol, and there was everybody else in between. Lincoln was in the middle. He did not drink, but he was against the prohibition of alcohol. He said that "we non-drunks do not deserve any particular credit," and he believed that "drinkers just may be our superiors."

Today, there is an ongoing controversy over the effects and use of alcohol versus the effects and use of marijuana (cannabis). Alcohol is legal for adults over 21. Use of marijuana is against federal law. However, more and more states are legalizing cannabis for medical purposes and several have made recreational use lawful. In effect, then, there is a major conflict between federal and state law on the issue of legalized marijuana. But, almost paradoxically, there is no controversy over the legal use of alcohol, which (according to numerous scientific studies) is far more addictive and dangerous than cannabis.

So where might Lincoln come down on the use of alcohol and the legalization of marijuana? I believe he would study the science carefully and put everything in a broad perspective. In my opinion, he would conclude that moderate use of alcohol is okay for most people. However, alcoholism is a disease, and those who are afflicted with it should not be condemned or ostracized. Rather, they should be treated as if they had any other illness — with medical expertise, compassion, and understanding. *[Lincoln would most likely feel the same way about people with a major drug addiction.]*

I also believe that Lincoln would conclude that medical science has demonstrated that marijuana is no more harmful than alcohol, perhaps even less so. Furthermore, cannabis has proven medicinal properties that relieve pain and symptoms related to a number of diseases and afflictions. Therefore, rather than being criminalized, marijuana should be legalized and regulated, just like alcohol. Lincoln would propose and support federal legislation to that effect so that there is no conflict between federal and state policy.

I am glad to know that there is a system of labor where the laborer can strike if he wants to! I would to God that such a system prevailed all over the world.

— Lincoln, in support of the
1860 New England Shoemakers' Strike
Hartford, Connecticut
March 5, 1860

ISSUES
Labor Unions and the Right to Strike
Income Inequality and the Minimum Wage
Big Business and Congressional Lobbying

6

The Tendency of Prosperity to Breed Tyrants

★ ★ ★

Ladies and gentlemen, I believe I lack the credentials to speak to such a distinguished group. I feel much like I did back when I was riding the circuit in Illinois and happened to cross paths with a woman on horseback along a narrow trail in the woods. I reined in my horse and pulled out to let her pass. But when the woman reached me, she halted her horse and looked at me for the longest time.

"Well, for heavens sake," she finally said. "I do believe you are the ugliest man I ever saw."

"Madam, I expect you're right," I replied. "But, you see, I just can't help it."

"No, you can't help it," she said. "But you might stay at home."

Abraham Lincoln sometimes used that little story to open a speech by poking fun at his homely appearance, and then followed up by modestly implying that his audience might have dug up a better speaker if he had stayed at home. Well, in the year and a half following his election loss for Illinois's U.S. Senate seat, the one thing Lincoln did not do much of was stay at home when he was asked to give a speech somewhere else. And in the aftermath of the debates with Stephen A. Douglas, he was quite literally bombarded with requests to speak, mostly by Republicans who now looked at him as a national spokesman for their cause.

In 1859 alone, Lincoln gave more than a dozen talks across the six Midwestern states of Ohio, Wisconsin, Illinois, Iowa, Indiana, and Kansas. In these speeches, Lincoln continued to hammer away at the slavery issue, because he still wanted it openly discussed across the land. "Slavery is doomed, and that within a few years," he said in Columbus. "Evil can't stand discussion. . . . What kills the skunk is the publicity it gives itself. What a skunk wants to do is keep snug under the barn — in the daytime, when men are around with shotguns."

During this speaking tour, Lincoln also began articulating the platform of his party with an eye on getting a Republican elected president of the United States in 1860. In Milwaukee, he took the opportunity of speaking before the Wisconsin State Agricultural Society to convey the Republican principle that one class of people does not have to be subservient to another. "Some [Democrats] say that nobody labors unless somebody owning capital . . . induces [them] to do it," said Lincoln. But others disagree, he continued, and say that "labor is prior to, and independent of capital; that, in fact, capital is the fruit of labor, and could never have existed if labor had not first existed. [Therefore], labor is the superior — greatly the superior — of capital." In other words, Abraham Lincoln was saying that those with a lot of money would be nowhere without the working people who earn it for them. He was speaking out against an ever-growing farm system run by a wealthy few land barons who believed that their low-paid laborers (or slaves, even) were better off this way than being allowed to sell their skills on the open market.

Lincoln went on to link farming with obtaining a good education. "No other human occupation opens so wide a field for the profitable and agreeable combination of labor with cultivated thought, as agriculture," he said. Lincoln then brilliantly made his case that all Americans should "cultivate" intellectual learning the same way farmers "cultivate" the soil. "Let us hope that by the best cultivation of the physical world, beneath and around us — and the intellectual and moral world within us, we shall secure an individual, social, and political prosperity and happiness — [one] that conforms to what must occur in a world less inclined to wars and more devoted to the arts and peace."

Lincoln was such a hit on his speaking tour of the Midwest that, by the fall of 1859, Republican newspapers in Illinois, Ohio, New York, and Pennsylvania were suggesting he would be a good candidate for president himself. Initially flattered, Lincoln modestly played down the idea. At the same time, however, he knew he had an outside shot at the nomination — *and was definitely interested* in that possibility. But Lincoln did not want to appear too anxious, so he decided to run something of a stealth campaign — below the radar of the more prominent and favored candidates. He did not, for instance, make a formal announcement of his candidacy. "I really think it best ... that no concerted effort ... should be made," he said to a friend. And, with a roar of laughter, he self-deprecatingly told a journalist, "Just think of such a sucker as me as President!" *[In those days, "sucker" was a good-natured slang term for an Illinoisan.]* Although outwardly reserved, Lincoln probably recalled what he said to a man who came up to him before one of the Lincoln-Douglas debates expressing concern that Douglas seemed confident of victory:

> You have seen two men about to fight? Well, one of them brags about what he means to do. He jumps high in the air, cracking his heels together, smites his fists, and wastes his breath try-

ing to scare everybody. You see the other fellow. He says not
a word. His arms are at his sides, his fists are closely doubled
up, his head is drawn to the shoulder, and his teeth are set firm
together. He is saving his wind for the fight, and as sure as it
comes off, he will win it or die a-trying.

Sure enough, Lincoln worked behind the scenes to craft a plan
to at least give himself a chance at his party's nomination. At the
request of newspaper editors, for instance, he wrote out several
short biographies, which were not only printed in the papers, but
were later turned into tens of thousands of pamphlets that emphasized his humble beginnings. Lincoln also sent dozens of letters to Republicans all over the country urging them to stay unified, to plan long term rather than only short term, and to think
national in scope rather than only local. "In every locality, we
should look beyond our noses," he urged, "and at least say *nothing* on points where it is probable we shall disagree."

Lincoln also collected old newspapers and edited the complete
texts of his debates with Douglas. Then he convinced a large publishing firm in Columbus, Ohio, to print a book entitled *Political Debates Between Hon. Abraham Lincoln and Hon. Stephen A.
Douglas, in the Celebrated Campaign of 1858, in Illinois.* The volume immediately became a best seller, with more than 30,000
copies sold in 1860 alone — and many of those were personally
autographed and given away by Lincoln himself. Additionally,
in an unprecedented effort to move public opinion his way, Lincoln became his own publisher by investing in a foreign-language
newspaper with German immigrant Heinrich Theodor Canisius.
The contract specified that Canisius would manage the paper and
keep "all incomes and profits." The *Illinois Staats-Anzeiger* (State
Advertiser) was published weekly in Springfield and designed to
reach the many German immigrants in America who had fled
persecution after the failed European revolutions of 1848. *[One
month after winning the Republican nomination, Lincoln relin-*

quished his ownership of the Staats-Anzeiger, *which ceased operations before he became president.]*

Another major element of Abraham Lincoln's campaign plan was to increase his personal visibility in the eastern United States. So when he received an invitation to speak at the Young Men's Central Republican Union of New York, Lincoln immediately accepted, and then laid out plans for a speaking tour of the Northeast. He was particularly excited about the chance to speak in New York City, not only for the large audience it would attract, but also because the leading Republican presidential candidate, Senator William Seward, hailed from that state. Furthermore, Lincoln would also be guaranteed solid press coverage, as two of the leaders of the sponsoring organization were the poet William Cullen Bryant and the editor of the *New York Tribune,* Horace Greeley.

On February 27, 1860, a capacity crowd of 1,500 Republicans (both men and women) paid 25 cents each to hear Abraham Lincoln speak at the Cooper Institute in Manhattan. Conscious that some New Yorkers might view him as a country bumpkin, and wanting to make a good impression, Lincoln meticulously researched and prepared what was to be one of the longest speeches he ever gave. He began by pointing out that Stephen A. Douglas had openly claimed that America's Founding Fathers had specifically stated that the federal government could not prevent the expansion of slavery. But with his lawyerly precision, Lincoln took the audience back to the American Revolution and proved Douglas wrong by demonstrating that "a clear majority" of the signers of the Constitution (21 of 39) *did not* favor the expansion of slavery, and that they *did not* forbid federal government action to stop it. He further pointed out that the only thing that would satisfy slavery proponents in the South would be if the opposition would "cease to call slavery wrong, and join them in calling it right." And finally, Lincoln ended his speech with an emotional rallying cry for all Republicans to stay strong and united:

Let us [not] be diverted by ... contrivances such as groping for some middle ground between the right and the wrong. . . . Neither let us be slandered from our duty by false accusations against us, nor frightened from it by menaces of destruction to the Government, nor of dungeons to ourselves. LET US HAVE FAITH THAT RIGHT MAKES MIGHT, AND IN THAT FAITH, LET US, TO THE END, DARE TO DO OUR DUTY AS WE UNDERSTAND IT.

When Lincoln finished, people in the audience leapt to their feet and gave him a sustained ovation. The next day's *New York Tribune* wrote that it was "one of the most convincing political arguments ever made in this city" and that "no man ever made such an impression on his first appeal to a New York audience." All four New York newspapers published the speech in its entirety, which led to it being picked up by other outlets across the country. And Horace Greeley personally saw to it that Lincoln's Cooper Institute speech was published in pamphlet form and sold nationwide (at four cents a copy).

Meanwhile, Lincoln headed north for Rhode Island, New Hampshire, and Connecticut. He gave at least one major speech a day (11 in total), pausing for a short rest in Dover, New Hampshire, to spend time with his 16-year-old son, Robert, who was attending nearby Phillips Exeter Academy. Many of the students attended Lincoln's Dover speech and, by one account, felt sorry for their classmate. "Isn't it too bad Bob's father is so homely?" they thought. He was "tall, lank, awkward, dressed in a loose, ill-fitting black frock coat, with black trousers, ill-fitting and somewhat baggy at the knees." And that was a fairly typical description of Lincoln when he was onstage. He had black, somewhat bushy hair that often wasn't combed. His face looked sad most of the time and was adorned with thick black eyebrows, a large nose, and a ruddy complexion. He had a disproportionately long neck, leaned forward when he walked, and often stood with his hands locked behind his back. But Lincoln was so effective at public speaking that people quickly forgot what he looked like.

Much of what Lincoln said on his New England tour was a rehash of the Cooper Institute address. But he also spent a good amount of time discussing the plight of organized labor, because one of the largest strikes in American history (prior to the Civil War) was currently taking place there. Twenty thousand shoe factory workers in Massachusetts had walked off their jobs and gone on strike for higher wages and better conditions. Both male and female workers listed demands, marched through the streets, and held mass demonstrations in a year that many historians mark as the beginning of the modern Industrial Revolution.

Lincoln, who read about the event in the newspapers and chatted about it with locals, came down on the side of the strikers. "I am glad to know that there is a system of labor where the laborer can strike if he wants to!" he said in Hartford. "I would to God that such a system prevailed all over the world." At the same time, however, this unannounced presidential candidate also made it clear that he would not assail big business. In New Haven, Lincoln remarked: "I don't believe in a law to prevent a man from getting rich. It would do more harm than good. So while we [the Republicans] do not propose any war upon capital, we do wish to allow the humblest man an equal chance to get rich with everybody else."

Taking a position between two seemingly opposing factions was a trademark of Abraham Lincoln's leadership style. He was a moderate, middle-of-the-road politician who could look at any issue and have empathy for both sides. While he was keenly aware that some financially successful people tended to think they were better than everybody else, he also understood that many others who had toiled up from poverty remained humble. So Lincoln continued to balance an individual *employee's* right to rise with an *employer's* right to grow a business. One side or the other didn't have to prevail, he believed. Both could win and prosper.

Overall, Abraham Lincoln was fairly consistent in maintaining this balance throughout his political career, even as president. As a matter of fact, businessmen who visited the White House often didn't know which man they would get — the pro-business Lincoln or the pro-labor Lincoln. One entrepreneur incurred the president's wrath after pitching him a moneymaking scheme. "No!" said Lincoln firmly. "Do you take the President of the United States to be a commission broker?" And when railroad rates were raised in New York after some transportation routes to the South were cut off, Lincoln chastised the businessmen responsible and urged the state's governor to use his power and influence to reduce the rates.

On the flip side, Lincoln frequently interceded on behalf of big business. When executives complained that they were not being paid in a timely fashion, he usually arranged for the payments. "The government can not afford to accept services and refuse payment for them," he said. Much of Lincoln's support of big business was grounded in the realization that such large companies helped fund the Union war effort through the taxes they paid. Amusingly, he even sent off one newly appointed tax assessor to the Wall Street district in New York with the following advice: "You are going on good missionary ground. [So] preach God and Liberty to the 'bulls' and 'bears,' and get all the money you can for the government."

Although Lincoln wanted to support both sides, when he was forced to pick one or the other, he usually came down in favor of the individual. Twice during his administration, workers went on strike in the Navy yards, delaying the completion of new ships. To one of those labor groups, Lincoln said: "I know the trials and woes of workingmen [and] I have always felt for them" — then he took their side and demanded that the contractors get the ships built on time.

Over and over again, President Lincoln emphasized his commitment to the common man's right to rise in the workplace. "The strongest bond of human sympathy, outside of the family relation, should be one uniting all working people, of all nations, and tongues, and kindreds," he wrote to the New York Workingmen's Association. And in his first annual message to Congress, Lincoln both repeated his support for average workers *and* issued them a cautionary warning to not relinquish their rights:

> No men living are more worthy to be trusted than those who toil up from poverty; none less inclined to take or touch [that] which they have not honestly earned. Let them beware of surrendering a political power which they already possess, and which if surrendered will surely be used to close the door of advancement against such as they and to fix new disabilities and burdens upon them till all of liberty shall be lost.

★ ★ ★

A little more than two months after Lincoln completed his speaking tour of New England, the Republican Party held its national convention (from May 16 to 18, 1860) in, of all places, Chicago, the largest city in Lincoln's home state. Although the unannounced candidate had finally given permission for a small group of close friends to work toward his nomination, most pundits did not give him much of a chance. After all, there were several already-announced candidates that seemed more qualified, and, besides, Lincoln seemed to have a penchant for losing national races.

One thing that the experts couldn't know, however, was the power of Lincoln's ability to forge and maintain personal relationships. And the group he had working for him at the convention burned with both personal devotion and loyalty to him. It included Judge David Davis (who rode the Eighth Circuit with Lincoln) and fellow lawyers Leonard Swett and Ward Hill Lamon. U.S. senator Lyman Trumbull, who had never forgotten Lincoln's magnanimity after losing the 1854 Senate seat, also provided enthusiastic support. These men would make good use of Chicago newspapers and citizens who wanted to see one of their own become president of the United States. They arranged for positive stories to be published frequently, and even packed the convention hall by printing up hundreds of fake admission tickets and giving them to Lincoln supporters. Ten days earlier, at the Illinois Republican State Convention in Decatur, they had also managed to dub their candidate "the Rail Splitter" by parading Lincoln's cousin, John Hanks, into the arena with two fence rails and a sign that read:

> ABRAHAM LINCOLN; The Rail Candidate; FOR PRESIDENT IN 1860; Two rails from a lot of 3,000 made in 1830 by Thos. Hanks and Abe Lincoln — whose father was the first pioneer of Macon County.

Although Lincoln's core group worked mainly behind the scenes, it was Lincoln, himself, who directed the larger political strategy. "My name is new in the field," he said, and "I am not the first choice of a very great many." So part of his strategy was to keep quiet as long as possible, "give no offense to others," and "leave them in a mood to come to us, if they [are] compelled to give up their first love."

While Lincoln did not appear eager for the nomination, the top four candidates were openly salivating at the possibility. Senator William H. Seward from New York was the overall favorite, followed by Ohio governor Salmon P. Chase, Pennsylvania senator Simon Cameron, and, finally, former U.S. representative Edward Bates of Missouri. Although Lincoln was not the first choice of most Republicans, he did have the unanimous backing of the delegates from Illinois, which was an important swing state. Furthermore, because he was not a major player on the national stage and had deliberately kept quiet up to the very last moment, Lincoln had made few political enemies. Meanwhile, the Rail Splitter's team worked frantically to secure those delegates who were Seward's political enemies, many of whom hailed from the New England states Lincoln had just visited.

When, on the first ballot, Seward failed to secure the necessary

233 votes to win, delegates began moving toward Illinois's favorite son. On the second ballot, Lincoln was in second place, only three votes behind. And on the third, Lincoln garnered 364 votes to win the nomination over Seward, who then moved to make the final count unanimous.

Abraham Lincoln was at home in Springfield when he heard the news — sitting in the offices of the *Illinois State Journal,* which had been receiving regular telegraph updates from Chicago. After receiving congratulations from the newspaper personnel, Lincoln left to go home and tell the good news to his family. Outside, he was immediately mobbed by neighbors shaking his hand and patting him on the back. "There's a little woman at our house who is interested in this," he said breaking away. "I'll go and let her see it."

As Lincoln started to walk home, however, a group of Irish immigrant laborers stood back out of respect, and began to applaud and cheer him. Lincoln stopped and smiled at them. "Gentlemen, you had better come up and shake my hand while you can," he said. "Honors elevate some men, you know."

Wise statesmen as they were, they knew the tendency of prosperity to breed tyrants, and so they established these great self-evident truths, that when in the distant future [should] some man, some faction, [or] some interest set up the doctrine that none but rich men, or none but white men, were entitled to life, liberty and the pursuit of happiness, their posterity might look up again to the Declaration of Independence . . . so that truth, and justice, and mercy, and all the humane and Christian virtues might not be extinguished from the land.

Abraham Lincoln, on the Founding Fathers
August 17, 1858

LINCOLN ON LEADERSHIP FOR TODAY

Labor Unions and the Right to Strike

The modern Industrial Revolution had its beginnings right about the time Abraham Lincoln became president. Labor unions began forming shortly after the Civil War ended and by the 1880s were major forces in America. The unions were originally created to protect people from unsafe working conditions, harsh treatment, and unfair compensation. During the Great Depression, they were given legal protection under the New Deal legislation of President Franklin Roosevelt and soon became politically allied with the Democratic Party and progressives in general. The post–World War II economic boom saw a vast expansion of labor unions, and by the late 1970s more than 20 million American workers had joined a union. But with that kind of membership, and the money and power that come with it, many union executives became corrupt. Strikes were called for little reason other than to increase union coffers, and legitimate business operations were sometimes seriously hampered. As a result, in the 1980s and 1990s, businesses rebelled across the board by funding campaigns to bust the unions. And gradually, as membership dropped, labor unions began to lose power and influence.

Today, pro-business conservatives control much of Congress and have great influence on the outcome of state and national elections. As a result, major policy has been created to significantly reduce the power of labor unions, or even eliminate them altogether. In 2011, for instance, the governor of Wisconsin (in an effort to help balance the state budget) pushed a bill through the state legislature eliminating the collective bargaining rights of most state public sector unions with regard to pay raises, health care, and pensions. The resulting protests from outraged state workers made national headlines and led to an unsuccessful recall election.

Abraham Lincoln's position in regard to workers going on strike for higher wages and better working conditions was clear and unwavering. He supported shoe factory workers in Massachusetts and wished "that such a system prevailed all over the world." And he insisted that "labor is the superior of capital," meaning that wealthy businesspeople would be nowhere without their laborers.

I believe if Lincoln were president today, he would reaffirm his stance that all employees in every industry should have the right to strike against poor wages or unfair working conditions, if they wish. Employees who want to join a union should be allowed to do so. Furthermore, governments (whether federal, state, or local) should not interfere in labor's right to negotiate with management in either the private sector or the public sector. And non–union members *should not* be required to pay union dues. In my opinion, Lincoln would sponsor federal legislation that respects both the rights of workers and the right of corporations to run a successful business. There must be a balance between the two.

Income Inequality and the Minimum Wage

These are two issues that Abraham Lincoln did not confront directly. The first national minimum wage was set in 1938 as part of the New Deal's Fair Labor Standards Act (which also established a 40-hour workweek). In Lincoln's time, income was more equally divided among the masses (excluding slaves, of course) — although statistics varied widely from region to region in the United States. According to historical studies (based on censuses and property records), the top 1 percent of U.S. households in 1860 generated 10 percent of the nation's income. Today, it's estimated that the top 1 percent generate 20 percent of the nation's income — and that same 1 percent receive 90 percent of yearly income gains.

Virtually every reputable economist today agrees that the gap between affluent people and those struggling to make ends meet is widening at unprecedented rates nearly everywhere. However, there is significant debate around causes and effects. Arguments are made for and against the causes being related to such things as (1) techno-logical advances eliminating traditional jobs in both manufacturing and service, (2) current tax rates favoring the wealthy, (3) stock markets being manipulated for quick and easy profits, and (4) the degree of greed among corporate executives. There is less disagreement regarding the immediate and long-term effects of the widening gap between rich and poor, which include (1) a shrinking middle class, (2) poverty on the rise, (3) increasing inequities in access to health care, education, and adequate compensation in the job market, (4) erosion of confidence in government, (5) danger to the long-term health of the economy, (6) despair for the future, and (7) whether or not the gap fosters political instability.

I believe Abraham Lincoln would conclude that the widening chasm between the haves and have-nots is unfair to average- and lower-wage earners. Recall that he once said, "I hold the value of life is to improve one's condition." I think Lincoln would also hold that an individual's right to rise and live the American dream is impeded if there is not a strong middle class and a solid economic structure to support it. Therefore, the federal government *must* provide a system that allows people to improve themselves.

Specifically, it's my opinion that Lincoln would sponsor legislation designed to halt the shrinking of the middle class and to lift people out of poverty. He would support the implementation of a fair and reasonable minimum wage (mandated by federal law) in order to both ensure adequate living conditions and maintain human dignity. An independent government committee should set the dollar amount, and a periodic increase in the minimum wage should be implemented to keep up with the cost of living and inflation. Government should also consider offering tax incentives to major corporations and small businesses to help out the communities in which they live. For instance, if a Michigan-based company helps to pay public teachers in Detroit, or helps replace lead water pipes in Flint, it would receive a generous tax credit.

Income "inequality" violates what Lincoln believed was the true promise of America. To him, it was about equality and fairness to all — "to afford all, an unfettered start, and a fair chance, in the race of life."

Big Business and Congressional Lobbying

Throughout history, there has been a natural human tendency for the rich to use vast resources to perpetuate their own interests, often at the expense of the lower classes and society in general. In Lincoln's day, there was an agricultural farm system run by a small number of land barons who believed that their low-paid laborers were better off working for them than being allowed to sell their skills in an open market. And they collaborated to keep wages low, to manipulate the system around them to their own best interests, and to influence government representatives (whom they often sponsored) to pass laws for their personal benefit.

Today, large corporations spend billions of dollars not only to influence decisions made at the highest levels of government, but also to influence the inner workings of Congress. Some industries employ not just one or two professionals for this purpose, but a hundred or more. These "lobbyists" not only influence legislation, they often are allowed to write part or all of the laws that benefit the industries of their employers, including those in health care, banking, telecommunications, defense contracting, energy, the environment, and on and on and on. The lobbyists, themselves, often argue that their services are indispensable, because congressional staffers are too poorly paid, or don't have the time or expertise to write responsible and informed legislation.

If Abraham Lincoln were here today, I believe he would see right through that manufactured smoke screen. Remember that he once tossed a man out of his office for proposing that the government enter a moneymaking scheme, saying: "No! Do you take the President of the United States to be a commission broker?" Make no mistake, Lincoln would be outraged at the undue influence lobbyists have on Congress. But what would he do to fix the problem?

First, I think it's important to note that Lincoln would realize it does more harm than good to wage war on big business. After all, major corporations drive the general economy and provide jobs for millions of Americans. Rather, he would probably concentrate on the specifics of the problem. However, I also think he would be tough on both the corporations and their lobbyists. He might sponsor and support federal laws that prohibit anyone associated with an industry group or corporation from ever writing legislation that might impact their own interests. In fact, such a bill might ban all lobbyists from walking the halls of Congress, from sponsoring private travel and gift giving to public officials, and eliminate all influence peddling in general. Lincoln might also budget more funding for the Congressional Research Service and Government Accountability Office, both of which provide service to members of Congress for researching and writing legislation.

If Abraham Lincoln, as president, could write the Emancipation Proclamation by himself, why can't a U.S. congressman or senator write their own bills? Our laws would certainly end up being shorter and more to the point, rather than being the massive, confusing, poorly written, and never-read volumes they tend to be today.

My advice is to keep cool. If the great American people will only keep their temper, on both sides of the line, the troubles will come to an end.

— Lincoln, on his way to Washington, D.C.,
to take the presidential oath of office
Pittsburgh, Pennsylvania
February 15, 1861

ISSUES
Any Immediate Crisis
The Confederate Flag

7

The Better Angels of Our Nature

★ ★ ★

FROM HIS NOMINATION in May to the presidential election in November, Abraham Lincoln made only one public appearance. He did not campaign. He did not barnstorm the country. He barely left Springfield. "It has been my purpose, since I have been placed in my present position to make no speeches," he said at that one rally in August 1860. "I appear . . . here at this time only for the purpose of affording myself the best opportunity of seeing you and enabling you to see me." Shortly thereafter, he wrote to a friend: "*Justice* and *fairness* to *all* is the utmost I have said or will say."

The Republican ticket of Lincoln and his vice presidential running mate, Senator Hannibal Hamlin of Maine, had solid backing from nearly all the Northern states. But the Democratic Party was hopelessly split. Northern Democrats had nominated Stephen A. Douglas to run for president, and Southern Democrats had chosen the current vice president, John C. Breckinridge, a Kentucky native. Additionally, former Tennessee senator John Bell became a contender when nominated by the newly formed Constitutional Union Party. Political reality, then, made it apparent that Lincoln would win the presidency if he did not create any controversy. So he refused all speaking engagements, and when asked to answer questions on specific issues, he would reply with something like "My published speeches contain nearly all I could willingly say."

On Tuesday, November 6, 1860, Americans across the land turned out in record numbers. *[Voter turnout that year was an astounding 81.2 percent.]* And though Abraham Lincoln was not even on the ballot in any Southern state, he won the election handily with 180 electoral votes by carrying (as predicted) every Northern state. *[The other three candidates totaled only 123 electoral votes combined.]* Lincoln also received the highest popular vote tally, although it was only a plurality, at 39.8 percent. Douglas came in second with 29.5 percent.

Reaction to Lincoln's victory ran the gamut from elation in the North to outrage in the South. South Carolina immediately began making noises about seceding from the Union, which was not a surprise since many Southerners had threatened to do just that if a Republican won the presidency — and then it would be the North's fault. "That is cool," said Lincoln when he heard the threat. "A highwayman holds a pistol to my ear and mutters through his teeth, 'Stand and deliver or I shall kill you, and then you will be a murderer!'"

Despite the festering ill will, Lincoln continued to stay quiet in Springfield, issuing only a few brief statements. "Let us at all times remember that all American citizens are brothers of a common country, and should dwell together in the bonds of fraternal feeling," he wrote on November 20, 1860. But Lincoln made no formal victory speech, and indeed would not make any formal remarks until his inauguration, which would be on March 4, 1861. That four-month span provided more than enough time for six Southern states to organize themselves into the Confederate States of America. South Carolina was, indeed, the first to secede (on December 20, 1860) followed by Mississippi (January 9, 1861), Florida (January 10, 1861), Alabama (January 11, 1861), Georgia (January 19, 1861), and Louisiana (January 26, 1861). Most of these states made it clear they were leaving the Union over slavery. South Carolina, for example, specifically mentioned in its secession declaration "the election of a man to that high office of president of the United States whose opinions and purposes are hostile to slavery." And Mississippi stated: "Our position is thoroughly identified with the institution of slavery — the greatest material interest of the world."

According to one witness, when Lincoln first heard the news of South Carolina's secession ordinance, "the President-elect did not experience any extraordinary shock. Timidity is evidently no element in his composition [because] it certainly does not make him any more willing to listen to compromises." And certainly, in this immediate crisis, nearly everybody had an opinion on what needed to be done. Moderates wanted to offer compromises on slavery so the Union could be held together. Hard-liners wanted no compromises at all, and some were itching for war. Lincoln, who really had no power to do anything as president-elect, did not panic. "My advice is to keep cool," he said. "If the great American people will only keep their temper, on both sides of the line, the troubles will come to an end."

Congress, however, made several last-ditch attempts to prevent disunion. Kentucky senator John J. Crittenden, for instance, proposed six constitutional amendments and four congressional resolutions that, if taken in total, would guarantee the permanent existence of slavery in the United States. And in the very last moments of the final congressional session, several Republicans lent

their support to a proposed irrevocable constitutional amendment prohibiting the federal government from ever interfering
with the institution of slavery.

In Springfield, Lincoln calmly reviewed these proposals and
listened to all the arguments pro and con. The pressure on him to
offer some sort of compromise to the Southern states was enormous. He was also well aware that although the issue of slavery
was the South's main reason for secession, he now had to be concerned with the more perilous issue of preserving the nation. After all, on March 4 he was going to take an oath to "preserve, protect, and defend the Constitution of the United States."

After carefully thinking things through, Lincoln refused to
separate the two issues or give up one for the other. "On the question of extending slavery under the national auspices, I am in-
flexible," he wrote to William Seward. "I am for no compromise
which *assists* or *permits* the extension of the institution on soil
owned by the nation." And Lincoln was going to "hold firm, as
with a chain of steel," on that point. Regarding the proposed compromises in Congress, Lincoln said he would "suffer death before
I will consent . . . to any such concession or compromise which
looks like buying privilege to take possession of this government
to which we have a constitutional right." More specifically, Lincoln rejected the Crittenden Compromise because "it acknowledges that slavery has equal rights with liberty." And after hearing
of Lincoln's objection, Republicans in the Senate tabled the entire
package.

The president-elect was equally unbending on allowing the
nation to be broken apart. "We have just carried an election on
principles fairly stated to the people," he wrote to a friend. "Now
we are told in advance the government shall be broken up, unless
we surrender to those we have beaten, before we take [office]. If
we surrender, it is the end of us, and of the government." To his
assistant, John Nicolay, he also said: "We must settle this question
now, whether in a free government, the minority have the right
to break up the government whenever they choose. If we fail it

will go far to prove the incapability of the people to govern themselves." Any compromise, he further pointed out, "would lose us everything we gained by the election. . . . The tug has to come, and better now, than any time hereafter."

A number of people around Lincoln at the time noticed what seemed to be a transformation in both his demeanor and physical appearance. "Instead of intimidating the President-elect, [secession] only made him firmer and more decided in his views on the reckless and unjustifiable attempt to break up the Union," noted one observer. "He will not give way to terror . . . and despair." And Thomas D. Jones, who had traveled to Springfield to sculpt a bust of Lincoln, noted that "about two weeks before [he] left for Springfield, the former Lincoln was no longer visible to me." Rather, Jones noted, he had become so determined, that "his face was transformed from mobility into an iron mask."

★ ★ ★

While dealing with the immediate secession crisis, President-elect Lincoln also found time to put together a presidential cabinet. And for starters, he was able to talk his four main rivals for the Republican nomination into accepting appointments. Lincoln made William H. Seward his secretary of state, Salmon P. Chase secretary of the Treasury, Simon Cameron secretary of war, and Edward Bates attorney general. When asked about this most unusual political move, Lincoln stated that he "needed the strongest men of the party in the Cabinet" and that he "had no right to deprive the country of their services."

Lincoln rounded out his appointments with Caleb B. Smith as interior secretary, Gideon Welles as secretary of the Navy, and Montgomery Blair as postmaster general. These seven men were not old cronies who were being rewarded with plum jobs. They were strong-thinking individuals who were leaders in their own right — all with egocentric personalities, and all with their own ideas about how the country needed to be run. Strategically, however, Lincoln couldn't have picked a better cabinet to provide a variety of opinions. Three were from northeastern states: Seward (New York), Welles (Connecticut), and Cameron (Pennsylvania). Two were from the Midwest: Chase (Ohio) and Smith (Indiana). And two were from slave states: Bates (Missouri) and Blair (who lived in Maryland). The group also consisted of both former Whigs and former Democrats, which could have led to a clash in political ideals. But when it was suggested that the more Democratic-leaning secretaries might have an edge in numbers, Lincoln replied: "You seem to forget that I expect to be there and, counting me as one, you see how nicely the cabinet would be balanced."

Over the next four years, Lincoln would have his hands full dealing with his cabinet members, all of whom seemed to be perpetually at war with each other either through personality disagreements, petty criticisms, or personal ambitions. It would be Lincoln, however, who would hold everybody together by building personal relationships with each, by accepting responsibility when things went wrong in their departments, and by coming to their rescue when they were criticized by the public. The truth is that Lincoln liked the members of his cabinet. He was a people person with exceptional people skills. In fact, Lincoln enjoyed interacting with others so much that he carved time out of each day for just that purpose — beginning in Springfield when he became president-elect and continuing throughout his entire presidency.

The president-elect's office in the Illinois State Capitol was always crowded with visitors. Everyone wanted to see him — for an autograph, to offer support, to ask for a government job, or to just shake his hand. And virtually every person who got in to see Lincoln would hear him spout out some sort of story or witty remark. When one young man, for instance, vowed to give his life for the president and the nation, Lincoln said he was reminded of a young soldier in the American Revolution who was going off to war, and his sweetheart made him a sash to wear into battle bearing the motto "Liberty or Death." He looked at it intently and then asked if she would change the wording to "Liberty or Badly Wounded."

There were also a number of politicians who visited Lincoln in Springfield to implore that he modify his hard-line positions on slavery and secession. To one official, he refused, stating that if he did so, he "would be as powerless as a block of buckeye wood." To another, he quoted one of Aesop's fables:

Do you remember the fable of the lion and the woodman's daughter? Well, Aesop wrote that a lion was very much in love with a woodman's daughter. The fair maid referred him to her father. The lion applied for the girl. The father replied: "Your teeth are too long." The lion went to a dentist and had them extracted. Returning, he asked for his bride. "No," said the woodman, "your claws are too long." Going back to the dentist, he had them drawn. Then he returned to claim his bride, and the woodman, seeing that the lion was now completely unarmed, beat out his brains.

May it not be so with me if I give up all that is asked?

Exactly one month before Abraham Lincoln was to be sworn in as president of the United States, a convention was convened in Montgomery, Alabama, to form the Confederate States of America. Delegates from the seceding states showed up on February 4, 1861, and a provisional Congress was seated. A resolution to design a new Confederate flag was quickly approved, and Mississippi senator Jefferson Davis was chosen as the Confederacy's new president. By February 8, 1861, the new Congress had adopted a provisional constitution. Similar to the U.S. Constitution, it provided for a Supreme Court and included the current 12 amendments. Unlike the U.S. Constitution, however, it made specific mention of the institution of slavery in several places. Article IV, Section 3(3), for example, read, in part: "In all . . . territory, the institution of negro slavery as it now exists in the Confederate States, shall be recognized and protected by Congress."

On February 11, 1861, Abraham Lincoln began a 12-day train trip that would take him through 8 states on his way to Washington, D.C. There were only three cars on the train, assigned to journalists, local dignitaries, and the Lincoln family, respectively. As the procession meandered its way through Illinois, Indiana, Ohio, Pennsylvania, New York, New Jersey, and Delaware, cheering citizens gathered all along the pre-published 1,900-mile route — and Lincoln had the train stop at every small town so he could step out on the rear platform and say a few words.

On that first day, Lincoln delivered brief remarks at Tolono and Danville, Illinois, and at Lafayette, Thorntown, and Lebanon, Indiana, before staying the night in Indianapolis, where he gave a longer speech from the balcony of his hotel.

On February 11, 1861, Alexander Stephens was inaugurated vice president of the Confederate States of America. [Recall that, in 1848–1849, Stephens had served in Congress as a representative from Georgia and, along with Lincoln, had been a member of the group calling themselves the Young Indians.]

On the second and third days of his trip (February 12–13, 1861), Lincoln passed through Lawrenceburg, Indiana, and Cincinnati and London, Ohio, before stopping at the state capital in Columbus, where 60,000 people greeted him before he addressed the Ohio legislature. Over the next five days, the president-elect's train went through 24 towns and cities in Ohio, Pennsylvania, and New York before stopping for the night in Albany, where (on February 18, 1861) he would formally address the New York legislature.

On February 18, 1861, Jefferson Davis was inaugurated president of the Confederate States of America. Among other things, Davis stated that "governments rest only on the consent of the governed," that separation from the Union was a "necessity, not a choice," and that it was "actuated solely by the desire to preserve our own rights and promote our own welfare."

From February 19 to 21, 1861, Lincoln passed through 11 towns in New York and New Jersey before stopping in Trenton to make a couple of short speeches to the New Jersey legislature. In the first address, he recalled how he had first learned of George Washington's crossing of the Delaware:

> Way back in my childhood, [during] the earliest days of my being able to read, I got hold of a small book [titled] "Weems's Life of Washington." I remember all the accounts given of the battlefields and struggles for the liberties of the country, and none fixed themselves upon my imagination so deeply as the struggle here at Trenton, New-Jersey.... I recollect thinking then that there must have been something more . . . that those men struggled for — something that held out a great promise to all the people of the world [for] all time to come. I am exceedingly anxious that this Union, the Constitution, and the liberties of the people shall be perpetuated in accordance with the original idea for which that struggle was made.

The next day, after passing through Wilmington, Delaware, Lincoln stopped in Philadelphia to speak at Independence Hall on George Washington's birthday (February 22, 1861). Here again, in the very place where the Declaration of Independence was signed, Lincoln invoked the history of the nation. "I am filled with deep emotion at finding myself standing here," he began. "I have never had a feeling politically that did not spring from the sentiments embodied in the Declaration of Independence," which, he went on to say, "gave promise that in due time the weights should be lifted from the shoulders of all men, and that *all* should have an equal chance." Finally, in a remarkable vow of commitment, Lincoln said: "I would rather be assassinated on [the] spot than to surrender that principle."

Later that same day, the president-elect traveled to Harrisburg, where he delivered a short speech to the Pennsylvania legislature. Then, due to the report of a possible assassination attempt in Baltimore, Lincoln left the procession and secretly traveled to Washington, D.C. (arriving at 6:00 a.m. on February 23, 1861).

On February 23, 1861, the people of Texas formally voted to secede from the Union, becoming the seventh state to join the Confederacy. The Texas secession ordinance specifically mentioned "the disloyalty of the Northern States . . . and the imbecility of the Federal Government." The Confederacy, it stated, was "established by the white race, for themselves and their posterity; that the African race [was] regarded as an inferior and dependent race, and in that condition only could their existence in this country be rendered beneficial or tolerable." The institution of slavery, it went on to state, "is abundantly authorized and justified by the experience of mankind, and the revealed will of the Almighty Creator, as recognized by all Christian nations."

On March 4, 1861, Abraham Lincoln was sworn in by Chief Justice Roger B. Taney as the 16th president of the United States. Seated on the platform with him were, among others, outgoing president James Buchanan, Vice President Hannibal Hamlin, Mary Todd Lincoln and the Lincolns' sons (Robert, Willie, and Tad), and Stephen A. Douglas and his wife, Adele. When Lincoln moved to the lectern, he took off his hat and looked around for a place to stash it. Douglas jumped up, took it from his old friend, and held Lincoln's hat for the entire speech.

In his inaugural address, Lincoln pointed out that the "only substantial dispute" between North and South was that "one section of our country believes slavery is right, and ought to be extended, while the other believes it is wrong, and ought not to be extended." However, he refused to recognize the newly formed Confederacy. "No state can lawfully get out of the Union [and] resolves and ordinances to that effect are legally void," he said. He further stated that any acts of violence "against the authority of the United States are insurrectionary or revolutionary."

Near the end of his remarks, Lincoln plainly threw down the gauntlet. "In *your* hands, my dissatisfied fellow countrymen, and not in *mine,* is the momentous issue of civil war," he said. "The government will not assail *you.* You can have no conflict, without being yourselves the aggressors."

But then Lincoln made an eloquent plea for peace:

> We are not enemies, but friends. We must not be enemies. Though passion may have strained, it must not break our bonds of affection. The mystic chords of memory, stretching from every battlefield, and patriot grave, to every living heart and hearthstone, all over this broad land, will yet swell the chorus of the Union, when again touched, as surely they will be, by the better angels of our nature.

On March 4, 1861, the Confederate flag, which became popularly known as the "Stars and Bars," was raised for the first time on the dome of the capitol building in Montgomery, Alabama.

★ ★ ★

Elected "by a mere accident," Abraham Lincoln found himself in a situation that, by modern standards, is almost unbelievable to contemplate. Seven states had seceded to form the Confederate States of America, and the South had taken control of the Mississippi River (lifeblood of the nation's commerce and trade), along with most federal forts, arsenals, government buildings, banks, and other financial institutions. There was also a dire national economic crisis taking place (spurred by the Financial Panic of 1857), which resulted in a national recession, thousands of business and bank failures, high unemployment, government budget deficits, and a skyrocketing national debt. The fractured United

States Congress had adjourned, having taken no action whatsoever, and James Buchanan had reportedly declared that he was the last president of the United States.

On paper, Abraham Lincoln was not qualified to be president. He had no formal education, no military experience, was a Washington outsider, had never been a senator or a governor or, for that matter, even held an executive leadership position of any kind. What was he going to do?

It is 8:00 a.m. on February 11, 1861, at the
train depot in Springfield, Illinois.
A thousand people have shown up to say good-bye.
Lincoln shakes many hands as he walks through the crowd.
He steps up onto the back platform of the last train car.
He removes his hat and asks for silence.
The men in the crowd remove their hats.
Lincoln speaks:

"My friends — No one, not in my situation, can appreciate my feeling of sadness at this parting. To this place, and the kindness of these people, I owe everything. Here I have lived a quarter of a century, and have passed from a young to an old man. Here my children have been born, and one is buried. I now leave, not knowing when, or whether ever, I may return, with a task before me greater than that which rested upon Washington. Without the assistance of the Divine Being who ever attended him, I cannot succeed. With that assistance I cannot fail. Trusting in Him who can go with me, and remain with you and be every where for good, let us confidently hope that all will yet be well. To His care commending you, as I hope in your prayers you will commend me, I bid you an affectionate farewell."

Lincoln, moved to tears, bows and turns to enter the train car.
The locomotive moves slowly out of sight.

LINCOLN ON LEADERSHIP FOR TODAY

Any Immediate Crisis

During his four years in office, President Lincoln was confronted with an almost unbelievable number of immediate and severe crises that, at any time, could have brought down the nation he had sworn to preserve, protect, and defend. From outright secession and rebellion by half the country to major Union losses in battle, threatened attacks on Washington, behind-the-scenes scheming by political enemies, international threats to side with the Confederacy, disruptions in the economy, border state atrocities, persistent lack of funds to pay for the war, congressional investigations, and the meddling of backseat drivers and Monday-morning quarterbacks — it was a never-ending string.

Genuine leaders, however, do not lose control. And Abraham Lincoln's unofficial 10-step approach to handling any immediate crisis can be an effective model for leaders in any field: (1) Keep cool. (2) Reassure everybody that all will yet be well. (3) Assemble your team of diverse, competent, and strong-thinking individuals. (4) Consider yourself a part of the team. (5) Gather information and analyze the situation. (6) Seek advice from all sides of the issue. (7) Encourage advisers to speak their minds so that you receive a wide range of options. (8) Take time to think and deliberate. (9) Even if a consensus is reached, reserve the right to take a firm stand and make the final decision yourself. (10) Communicate your decision to everybody involved.

The Confederate Flag

When the South seceded from the Union to form the Confederate States of America, its bottom line was to preserve the institution of slavery — with a sincere belief that states' rights provided the legal authority to do so. Today, many Southerners honestly view the Stars and Bars as a symbol of Southern pride and of their cultural history.

Others, especially minorities, view it with disdain as a symbol of racism.

Major controversy was reignited in June 2015 when a white gunman murdered nine black people during a prayer meeting at the Emanuel African Methodist Episcopal Church in Charleston, South Carolina. Photographs with the shooter brandishing the Confederate flag and burning the American flag ignited a national firestorm over public display of the Stars and Bars. One side wanted to ban it from being flown on state or federal government grounds and have it removed as a symbol of any state. Others didn't want any changes at all, arguing that just because one man on the lunatic fringe displayed the Confederate flag as a sign of racism, its historical importance as a symbol of Southern pride was not completely negated.

So if Abraham Lincoln were here today, on which side of this issue would he come down? In my opinion, he would first deplore the violence that took place at the Charleston church and would publicly mourn for the victims and their families. Then I believe he would point out that there is a historical element to this issue that must not be ignored. In a classic personal struggle between the better and darker angels of our nature, many Southerners fought to preserve slavery, while sincerely believing in the value and integrity of states' rights. And as Lincoln said of the South in his second inaugural address, "Let us judge not that we be not judged."

During his lifetime, Abraham Lincoln accommodated as much tolerance for dissent as any human being can muster. On this modern issue, I don't think he would give in to a minority perspective just because it was politically expedient to do so. Rather, he would most likely stake his ground on principle, and then compromise to support that principle. Accordingly, the 10th Amendment to the U.S. Constitution reads: *"The powers not delegated to the United States by the Constitution, nor prohibited by it to the States, are reserved to the States respectively, or to the people."* So in a country like ours, how far can the federal government go in telling a state what to do?

My sense is Lincoln would feel the anguish and pain of people who view the Confederate flag as racist, but he would also place the issue in a larger context. This is one of those humble lessons in democracy. Often, people say things we strongly object to, or disagree with, or find completely wrong in some form or another. But we still must accommodate the overall spirit of the Union when we disagree or don't get our way. This is a measure of our individual capacity to coexist. I believe Lincoln would allow the states to make their own decisions on this subject. He would not issue a "king's proclamation" that the Confederate flag not be flown publicly — because, if he were to do so, then there would be no point in the American Revolution (which was waged against tyranny of the individual) ever having been fought in the first place.

You, gentlemen, come here to me and ask for peace on any terms, and yet have no word of condemnation for those who are making war on us. You express great horror of bloodshed, and yet would not lay a straw in the way of those who are organizing in Virginia and elsewhere to capture this city. The rebels attack Fort Sumter, and your citizens attack troops sent to the defense of the Government, and the lives and property in Washington, and yet you would have me break my oath and surrender the Government without a blow. There is no manhood or honor in that. . . . Go home.

— Lincoln, to a group of 50 citizens from Baltimore
April 22, 1861

ISSUES
Presidential Executive Orders
Domestic Terrorism
Gun Control

8

With Firmness in the Right

★ ★ ★

THE FIRST THING that was handed to me after . . . the inauguration," Lincoln told a friend, "was the letter from Major Anderson [at Fort Sumter] saying that their provisions would be exhausted before an expedition could be sent to their relief."

Major Robert Anderson and his 85 men were under siege by more than 3,000 Confederate troops in the middle of Charleston Harbor at Fort Sumter, the only federal installation in South Carolina still in U.S. government hands. Over the next few weeks, the new president met repeatedly with his cabinet and the nation's top military commander, General Winfield Scott, to gather facts, verify information, and confer. "I see no alternative but surrender," Scott told the president. He also said he had already drafted a letter ordering Major Anderson to do just that, and further informed Lincoln that, in his opinion, it would take a force of 25,000 to relieve Fort Sumter. *[At the time, the entire federal army consisted of only 16,000 men.]* The consensus of the cabinet, too, was that the fort had to be surrendered — and Secretary of State Seward had even taken the initiative (without informing Lincoln) of trying to arrange a peaceful evacuation.

Lincoln, however, refused to surrender. In his inaugural address, he had pledged to the North that he would "hold, occupy, and possess the property and places belonging to the government." Moreover, he had assured the South that "the government will not assail *you*" and that "you can have no conflict, without being yourselves the aggressors." So Lincoln was boxed in by his own promises. He *would not* surrender and he *could not* hold the fort by force.

To buy some time, Lincoln ordered General Scott to reevaluate the situation. Then he began considering all his options and their consequences. "To abandon [Fort Sumter]," he concluded, "would be utterly ruinous [and] could not be allowed." But any kind of aggressive military operation would enrage the South and probably lead to the secession of more states. That, too, would create a problem, because Lincoln absolutely had to keep the border states (Kentucky, Maryland, and Missouri) in the Union, or he would "lose the whole game." So what was he going to do?

On his own, Lincoln came up with a creative alternative that had not really been discussed or considered. He would neither surrender the fort nor deploy reinforcements. Rather, he would send only supplies to the garrison, *and* he would let both the governor of South Carolina and the American press know in advance what he was going to do. President Lincoln, now acting forcefully as the nation's commander in chief, set the entire operation in motion on April 6, 1861. The decision about whether to start a war would be in Southern hands.

In Charleston Harbor on the afternoon of April 11, 1861, Confederate general P.G.T. Beauregard sent a communiqué to the Union forces demanding an immediate evacuation of the fort. Major Anderson steadfastly refused. So at 4:40 a.m. on April 12, barely an hour after the first ships from the Union relief expedition arrived on the outskirts of Charleston, Confederate batteries opened fire on Fort Sumter. And after 34 hours of continual bombardment, Major Anderson surrendered his garrison, the American flag was lowered, and the Confederate flag was raised.

The South had fired the first shots of the Civil War — and public opinion in the North would be on Lincoln's side.

★ ★ ★

On the very day that Fort Sumter fell, three delegates from Virginia (which was considering a declaration of secession) called on President Lincoln and asked him what policy he intended "to pursue in regard to the Confederate States." His answer was brief, frank, and in writing. Now that "an unprovoked assault" had been made and, with it, "the commencement of actual war against the Government," wrote Lincoln, "[he would] in every event . . . repel force by force." Lincoln's response was remarkable given the fact that he really had no means at his disposal to back it up. "We were entirely unprepared for such a conflict," recalled Secretary of War Simon Cameron. "[We were] absolutely without even the simplest instruments with which to engage in war."

Fearless and determined, however, Lincoln responded boldly to the crisis. He called his cabinet together on April 14 and met with them at all hours for days on end. Almost immediately, Lincoln used his executive power under the Constitution to call out 75,000 members of the various state militias. *[The number was recommended by General Winfield Scott, and the states of Massachusetts, New York, Maine, and Indiana quickly responded.]* Then, because the 1795 Militia Act authorized service for only 30 days after the beginning of the next congressional session, Lincoln set the date of July 4 to call Congress into special session. That decision also suited Lincoln, because he didn't have time for a debate. It gave him nearly three full months to act on his own.

Shortly after word reached Washington that Virginia delegates had voted (on April 17, 1861) to secede from the Union pending a vote of the people, Lincoln instituted a naval blockade along the coasts of the states in rebellion. "A competent force will be posted so as to prevent entrance and exit of vessels from the ports," the order read. Once again, the Union did not have the means to enforce such a blockade, which constituted more than 3,000 miles of Atlantic Ocean and Gulf of Mexico coastline, and included the major ports of Charleston, Mobile, and New Orleans. Then, the very day that Lincoln signed the blockade order, a mob of Confederate sympathizers in Baltimore attacked troops from Massachusetts on their way to defend the nation's capital. *[Nine soldiers and a dozen civilians were killed in the fighting.]* Railroad bridges were also burned and telegraph lines cut between Baltimore and Washington by, as Lincoln phrased it, "organized and combined treasonable resistance in the State of Maryland."

With Union troops stalled outside Baltimore and rebellion fever rising all around him, Lincoln barely blinked. He convened his cabinet again on Sunday, April 21, 1861, and, this time, took a series of unprecedented executive actions, which included spending money without the approval of Congress. "It became necessary for me to choose whether . . . [to] let the government fall at once into ruin," he later wrote, "or whether, availing myself of the broader powers conferred by the Constitution in cases of insurrection, I would make an effort to save it." And make an effort he did. At that cabinet meeting, Lincoln ordered all the necessary tools of war to be purchased, including weapons, munitions, transports, and ships. And because the government departments that would carry out his orders "contained so large a number of disloyal persons that it would have been impossible" to get it done through them, Lincoln directed Secretary of the Treasury Chase to give $2 million to three trusted New York businessmen to arrange for most of the purchases.

The very next day (Monday, April 22, 1861), a host of government workers walked off their jobs in Washington and headed south. Just two days earlier, Virginia's Robert E. Lee had resigned his commission to go and fight for the Confederacy, as would nearly one-third of the Union army's officers. Also on April 22, President Lincoln received at the White House a group of 50 interdenominational religious people from Baltimore, who innocently asked him to recognize the Confederacy and keep Union troops out of their city. In a rare display of anger, but a forceful display of resolve, Lincoln blasted the group: "You, gentlemen, come here to me and ask for peace on any terms, and yet have no word of condemnation for those who are making war on us," he said. "You express great horror of bloodshed, and yet would not lay a straw in the way of those who are organizing in Virginia and elsewhere to capture this city. The rebels attack Fort Sumter, and your citizens attack troops sent to the defense of the Government, and the lives and property in Washington, and yet you would have me break my oath and surrender the Government without a blow. There is no manhood or honor in that. . . . Go home . . . and tell your people that if they attack us, we will return it, and severely."

During those tense, perilous five days after the Baltimore riots, Washington, D.C., was left virtually defenseless, trapped between two slave states—Maryland to the north and Virginia to the south. Railroad travel was halted, roads were blocked, postal deliveries were stopped, and telegraph lines were severed. To send and receive information, Lincoln had to dispatch individual riders, but many of them were captured or killed along their routes. And the information that did make it through led to a palpable fear that the Confederacy was making plans to attack Washington.

Although Lincoln maintained a strong outward appearance

of firmness and conviction, those closest to him could see that he was terribly concerned. On the afternoon of April 23, 1861, for example, the president's assistant, John Hay, observed Lincoln "walking the floor alone in silent thought for nearly half an hour." Then he stopped and took a long look out the second-story window. From there, he could see a Confederate flag flying in Alexandria across the Potomac River. But he could not see any Union troops. "Why don't they come?" he asked. "Why don't they come?"

On April 25, 1861, the *New York Times* published an editorial that represented the North's growing fear that Washington was going to fall and that Abraham Lincoln was not up to the job. "Wanted: A Leader!" was the title.

> In every great crisis, the human heart demands a leader that incarnates its ideas, its emotions, and its aims. Till such a leader appears, everything is disorder, disaster, and defeat. The moment he takes the helm, order, promptitude, and confidence follow as the necessary result. When we see such results, we know that a hero leads. No such hero at present directs affairs.

The very afternoon that editorial was published, troops from the Seventh New York Regiment arrived in the city and marched down Pennsylvania Avenue to the White House. And over the next several days, other Union troops arrived, including 700 from the Sixth Massachusetts Regiment that had been attacked in Baltimore.

Washington, D.C., was saved — at least for the moment.

★ ★ ★

Once the nation's capital had gained military protection, President Lincoln made several more major decisions. He cut the telegraph lines from Richmond to Washington, suppressed postal service in and out of the Southern states, and reestablished the train routes up to Baltimore. And on April 27, 1861, Abraham Lincoln took one of the most dramatic steps any American president had ever taken — he suspended the writ of *habeas corpus.*

Because Virginia had all but joined the Confederacy, land travel routes to Washington were now forced to go through Maryland. And when some state officials threatened to destroy the railroad tracks between Annapolis and Philadelphia in order to disrupt the flow of troops and supplies, Lincoln sent the following dispatch to General Winfield Scott:

> To the Commanding General of the Army of the United States:
>
> You are engaged in repressing an insurrection against the laws of the United States. If at any point . . . between Philadelphia and Washington . . . you find resistance which renders it necessary to suspend the writ of Habeas Corpus for the public safety, you . . . are authorized to suspend that writ.
>
> ABRAHAM LINCOLN

The writ of *habeas corpus,* specifically mentioned in the Constitution, is a fundamental protection against illegal imprisonment and requires any individual arrested to be brought before a judge or court to show just cause. But as he later wrote, Lincoln suspended the writ "to arrest and detain, without resort to the ordinary processes and forms of law, such individuals as he might deem dangerous to the public safety." It was the first time an American president had ever done so. Lincoln did not make the suspension public, nor did he inform the Supreme Court. Before Chief Justice Roger B. Taney found out about it, three more states had seceded from the Union (Arkansas on May 6, North Carolina on May 20, and Virginia made it official on May 23). *[Tennessee would soon join them on June 8.]*

After Taney was petitioned by Maryland militia lieutenant John Merryman (who had been arrested and charged with treason for destroying railroad bridges), he issued an order (on May 26, 1861) demanding that the commander of Fort McHenry produce Merryman in his courtroom the next day. But the commander refused, citing President Lincoln's suspension of the writ. At that point, Taney, who had penned the *Dred Scott* decision and was no friend of Lincoln's, went ballistic. On June 1, he issued a lengthy Supreme Court opinion that railed against Lincoln for abusing his presidential powers and insisted that only Congress had the authority to suspend *habeas corpus.* The only response Lincoln had was to ask Edward Bates to handle the matter, and the attorney general responded with a 26-page opinion justifying the president's action.

Not only did Lincoln blow off Chief Justice Taney, he continued to suspend *habeas corpus* as he deemed necessary. The Democrats in Congress, of course, attacked his actions by charging that they were "unwarranted by the Constitution and laws of the United States and a . . . usurpation of power never given up by the people." But pro-Union newspapers supported Lincoln in print, which led to a major public debate on the issue. Finally, on March 3, 1863, Republicans in Congress managed to pass the Habeas Corpus Suspension Act, which authorized the president to suspend the writ when necessary. It also indemnified Lincoln for his past suspensions. Six months later (on September 15, 1863), Lincoln suspended *habeas corpus* throughout the entire country. And over the course of the war, the Lincoln administration also infringed on American civil liberties by, among other things, imprisoning one-third of the Maryland legislature so it could not vote to secede, shutting down pro-Confederacy newspapers in the Northern states (sometimes imprisoning publishers and reporters), declaring martial law in various locations, and trying civilians in military courts.

★ ★ ★

On June 3, 1861, Stephen A. Douglas died unexpectedly from typhoid fever at the age of 48. Lincoln wept openly upon hearing the news. Then he had the White House decorated in black crepe to mourn the loss of his longtime friend and honor his memory.

★ ★ ★

When Congress met in special session on July 4, 1861, President Lincoln defended and explained his actions over the previous three months. Regarding the suspension of *habeas corpus,* he pointed out that Article I, Section 9, of the U.S. Constitution read that "the privilege of the writ of *habeas corpus* shall not be suspended, unless when in cases of rebellion and invasion the public safety may require it." He also noted that "the Constitution is silent as to who is to exercise the power." But as president, and with Congress out of session, Lincoln had been in the best position to take action. "I believe that by these and similar measures taken in that crisis," said the president, "some of which were without any authority of law, the government was saved from overthrow."

In that address, Lincoln also made another call for troops, asking Congress to authorize 400,000 more men at a cost of $400 million. *[Congress responded by giving Lincoln $500 million for 500,000 men.]* And he repeatedly tried to establish a strategic sense of mission and a higher calling to inspire the congressmen, senators, and American people in general:

> This is essentially a People's contest. On the side of the Union, it is a struggle for maintaining in the world, that form and substance of government whose leading object is to elevate the condition of men — to lift artificial weights from all shoulders — to clear the paths of laudable pursuit for all — to afford all, an unfettered start, and a fair chance, in the race of life.

By the time this special session of Congress convened, the ranks of the Union army had swelled considerably as most of Lincoln's first call for 75,000 troops had arrived and were assembled on the banks of the Potomac River. Pressed by overconfident legislators and Lincoln, himself, military commanders began making plans for an attack on the Confederate army camped 32 miles away near Manassas, Virginia. Finally, on July 21, 1861, General Irvin C. McDowell led what he thought was going to be a surprise attack there. But Confederate generals P.G.T. Beauregard and Stonewall Jackson were tipped off in advance by a spy and responded by routing the poorly trained Union soldiers, who fled in disarray back to Washington.

Bull Run (as it came to be known in the North) was the first major battle of the Civil War. Eighteen thousand soldiers on each side had engaged, and many casualties were sustained. All of a sudden, a stark reality hit Northerners everywhere. This conflict was not going to be over in three or even six months, as many had predicted. It was going to be long and bloody, *and* there was a real possibility that the Union might lose to the Confederacy. According to D.C. resident and poet Walt Whitman, a defeatist panic set in and people were saying "it was useless to fight." "The talk . . . in and around Washington after Bull Run," wrote Whitman, "was loud and undisguised for yielding out and out, and substituting the southern rule, and Lincoln promptly abdicating and departing." There was also a genuine fear that the Confederate army would turn and mount a major assault on the nation's capital while they had momentum on their side. President Lincoln was even urged to move his family out of the city, but Mary would not leave without her husband—and the president wasn't going anywhere.

When Lincoln first heard of the loss, John Hay remembered that "he listened in silence without making the slightest change of feature or expression, and walked away to army headquarters." Lincoln remained stoic, because he did not want to cause his people any undue worry, which might have occurred had he fallen apart. Essentially, the president was showing the face his team needed to see.

Looking long term, Lincoln planned to organize the vast resources of the Union. After all, the North had a population of 22 million compared to the South's 9 million (4 million of whom were slaves). Their manufacturing superiority was also enormous, with the North manufacturing 97 percent of the nation's firearms and 94 percent of its iron. Despite these sheer numbers, however, Lincoln had warned of overconfidence. He knew public opinion would carry more weight than statistics, and besides, "man for man, the soldier from the South will be a match for the soldier from the North."

Bull Run was a very serious defeat, but in Lincoln's mind, it was only one loss. The war was just beginning, and he knew he had better get busy to turn things around. As a matter of fact, the forceful actions President Lincoln took after the Battle of Bull Run were the beginning of a pattern he would frequently use after the Union lost a battle. The strength and tenacity of his executive leadership in this regard was astonishing. Abraham Lincoln seemed to draw more strength and determination from every defeat.

Two days after Bull Run (on July 23, 1861), Lincoln took the following actions:

1. He drafted a memo ordering the untrained troops to "be constantly drilled, disciplined, and instructed."
2. He relieved McDowell and put General George B. McClellan in command of the Army of the Potomac, with orders to reorganize, train, and build a stronger army.
3. He called for an additional half a million new troops (over and above the half a million Congress had already authorized).
4. He laid out specific military plans to (a) send reinforcements to Fort Monroe and the Shenandoah Valley in Virginia; (b) retake Manassas and hold it permanently; (c) undertake joint land and water movements from Cairo, Illinois, to Memphis, Tennessee, and from Cincinnati, Ohio, to East Tennessee; (d) keep the city of Baltimore in Union hands; and (e) strengthen the blockade of Southern ports.

Lincoln next turned his attention to the troops, themselves. He headed out in a carriage with Secretary of State Seward to visit the regiments in the city and those camped on the Virginia side of the Potomac. One reporter wrote that the president waded into the crowds of soldiers and shook hands with as many of them as he could: "He goes at it with both hands, and hand over hand, very much as a sailor would climb a rope."

Lincoln also stopped and chatted with the men. He swapped stories to lighten the mood, and then listened as they told him about the battle. The president thanked them for their service and promised they would get all the food and supplies they needed. He further gave them spontaneous pep talks whenever the opportunity arose. Colonel (later General) William Tecumseh Sherman remembered that "Lincoln made one of the neatest, best, and most feeling addresses I ever listened to — referring to our disaster, the high duties that still devolved on us, and the brighter days to come."

In the days and months that followed, President Lincoln continued to visit the field as often as he could, and in his conversations with the soldiers, it became clear that his message was starting to get through. They were beginning to believe — not only in themselves, but in the strength of their leader.

★ ★ ★

Several months after the Battle of Bull Run, Lincoln boarded the five-gun Treasury cutter *Miami* to travel via the Potomac River and Chesapeake Bay down to Fort Monroe on the tip of the Virginia Peninsula. On that trip, the president grabbed an axe on deck and, according to one witness, demonstrated that "he possessed the strength of a giant." Lincoln "held it at arm's length at the extremity of the [handle] with his thumb and forefinger, continuing to hold it there [horizontally] for a number of minutes. The most powerful sailors on board tried in vain to imitate him."

"When I was eighteen years of age I could do this," Lincoln said, "and I have never seen the day since that I could not do it."

LINCOLN ON LEADERSHIP FOR TODAY

Presidential Executive Orders

Because Abraham Lincoln was confronted with an open and armed rebellion, something the Constitution had not specifically provided for, he was forced to be creative and bold. First, he purposely did not call Congress into session for three months, because he did not have time to debate. Then he issued a series of unprecedented executive orders, in which he spent money without the approval of Congress, called up troops, and suspended the writ of *habeas corpus* (the first time a U.S. president had ever done so). At that moment of crisis, Lincoln's highest priority was to preserve the Union, which ultimately confers all our rights of citizenship. So he strategically chose to deny individual rights in order to preserve the Union. But he did so only on a temporary basis. As Lincoln eventually told Congress, all rights would be restored after the rebellion was put down. He also asked the legislative branch to grant him retroactive approval for his executive actions, which they did.

Presidential executive orders are legal tools that have been part of American government since the days of George Washington. Initially, they were basically directives issued to various administration departments. With time, however, they have been employed to further a president's national policy. Although executive orders have the full force of law, they may not directly contravene congressional bills and must have some constitutional basis. Both the legislative and judicial branches are provided remedies to counter a president's executive order, in that Congress has the power to override and the Supreme Court to invalidate.

In 2014, President Barack Obama signed a number of executive orders banning the deportation of millions of immigrants residing in the country without proper credentials. These orders were framed as directives to departments that fell within the sphere of authority of the executive branch, did not strip the legislative or judicial branches of any power or responsibility, and were temporary in that they pertained only to the individuals involved — nor did they alter immigration law. Obama also issued other executive orders designed to work around a recalcitrant U.S. Congress on such issues as regulation of greenhouse gas emissions, renewable energy, and health care.

In my opinion, Abraham Lincoln would have backed Barack Obama on the issuance of these orders. Like Lincoln, Obama was confronted with something not really seen before — in this case, a legislative branch that would take no action due to dogmatic idealism and/or the influence of special interest groups. It is a matter of record that such legislators would take no action proposed by Obama, even if they had been previously in favor of it. So Obama had to be innovative if he was going to get anything done at all. I think Lincoln would have admired that.

Presidents of the United States are entitled to use every bit of latitude, flexibility, and authority the Constitution provides, especially when they determine that decisive action absolutely needs to be taken. Not hesitating to take bold and creative action is a mark of good leadership.

Domestic Terrorism

During the early days of the Civil War, President Lincoln was faced with significant outbursts of public violence. Things were especially bad in Baltimore, which is only 45 miles from Washington. Overall, Lincoln took bold and decisive actions to counter the insurgencies. He did so quickly and did not hesitate to use military force. Indeed, throughout his tenure as president, Lincoln was faced with the potential dissolution of the Union, and, certainly, a full-fledged civil war can be categorized as "domestic terrorism."

Today, *global* terrorism threatens every peace-loving nation in the world and, as such, vaults the issue to the forefront of debate and decision. Since the 9/11 attacks and the rise of al-Qaeda, ISIL (or ISIS), and other terrorist groups, the United States (largely through the actions of President George W. Bush) has responded forcefully by, among other things, creating the Department of Homeland Security, ramping up domestic and international intelligence efforts, and mobilizing the Department of Defense to strike terrorists in their base areas of operation (part of the Bush Doctrine).

While most Americans applaud and support strong federal action to prevent domestic terrorism, controversy exists regarding its scope and expense. Specific areas of concern include (1) an unchecked massive expansion of U.S. intelligence operations, including authorization by the National Security Agency (NSA) to eavesdrop (via e-mail, texts, phone calls, etc.) on citizens within the United States; (2) actual costs of operations not being revealed or open to public scrutiny; (3) the general perception that untold billions of federal dollars are unaccounted for or spent without regard to the source of funds or adding to the federal deficit; and (4) whether the Bush Doctrine was necessary or simply a means of promoting war and the special interests that profit from it.

In my opinion, if Abraham Lincoln were alive today, he would still take the position that a president's top priority is to preserve, protect, and defend the Union, whatever it takes. He would certainly say that any kind of domestic terrorism is unacceptable, and that the government must act to prevent it and hold perpetrators accountable. I believe he would also say that the civil liberties of American citizens must never be violated except in times of extreme danger, and even then, the U.S. Congress must be on board or at least informed.

Gun Control

Although Abraham Lincoln was not an avid hunter, he knew his way around guns. As president, he inspected all kinds of new weapons for possible use in the war effort, often inviting inventors of new repeating rifles to Washington so he could test them in target practice on the White House grounds. Lincoln even took a Gatling gun into a cabinet meeting one time.

Today, the wording of the Second Amendment to the Constitution is much in debate. *["A well regulated Militia being necessary to the security of a free State, the right of the people to keep and bear*

Arms, shall not be infringed."] One side takes the position that the clause "the right of the people to keep and bear Arms" provides the right to own and carry any kind of gun anytime and anywhere. The other side disagrees and states that this clause applies only to the previous wording regarding "a well regulated Militia."

I believe if Lincoln were here today and we asked him if American citizens have a general right to keep and bear arms, he would say, "Of course. That's a given." Then he might try to explain to us why the Founding Fathers felt they needed to address this issue in the Bill of Rights at all. The nation was brand-new back then, still a frontier with ragged borders that had to be protected. What if the British invaded from Canada or there was some sort of an uprising? They had to reserve the right of the federal government to muster an army. So the object of the Second Amendment was most likely to address "a well regulated Militia," and, in turn, the clause "the right of the people to keep and bear Arms" is related to the militia. I believe that's the way Abraham Lincoln probably viewed it back in his own time. But what would be his position if he were here today?

In my opinion, Lincoln would say that every American citizen has the right to own a pistol or a rifle for protection and hunting. I believe he'd also say that the government needs to protect its citizens from deviant members of society taking assault weapons into theaters, schools, or other public places and opening fire. My sense is that he would be in favor of both federal and state governments regulating all weapons that are designed to kill mass numbers of people.

It is very painful to me that you in Missouri cannot, or will not, settle your factional quarrel among yourselves. I have been tormented with it beyond endurance for months. . . . Neither side pays the least respect to my appeals to . . . reason.

— Lincoln, to a group of Missouri radicals who asked him to relieve General John M. Schofield from command of the Department of the West
May 15, 1863

ISSUES
Foreign Affairs and International Relations
Balancing Extreme Factions

9

The Middle Ground

★ ★ ★

Sixteen-year-old Julia Taft heard a terrible racket coming from one of the rooms of the White House. Opening the door, she found the president lying on the floor, with her two brothers (Bud, age 12, and Holly, 8) and Lincoln's two sons (Willie, 11, and Tad, 8) trying to hold him down. Willie and Bud had hold of his hands, Tad and Holly were sprawled over his feet and legs, and Lincoln, obviously enjoying the tussle, had a broad grin on his face. "Julie," shouted Tad, "come quick and sit on his stomach!"

★ ★ ★

Great Britain was angry. Its ministers said it was an illegal act and a clear violation of their neutrality. They threatened war, and to prove they were serious, 8,000 new British troops were ordered to Canada. They also demanded that the United States back down, apologize, and make reparations.

But Americans didn't want Lincoln to back down. Coming right after Bull Run, the general public viewed it as a Union victory. The heck with the British, some said. Let's fight them, too.

So what was everybody all excited about?

On November 8, 1861, Captain Charles Wilkes, of the American warship *San Jacinto,* captured two Confederate diplomats on their way to Europe in an effort to secure support and aid. The only problem was that Wilkes forcibly pulled them from the British mail steamer *Trent* in international waters near the Bahamas. The two men, James Mason of Virginia and John Slidell of Louisiana, were then claimed as contraband, moved north, and thrown into the stockade at Fort Warren in Boston Harbor.

President Lincoln stayed calm and pulled his cabinet together to evaluate the situation. After several heated meetings, he came to the conclusion that what Captain Wilkes had done *was,* in fact, a violation of international law, and that the U.S. really didn't have a leg to stand on. Furthermore, Lincoln realized what would happen if the United States got into a war with Great Britain: tens of thousands of redcoats coming down from Canada; the British navy breaking the blockade of Confederate ports; the South having one or more foreign allies *[France had promised to back whatever decision Great Britain made in the matter];* and the American Civil War then turning into a full-fledged international conflict. The consequences were simply too horrible to contemplate. So Lincoln decided not to have "two wars on his hands at a time," and in the end, he directed Secretary of State Seward to send a letter to Great Britain's prime minister admitting that Captain Wilkes had, indeed, violated international law and that Mason and Slidell would be "cheerfully liberated."

The president then turned his attention toward stabilizing America's relationship with Great Britain and working on British public opinion. And there was plenty to work on, because the Union's blockade had cut off shipments of Southern cotton to English clothing mills, which resulted in hundreds of workers being laid off. As part of Lincoln's sustained campaign, he personally wrote letters to be read at public meetings in England. "Through the actions of our disloyal citizens, the workingmen of Europe have been subjected to a severe trial," he stated in one document, and then complimented the English on a "sublime Christian heroism which has not been surpassed in any age or in any country." In notes for another letter, Lincoln made a subtle reference to the Gospel of Matthew by writing that "the family of Christian and civilized *nations*," and "all Christian and civilized men everywhere," should reject the Confederacy's principle of building a nation based on human bondage. [Italics added.] Lincoln made this last statement because he knew that Britain was a Christian nation and that public opinion there was fervently abolitionist. "I cannot imagine that any European power would dare to recognize and aid the Southern Confederacy if it became clear that the Confederacy stands for slavery and the Union for freedom," the president told a friend.

To that end, Lincoln directed Secretary of State Seward to begin negotiating with the British ambassador to the United States, Richard Lyons, for a treaty with Great Britain that would take aggressive measures to suppress the Atlantic slave trade. And once the Seward-Lyons Treaty was completed and signed, Lincoln asked the U.S. Senate to quietly ratify it, which they did on April 25, 1862. Lincoln also acted pragmatically to counter Britain's loss of revenue in the cotton trade by having the War Department purchase vast quantities of British goods, including ships, armaments, iron, uniforms, and wool blankets. In turn, Great Britain purchased American corn and flour. So by utilizing moral reasoning combined with economic incentives, Abraham Lincoln was not only able to avoid a war with Great Britain over the *Trent* affair, he effectively increased goodwill between the two nations. Not bad for a green president who had no prior experience in foreign affairs or world politics. As a matter of fact, Lincoln had never even set foot outside the United States. *[Diplomats Mason and Slidell were unsuccessful in their attempts to persuade Britain, France, or any other European nation to ally with the Confederate cause, or even recognize the Confederacy as an independent nation.]*

When it came to foreign affairs in general, Lincoln did not become overly isolationist, which would have been a natural tendency during a raging civil war. Rather, he monitored events overseas, largely through Secretary of State Seward, and was always ready to take action (or not take action), if necessary. When France's emperor, Napoleon III, for instance, made a play for Mexico by setting up a puppet regime there, Lincoln maintained neutrality and assured the French that the United States had no intention of intervening. And when Napoleon III later suggested that representatives from both the Union and Confederacy meet at a neutral site to discuss either reunification or permanent separation as two nations, Lincoln immediately rejected the idea.

With Seward leading the way, the president also encouraged American businessmen to pursue overseas opportunities with other countries. In time, such forays began to pay off. Plans were made for overland telegraph lines through the Bering Strait and Russia. And in addition to the new transatlantic cable, designs were completed for more telegraphic communications between America and Europe. Additionally, international trade picked up in Oregon and California, which were still in the Union and far away from the fighting. Secretary of State Seward also set up a brisk communications network with every important nation around the world, which Lincoln reported on in his regular messages to Congress. He mentioned, for instance, "efforts as were in my power have been used to . . . avert a threatened war between Peru and Spain," and that the "rebellion in China has at last been suppressed, with the cooperating good offices of this Government and of the other Western commercial states." Over the four years of his presidency, Lincoln also mentioned progress on communications and/or negotiations with dozens of nations around the world, including Costa Rica, Colombia, Chile, Argentina, and Japan, to name just a few. Lincoln even asked Congress to formally recognize and support the black nations of Liberia in Africa and Haiti in the Caribbean, something the previous Congress, hamstrung by Southern opposition, would never have dreamed of doing. *[Haiti was a nation of former slaves that had been seeking recognition in the Western Hemisphere since it declared independence in 1804.]*

Lincoln had Seward to help him maintain balance among nations so none took sides with the South or otherwise interfered in the American Civil War. However, he took personal charge when it came to balancing radical factions in the border states of Maryland, Kentucky, and Missouri — and *that* was one of the most difficult tasks any American president has ever undertaken. If all three of these states left the Union, the Confederacy's border would move north to the Ohio River, its population would increase by nearly 50 percent (not including another 420,000 slaves), and its manufacturing capacity would almost double. If only Maryland left, Washington, D.C., would be geographically isolated and, in all likelihood, have to be abandoned. If only Kentucky left, control of the Ohio River's shipping would be in dispute. And if only Missouri left, access to the northwest territories by the Missouri River would be cut off, and the Confederacy would control the Mississippi River up to St. Louis. From the beginning, Lincoln was well aware of the consequences of losing the border states. "These all against us, and the job on our hands is too large for us," he said to a friend in 1861. "We would as well consent to separation at once." But he may have been unprepared for the magnitude of the challenge that confronted him, because Maryland, Kentucky, and Missouri were slave states, and all three had mini civil wars raging internally.

After the first suspension of *habeas corpus* in Maryland, Lincoln sought to ease tensions there by writing a letter to the *Baltimore American* stating that "no arrest has been made, or will be made, based on substantial and unmistakable complicity with those in armed rebellion against the Government of the United States." And when General Winfield Scott recommended that anti-Union members of the state legislature be arrested prior to a meeting to vote on secession, the president held off. "I think it would not be justifiable," he responded. "First, they have a clearly legal right to assemble; and, we can not know in advance that their action will not be lawful and peaceful. Secondly, we cannot permanently prevent their action." So Lincoln took a "wait and see" position, and, sure enough, the Maryland legislature eventually voted against secession.

In Kentucky, Lincoln received some unexpected help from the Confederacy when it violated the state's proclamation of neutrality by sending in troops to Columbus to control traffic along the Mississippi River. General Ulysses S. Grant was then ordered to move his troops from Cairo, Illinois, to Paducah. In response, the state legislature passed a resolution ordering only the Confederate troops out of the state, and then raised the United States flag over the state capitol in Frankfort. While a major movement to secede never really took hold in Kentucky, Lincoln cemented its place in the Union when, in 1863, he allowed General Ambrose E. Burnside to proclaim martial law and imprison Democratic candidates in order to help elect a pro-Union governor.

Overall, the problems President Lincoln faced in Maryland and Kentucky were mild compared to the nightmare he encountered in Missouri. It all began in the first three months after Fort Sumter when pro-slavery governor Claiborne Jackson ordered the state militia to prepare to fight for the Confederacy. But acting on his own authority, a young Union captain named Nathaniel Lyon (in charge of the Union arsenal in St. Louis) attacked and defeated the militia. Lincoln immediately promoted him all the way up to brigadier general, and Lyon then marched to Jefferson City and forced Governor Jackson and other pro-Confederate officials out of the capital. Essentially, Lyon led a coup d'état that was sanctioned by Lincoln. Shortly thereafter, the state legislature voted against secession, affirmed Missouri's neutrality, and appointed pro-Union Democrat Hamilton Gamble as provisional governor. *[General Nathaniel Lyon was killed at the Battle of Wilson's Creek on August 10, 1861. He was the first Union general to lose his life in the Civil War.]*

The next major Missouri headache Lincoln experienced took place about a month after he placed former 1856 Republican presidential candidate General John C. Frémont in charge of the Department of the West (responsible for Missouri and the Northwest). Without consulting the president, Frémont issued a proclamation placing Missouri under martial law, which subjected civilians to military trials and confiscation of personal property—including slaves, which Frémont ordered set free. Lincoln quickly asked Frémont to revise the order by eliminating the emancipation portion. But the stubborn general refused, so Lincoln relieved him of command and rescinded his order. Abolitionist newspapers that had hailed Frémont's proclamation now castigated the president. But Lincoln would not back down and gave two reasons for his action. First, he was not going to allow a subordinate to act as president. Frémont's proclamation, Lincoln said, "is simply dictatorship. It assumes that the general may do anything he pleases. . . . I cannot assume this reckless position, nor allow others to assume it on my responsibility." Second, Lincoln realized (while Frémont did not) that the balance of power in Kentucky was at stake. In fact, key Kentuckians had warned of the legislature turning against the Union if Frémont's order was allowed to stand. So Lincoln rescinded it and made sure all the newspapers knew he had done so.

A year later, when General David Hunter (as commander of the Department of the South) issued a similar order freeing slaves in Florida, Georgia, and South Carolina, Lincoln rescinded that one, too. This time, he pointed out that, as president, only he could take such an action (emancipate slaves), and he would do so only if it became "a necessity indispensable to the maintenance of the government." Lincoln took heat for this action as well, in particular from Salmon P. Chase. But the president sternly rebuked his fierce abolitionist secretary of the Treasury. "No commanding general shall do such a thing, upon *my* responsibility, without consulting me," the president told Chase.

Both the Frémont and Hunter proclamations were extreme actions that had a very real possibility of endangering the balancing act Lincoln was performing in regard to the border states. And looking at the big picture, which individual generals could not do, only he could determine when the timing would be right for a major action like an emancipation proclamation.

As the war progressed, Lincoln's problems in the "Show Me State" worsened. "I am having a good deal of trouble with Missouri matters," he wrote in January 1863. "One class of friends believe in greater severity and another in greater lenience in regard to arrests, banishments, and assessments. As usual in such cases, each questions the other's motives." In this letter, the president was referring to pro-Union supporters who had divided themselves into competing factions. The "Charcoals" were radicals bent on the total abolition of slavery and severe treatment of rebel sympathizers. On the other side were the "Claybanks," who were moderate Republicans and War Democrats that favored a return to the United States as it was before secession (with slavery intact). Both factions wanted the president's support, but Lincoln refused to back either side. "I have stoutly tried to keep out of the quarrel, and so mean to do," he said in an internal memorandum. Lincoln also wrote to the radical Missourians personally: "It is very painful to me that you in Missouri cannot, or will not, settle your factional quarrel among yourselves. . . . Neither side pays the least respect to my appeals to . . . reason." And predictably, because Lincoln stayed neutral and would not support either side, *both factions* then attacked him.

As the months passed, the two factions only became more belligerent toward the president. In the fall of 1863, for example, a group of Charcoals traveled all the way to Washington to demand that Lincoln dismiss General John M. Schofield (then in command of Union forces in Missouri) for being too kindly toward Confederate sympathizers. Several months earlier, Lincoln had expressed some frustration with Schofield after the arrest of a Democratic newspaper editor. "I regret to learn of the arrest," he had written. "I fear this loses you the middle position I desired you to occupy." This time, however, after listening for two hours to complaints regarding Schofield, Lincoln took the general's side. He acknowledged that there were problems in Missouri but was not convinced that the Union command was causing them. Lincoln explained that in a war, "deception breeds and thrives. Confidence dies and universal suspicion reigns." The president then sent the Missourians on their way, later telling an aide: "I cannot do anything contrary to my conviction to please these men, earnest and powerful as they may be." And to Schofield, Lincoln offered some sage advice: "If both factions, or neither, shall abuse you, you will probably be about right. Beware of being assailed by one, and praised by the other."

In the end, Lincoln could not make any progress with the problems in Missouri, so he allowed his generals to use force. He endorsed General War Order No. 11, for instance, which was issued after the pro-slavery Missourians known as Quantrill's Raiders rode into Lawrence, Kansas, and killed nearly 200 men and boys, simply because the town was known for its anti-slavery stance. Order No. 11 declared martial law and forced partial evacuation of four rural counties in western Missouri. But Lincoln issued Schofield a moderating warning to proceed carefully:

> Under your recent order, which I have approved, you will only arrest individuals and suppress assemblies, or newspapers, when they may be working palpable injury to the military in your charge. In no other case will you interfere with the expression of opinion in any form, or allow it to be interfered with violently by others. In this, you have a discretion to exercise with great caution, calmness, and forbearance.

"Caution, calmness, and forbearance" might be used to describe Abraham Lincoln, himself, in balancing factions and extremes — whether among nations or states. Although, in the end, he had "no friends in Missouri," as he told Attorney General Edward Bates, he was at least able to keep all three border states in the Union. And the way he handled Missouri (using force only as a last resort) was a good example of how he kept political factions such as abolitionists, radical and conservative Republicans, and Northern Democrats together on a national scale — all in the midst of a raging civil war.

Secretary of State William Seward, a large part of whose job was to keep a balance of power in the world, marveled at Lincoln's skill in this area. "Somebody has to be in a position to mollify and moderate," he said. "That is the task of the president . . . [and Lincoln] is wise and practical." The president, himself, was more modest, but nonetheless proud of his achievements. "I may not have made as great a President as some other men," he told a friend, "but I believe I have kept these discordant elements together as well as anyone could."

Early one morning, sixteen-year-old Julia Taft arrived at the White House and went looking for Mrs. Lincoln and the boys. Wandering into the president's sitting room, she saw Lincoln sprawled out in his big easy chair with an old worn Bible on his lap and staring out the window. [Lincoln usually read the Bible first thing every morning.] When she went over to say good morning, the president (continuing to look out the window) clasped her hand and greeted her absent-mindedly. She paused and followed his gaze out the window, but could only see the tops of some trees. Thinking it would not be polite to pull back, Julia just stood there holding the president's hand as he remained deep in thought. After a while, her arm was just beginning to ache when, finally, Lincoln turned to her with a startled look. "Why, Julie," he said, "have I been holding you here all this time?" He then released her, and she ran off to find the boys.

LINCOLN ON LEADERSHIP FOR TODAY

Foreign Affairs and International Relations

When Abraham Lincoln took the presidential oath of office in 1861, he had no prior experience in foreign affairs or world politics. In fact, he had never even set foot outside the United States. Yet, even in the midst of a civil war, Lincoln went against a natural tendency to become isolationist and, instead, directed a savvy and robust program of international relations through Secretary of State Seward. His first priority was to maintain a balance among nations so that none (especially Britain or France) took sides with the Confederacy. In Great Britain's case, for example, Lincoln combined moral reasoning with economic incentives to ensure neutrality. He negotiated a treaty to suppress the Atlantic slave trade, and then set about working on British public opinion using the media and his own personal letters. He also directed the purchase of vast quantities of British goods and, in turn, sold Britain much-needed corn and flour. Moreover, Lincoln encouraged American businessmen to pursue overseas opportunities with other nations, which led to more international trade and better communications with Europe.

Today, through the executive branch of government, the president takes the lead in foreign affairs and international relations, mostly through the efforts of the Department of State. The legislative branch serves mostly to advise and ratify or disapprove of foreign policy agreements. Major controversy exists between conservatives and progressives about whether or not to negotiate with foreign governments considered to be hostile or adversarial. For instance, the Republican administration of George W. Bush declined to enter into nuclear arms negotiations with Iran or North Korea, while the Democratic administration of Barack Obama was open to the pursuit of such discussions and, in fact, did secure a controversial agreement with Iran.

I believe if Lincoln were here today, he would say that in a modern world with instant communications and virtual borders, it is unwise for any national leader to pursue an isolationist agenda. He would advise us to work hard at maintaining relations with friendly nations. And because silence stokes paranoia among lesser leaders, we should work even harder to initiate, build, and maintain relations with unfriendly nations. Only through dialogue and negotiation can understanding begin to take hold. Even strained discussions are preferable to no communication at all, because without them, there is no real chance to improve relations and avert potential war. Today's Lincoln would work hard to meet with foreign leaders and to build personal bonds with as many as possible. He would forge alliances, negotiate treaties, encourage international business agreements, and aggressively strive for open and peaceful relations among the United States and all nations.

Balancing Extreme Factions

As president, Lincoln had to balance a wide array of competing political factions, such as abolitionists with slaveholders, conservatives and radicals in Congress, and extremists in the border states of Maryland, Kentucky, and Missouri. It was an amazing juggling act, and he was only able to pull it off (1) by stepping back and looking at the big picture and (2) by consistently being a centrist. Perhaps his most revealing statement in this area was made to Missouri commander General John Schofield, to whom he said, "I fear this loses you the middle position I desired you to occupy."

Lincoln understood that extremism is part of human nature, and that, in any society, people will instinctively organize themselves into small, dissenting groups. The key word here is "small," because far-left-wing or far-right-wing political factions generally do not represent the majority of citizens. Rather, they are located on the ends of the organizational bell curve — and in order to increase their numbers, will often attempt to attract moderates and uncommitted individuals from the much larger (and quieter) middle. "A free people," said Lincoln in 1852, "in times of peace and quiet — when pressed by no common danger — naturally divide into parties."

Today, both major political parties have embraced the extremes of political ideology. Controversy swirls around exactly why it has happened, but some of the better scholarly reasoning suggests it is caused by voter anger, alienation, economic disadvantage, prejudice, dogmatic ideology, and just plain fear. Regardless of what has caused this polarization, the real issue is how to handle it.

I really believe that if Abraham Lincoln were here today, he would do exactly the same thing he did during the Civil War. He would plow right down the middle and search for as much common ground as possible. Rather than ignore representatives of extreme factions, he would meet with them, listen to their positions, treat them with respect, and try to engage them in a dialogue. He would be straightforward and clear as to his position, and would first appeal to reason — knowing full well that unreasonable people cannot be reasoned with. And Lincoln would advise us not to be bullied or intimidated into taking a position on either side. "[Let] nothing turn you to the right or the left," he once said. Of course, neither side will be happy with such a stance. But Lincoln would also say that "if both factions, or neither, shall abuse you, you will probably be about right," which is true, because the largest group of voters is in the middle. And that's who leaders really have to work on.

Pulling people back from the extremes is one of the most difficult jobs a leader can undertake. Presidents, in particular, have to look after *all the people* — the *entire* organization. In order to win over the majority, they must constantly communicate their messages and positions — and use every effective media outlet or communication device at their disposal. Leaders must seek to persuade and inspire rather than command or dictate. They must be positive rather than negative, include rather than divide, preach hope rather than stoke fear. Many people will be won over, but in truth, the most extreme among us may never change their positions. In such cases, once every other option has been tried, some form of force may have to be used.

If all men were just, there still would be *some,* though not *so much,* need for government.

— Lincoln, written notes to himself
July 1, 1854

ISSUES
Big Versus Small Federal Government
The IRS and Taxes
A Balanced Budget and the National Debt
Veterans Affairs

10

No Less Than National

★ ★ ★

LINCOLN'S CABINET OFTEN seemed dysfunctional. The secretary of state didn't like the secretary of war. The secretary of the Navy couldn't get along with the secretary of state. The postmaster general didn't like anybody, and they didn't like him. The secretary of the Treasury was always threatening to resign. Often, they wouldn't speak to each other. One adamantly refused to attend meetings if another was present. Sometimes the infighting was passionate and heated.

If Lincoln didn't expect such turmoil, he should have. After all, he had selected some of the brightest, strongest-minded people in the country, each of whom was a leader in his own right, most of whom had run for president, and all of whom believed, at first, that Abraham Lincoln was not up to the job. The attorney general, for instance, wrote in his diary that the president "lacks will and purpose and I greatly fear he has not the power to command." The secretary of the Navy pointed out that Lincoln "never had experience in administering the Government — State or National." And the secretary of state even suggested that he, rather than the president, should be allowed to make certain executive-level decisions. The price that Lincoln had to pay for not surrounding himself with yes-men was dealing with the egos, arrogant personalities, and overbearing behaviors of these high-strung individuals.

Most executives don't choose such people as their top advisers. But Lincoln was smart enough, confident enough, and secure enough to work with people who thought differently than himself. Not really knowing any of his cabinet members before being elected president, Lincoln first set out to build personal relationships with each. But because that would take some time, he repeatedly laid down the law to let them know who was in charge. To quell jockeying for position and maneuvers designed to oust one or the other, Lincoln let it be known that "I propose continuing to be myself the judge as to when a member of the Cabinet shall be dismissed." He told them all that "it would greatly pain me to discover any of you endeavoring to procure another's removal. . . . Such endeavor would be a wrong to me, and much worse, a wrong to the country."

Over the course of his presidency, Lincoln was not afraid to fire a subordinate when he deemed it necessary. Early in 1862, he relieved Simon Cameron in part because of irregularities in the War Department. The secretary, himself, had not engaged in graft, and the president leapt to his defense by writing a letter to Congress explaining the nation's dire situation after the fall of Fort Sumter and that both he and the entire cabinet "were at least equally responsible . . . for whatever error, wrong, or fault was committed." Lincoln further attempted to maintain a friendship with Cameron by appointing him U.S. ambassador to Russia. But perhaps a more relevant reason for Lincoln's removal of Cameron was the fact that this secretary of war frequently stoked disharmony among the team. Actually, a few years later, Lincoln would request Postmaster General Montgomery Blair's resignation for much the same reason. As he told a colleague, "The dismissal of Blair . . . would reconcile all parties and rid the Administration of irritating bickerings."

With the position of secretary of war vacant, Secretary of State Seward and Secretary of the Treasury Chase recommended Edwin M. Stanton for the post. Lincoln must have winced at the suggestion, because this was the very same lawyer from Pennsylvania who had mistreated him back in 1855 when both were members of the legal defense team in the famous McCormick reaper case. Although "roughly handled by that man," Lincoln had been impressed with Stanton's argument in court, which helped to win the lawsuit. And certainly, as Seward and Chase conveyed to the president, Stanton was a patriot and an extraordinarily hardworking and competent individual. Still, Lincoln had doubts, especially when others told him that his prospective nominee was arrogant, ill-tempered, difficult to get along with — and a Democrat, to boot. *[Stanton had served as President James Buchanan's attorney general.]*

In the end, Lincoln realized that the War Department needed the leadership of a strong individual, and if his secretaries of state and the Treasury wanted Stanton on their team, he was going to grant their wish. "You know the War Department has demonstrated the necessity for a Secretary of Mr. Stanton's great ability," Lincoln told a friend, "and I have made up my mind to sit down on all my pride [and] a portion of my self respect, and appoint him to the place."

As the months went by, many complaints were lodged about the secretary of war, mostly due to Edwin Stanton's acerbic personality. "Folks come up here and tell me that there are a great many men in the country who have all of Stanton's excellent qualities without his defects," the president told one acquaintance. "All I have to say is, I haven't met 'em [and] I don't know 'em!" Another time, when a lower-level official in the department began to complain about Stanton, Lincoln quickly shut him down. "Go home, my friend, and read attentively the tenth verse of the thirtieth chapter of Proverbs!" *["Accuse not a servant unto his master lest he curse thee, and thou be found guilty."]*

The fact is that Stanton was great at his job. So Lincoln supported him through thick and thin — even when General George McClellan publicly attacked the secretary of war over a disagreement about the total number of Union troops. After the press picked up McClellan's cause and started calling for Stanton to be fired, Lincoln walked over to an outdoor Union meeting on the steps of the Capitol (where newspaper reporters were sure to be present) and made a public statement:

> *There has been a wide-spread attempt to have a quarrel between Gen. McClellan and the Secretary of War. Now, I occupy a position that enables me to observe [that] these two gentlemen are not nearly so deep in the quarrel as some pretending to be their friends [say]. Gen. McClellan's attitude is such that, in the very selfishness of his nature, he cannot but wish to be successful, and I hope he will. . . . Sometimes we have a dispute about how many men Gen. McClellan has. . . . The basis for this is, there is always a wide difference . . . between the grand total on McClellan's rolls and the men actually fit for duty. . . . Gen. McClellan has sometimes asked for things that the Secretary of War did not give him. Gen. McClellan is not to blame for asking what he wanted and needed, and the Secretary of War is not to blame for not giving when he had none to give. And I say here, as far as I know, the Secretary of War has withheld no one thing at any time in my power to give him. . . . I believe he is a brave and able man, and I stand here, as justice requires me to do, to take upon myself what has been charged on the Secretary of War.*

Also on the platform when the president made these remarks were three other members of the cabinet (Bates, Blair, and Chase), who may have conveyed Lincoln's words to Stanton and the rest of the team. With acts like this, Lincoln was able to win the loyalty of his cabinet. In addition to accepting blame for things gone wrong, the president generously doled out credit for any and all achievements in his secretaries' respective departments. And with an action-oriented leader like Abraham Lincoln in charge, there would be a lot of credit to share over the course of the next four years, in part because his administration did not have to face a hostile Congress.

Because nearly all representatives of the Southern states had left for the Confederacy, the Republican Party was now in control of both the House and Senate. First as a Whig, and then as a Republican, Lincoln had always favored a strong federal government to promote economic progress for all Americans. Upon re-entering politics in 1854, he had declared his goal to be "no less than National in all the positions I may take." He further stated that "the legitimate object of government, is to do for a community of people, whatever they need to have done, but cannot do . . . for themselves — in their separate and individual capacities." More specifically, Lincoln pointed out that included anything requiring "combined action, [such as] public roads and highways, public schools, charities, pauperism, orphanage, estates of the deceased, and the machinery of government itself." Although Lincoln also cautioned that "success does not depend *as much* on external help as on self-reliance," he also pragmatically noted that "if all men were just, there still would be some, though not so much, need for government."

In the past, these Whig/Republican ideas had always been blocked by conservative states' rights advocates. But realizing the Civil War had created a most unusual situation in the halls of the federal government, Lincoln became determined to make the most of it and seize his opportunity to enact vigorous change — change that he had been hoping to see for more than 30 years. Of course, to get anything done, the president would need a lot of help, in part because time had to be spent fulfilling his role as commander in chief of the armed forces. So Lincoln strategically set out to collaborate with Congress and delegate to his cabinet.

He told Congress, for instance, that "we can succeed only by concert," and that it was time to combine creative thinking with bold action. "It is not, 'can *any* of us *imagine* better,'" said Lincoln, "but 'can we *all* do better?'" Maine senator William P. Fessenden immediately took the lead in Congress by vowing "to make the most of our time, for no one knows how soon this country may again fall into a Democratic [Party quagmire]."

Additionally, Lincoln told his cabinet secretaries that they were going to run their own areas without interference from him. He planned to set the overall direction, but then let the experts and leaders in their various fields do the rest. John Hay, Lincoln's assistant, once noted that "[the president] generally delegated to Mr. Chase exclusive control of those matters falling within the purview of his department." And it was Chase's Treasury Department where Lincoln would not only begin to change the government (in concert with Congress), but also where some of the Lincoln administration's most profound and long-lasting economic innovations would be made. They included the following four major initiatives.

Federal Income Tax and Creation of the First Internal Revenue Service

In order to fund the Union war effort and reduce the national debt, Congress passed, and the president signed, the Revenue Acts of 1861 and 1862, which created the position of commissioner of internal revenue and implemented the first federal income tax in United States history. In a graduated system, all citizens earning more than $800 per year were assessed a flat 3 percent tax, and those making more than $10,000 were taxed at 5 percent. (Citizens earning less than $800 paid no income tax.) Excise taxes were also levied on American businesses, along with the first sales taxes on the public. *[The income tax was repealed after the Civil War, but reinstated in 1913 upon ratification of the 16th Amendment to the Constitution.]*

Protective Tariffs

Secretary Chase worked closely with Vermont congressman Justin Morrill to pass a new tariff act in mid-1862 that dramatically increased duties on imported goods. And over the course of Lincoln's first term, additional tariff increases resulted in rates being raised up to 48 percent. Prior to 1861, the United States had one of the lowest tariff rates in the world. These increases not only helped fund the Union's war effort, but were the beginning of indisputable federal government protection for American business and industry. Modern historians generally agree that with such legislation, the Lincoln administration set the stage for the future growth of the modern Industrial Age.

National Paper Currency

Rather than take out a lot of high-interest loans from European banks, the Lincoln administration chose to create an independent debt-free currency. The Legal Tender Act of 1862 established the first national paper money in American history. It authorized an initial issuance of $150 million in "greenbacks," which could be used for payments to the federal government. Credit created by this paper money helped finance the war effort. In addition, the federal government allowed people to use greenbacks in purchasing newly issued war bonds, which accrued interest that was paid in gold. Of particular importance is that the new national currency generated no debt for the United States government. *[Modern Federal Reserve notes generate debt through the purchase of government bonds.]*

National Banking System

The National Banking Acts of 1863 and 1864 created a network of national banks for the first time since Andrew Jackson allowed the Second Bank of the United States to expire in 1836. The new system provided for the further development of a unified national currency backed and secured by the government. It also established federal regulation and supervision of all national banking. President Lincoln lobbied actively for the passage of these bills in Congress, which he said were to protect "honest trade and honest labor" and "furnish to the people a [safe] currency." By the end of the war, hundreds of national bank branches were in operation, mostly converted from former state banks. The Lincoln administration's new network became a blueprint for the future of America's modern banking system.

Four additional pieces of major legislation originated during the Lincoln administration, this time largely from a cooperative undertaking between Congress and the Department of the Interior. Both Secretary Caleb B. Smith and Assistant Secretary John Palmer Usher followed Abraham Lincoln's direction and helped create the following acts of Congress.

Homestead Act

The Homestead Act of 1862 promised 160 acres of surveyed government land to any adult citizen who agreed to farm, improve, and live on the land for five years. Essentially, this legislation provided for the privatization of federally owned land to promote development and growth in the western territories of the United States. As a result, millions of acres were given away and tens of thousands of new farms were created by Americans migrating west.

Transcontinental Railroad

Also aiding in the development of the West was the Pacific Railroad Act of 1862, which provided federal subsidies for the construction of a transcontinental railroad and telegraph line (from the Missouri River to the Pacific Ocean). The Union Pacific and Central Pacific railroad companies were awarded approximately 25 acres of land for every mile of track built *and* they were issued 30-year government bonds to finance construction. Once completed, the transcontinental railroad opened West Coast trade from Asia and East Coast trade from Europe to the rest of the continental United States. And along the new tracks came massive commercial and industrial development. *[The 1,907-mile route was completed when the Union Pacific and Central Pacific Railroads met at Promontory Summit, Utah, on May 10, 1869.]*

Land-Grant Colleges

The Land-Grant College Act of 1862, introduced by Vermont congressman Justin Morrill, gave every state 30,000 acres of government land for each senator and representative in Congress. That land was then sold and the proceeds used to create colleges and universities for the study of agriculture, engineering, and military science. Over time, more than 17 million acres were apportioned. These federal government grants provided the framework for a new system of higher education in the United States, essentially making an affordable education available for the average American.

The Department of Agriculture

On May 15, 1862, President Lincoln established the United States Department of Agriculture (USDA) on a non-cabinet-level status, independent of the Department of the Interior. Because more than half of America's population lived and worked on farms, Lincoln called the USDA "peculiarly a people's department" that would serve the best interests "of a large class of our most valuable citizens." During the Civil War, the new department accumulated crop statistics and distributed them to farmers, which helped them receive fair market prices. Over the next quarter of a century, the Department of Agriculture became one of the most valued agencies of the federal government. *[The USDA was elevated to cabinet-level status in 1889.]*

These achievements of the Lincoln administration and 37th and 38th United States Congresses were all the more remarkable when viewed in context with Abraham Lincoln's previous positions and statements on the same issues. For instance, in 1832, as a first-time candidate for office, he said, "I am in favor of a national bank . . . , the internal improvement system . . . , and a high protective tariff." Also in 1832, he backed the building of railroads throughout Illinois, because they were "a never-failing source of communication between places of business remotely situated from each other." In 1837, Lincoln created a government partnership with business and industry to begin the process of building those Illinois railroads. In 1839, he supported a government-regulated national bank. "No duty is more imperative on the [United States] Government than the duty it owes the people of furnishing them a sound and uniform currency," he said. And when the effects of the Financial Panic of 1837 finally took hold, Lincoln suggested purchasing all federally owned public land in the state and then selling it to the public. He also introduced a bill in the 1838–1839 Illinois legislature that proposed generating revenue through a graduated property tax plan in which the wealthy carried a higher share of "the burden." And "upon the subject of education," he said he viewed it "as the most important subject which we as a people can be engaged in." Finally, in 1859, in an address to the Wisconsin State Agricultural Society, Lincoln stated that "no other human occupation opens so wide a field for the profitable and agreeable combination of labor with cultivated thought, as agriculture."

Moreover, as president, Lincoln didn't stop there when it came to promoting his old agenda. He never forgot his failed attempt (as a member of the U.S. Congress in 1849) to end slavery in the nation's capital. Nor did he ever waver on his support for servicemen in the American military, whether they were ordered into battle for what he believed to be an unjust cause (such as President Polk's war with Mexico) or a just cause (such as his own during the Civil War). Accordingly, as president, Lincoln worked with Congress to secure two more pieces of major legislation.

Abolition of Slavery in Washington, D.C.

Lincoln worked closely with Massachusetts senator Henry Wilson to help craft the District of Columbia Compensated Emancipation Act, which he signed into law on April 16, 1862. The law immediately freed approximately 3,000 slaves then living in the nation's capital and provided $1 million to compensate owners. Upon signing the act, Lincoln wrote to Congress that he "never doubted the constitutional authority of Congress to abolish slavery" and that he always "desired to see the national capital freed from the institution in some satisfactory way." Lincoln's freeing of the slaves in Washington, D.C., predated and set the stage for his preliminary and final Emancipation Proclamations (issued on September 22, 1862, and January 1, 1863, respectively).

Taking Care of Veterans

On July 14, 1862, President Lincoln signed into law the Veterans Pension Act, which "provided eligibility to every person in military or naval service since March 4, 1861 [the day Lincoln took office], their widows, orphans, and other dependents." For a time during the Civil War, the section of the War Department that administered veterans' pensions accounted for almost half of the federal budget. The stage for future federal government support of the men and women who serve in the United States armed forces was set, in part, by Abraham Lincoln's actions during the Civil War. *[The Veterans Bureau (created on August 9, 1921) became the Veterans Administration (on July 21, 1930) and was elevated to cabinet-level status as the Department of Veterans Affairs (on March 15, 1989).]*

★ ★ ★

President Abraham Lincoln, his cabinet secretaries, and the United States Congress worked together to achieve *the largest ex-*

pansion of federal power in American history (up to that point in time). Their collaborative, decisive actions helped finance the Civil War, strengthen the economy, and set the stage for further development of the entire nation. Of course, while the president was pursuing his legislative agenda, anti-Lincoln Republican radicals and opponents in the Democratic Party fought him at every turn. But being the pragmatic politician he was, Lincoln expected it, handled it, and didn't let it bother him. Essentially, he unwaveringly maintained his agenda, cooperated with those who supported him, and simply "plowed around" those who did not.

Perhaps the most remarkable aspect of the Lincoln administration's legislative achievements is that the results actually could be seen in his own time as president, and Lincoln, himself, knew it to be true. As he said in his December 6, 1864, annual address to Congress:

> It is of noteworthy interest that the steady expansion of population, improvement, and governmental institutions over the new and unoccupied portions of our country have scarcely been checked, much less impeded or destroyed, by our great civil war, which at first glance would seem to have absorbed almost the entire energies of the nation.

Any historian, serious student, or even amateur fan of Abraham Lincoln has to recognize that the 16th president could not possibly have achieved such an astonishing legislative record all by himself. He did it, in part, by working with his team. And that started when he placed in his cabinet some of the country's most talented and outstanding leaders, even though most were once his adversaries. Rather than being jealous of their abilities, Lincoln treated them kindly and decently, and formed friendships with all of them. He gave credit where credit was due, accepted responsibility for failures, and came to their defense when they were attacked. And, in turn, nearly all responded by working hard, being loyal, and trusting Lincoln to do the right thing.

Lincoln's old friend and ally Illinois congressman Owen Lovejoy once persuaded the president to issue an order transferring some troops to help with a local project. But when Lovejoy took the order over to the War Department, Secretary Edwin M. Stanton refused to honor it, calling the president "a damned fool" for approving it. Lovejoy then went back to the White House and relayed the message.

"Did Stanton really say I was a damned fool?" asked Lincoln.

"He did, sir, and repeated it," replied Lovejoy.

After a momentary pause, Lincoln looked up and said, "Well, if Stanton said I was a damned fool, then I must be one, for he is nearly always right, and generally says what he means. I will step over and see him."

LINCOLN ON LEADERSHIP FOR TODAY

Big Versus Small Federal Government

Abraham Lincoln always favored a strong federal government and, while president, did indeed preside over the largest expansion of federal power in American history (up to that point in time). He created the national banking system to "furnish to the people a [safe] currency" and to ensure "honest trade and honest labor." In order to promote economic development and growth, he awarded federal subsidies for construction of a transcontinental railroad and telegraph. He gave away federally owned land, which was sold by the states to create colleges and universities.

Overall, Lincoln's massive expansion of the federal government helped finance the Civil War, reduce the national debt, strengthen the economy, and set the stage for future economic development. And amazingly, as Lincoln noted near the end of the war, the nation's "steady expansion" had "scarcely been checked, much less impeded or destroyed, by our great civil war."

Today, the federal government consists of more than 400 agencies that employ a little more than 4 million people (including the armed forces), which is slightly less than 2 percent of the total United States workforce. Controversy going back to the days of Hamilton and Jefferson continues to rage over whether the United States should have a big or small federal government. Those against a strong federal government argue that it breeds inept and wasteful spending, inhibits capitalism and free markets, provides poorer service than the private sector, and interferes with states setting their own social standards. Those in favor say it is necessary to provide regulation of capitalism and markets, the federal services keep prices down, and the federal government provides a collective and consistent moral compass for the entire nation.

Were Abraham Lincoln here today, I believe he would still be "no less than National." As he once said, "The legitimate object of government, is to do for a community of people, whatever they need to have done, but cannot do ... for themselves — in their separate and individual capacities." That being said, I'm sure Lincoln would continue to employ the vast resources of the nation to promote economic progress for all, maintain a strong national defense, and provide protections for the American people in terms of safe food, water, living conditions, and the like.

The IRS and Taxes

In order to fund the Union war effort and to reduce the national debt, the Lincoln administration created the position of internal revenue commissioner (precursor to the present-day Internal Revenue Service) and implemented the nation's first federal income tax. A simple three-tier graduated tax system was put in place, where the poor paid nothing and the rich paid the most. Excise taxes were also levied on American businesses, along with the first sales tax on the public.

Today, the Internal Revenue Service (IRS) is a branch of the Department of the Treasury. It employs approximately 90,000 people, has an operating budget of about $11 billion, and collects more than $2 trillion in revenue each year. It is also one of the most unpopular and feared agencies within the federal government. In fact, many conservative extremists have called for the complete abolishment of the IRS. This position is largely grounded in the complexity of federal tax laws, the agency's reputation for lack of compassion for average American taxpayers, its favoritism toward big business, and its understaffed bureaucratic departments that don't communicate with each other.

Were Abraham Lincoln here today, I believe he would maintain that the Internal Revenue Service is a necessary arm of the Department of the Treasury. But he would also conclude that individual income and corporate tax laws have become far too complicated and, in some cases, outrageously unfair — especially in regard to individuals and small business owners.

In my opinion, Lincoln would not abolish the IRS, but would give it a major overhaul. He would try to revamp and simplify the nation's entire tax system and imbue it with fairness and respect for the average American citizen. Income taxes would be made on a flat-rate assessment, with graduated increases for the wealthiest among us, because they can bear "the burden," while the poor cannot. He would lower corporate tax rates for manufacturing companies that agree to keep jobs in the United States — and he would provide tax credits for those that help their communities fund internal improvements and social programs. I believe his overall position would be this: If the federal government successfully creates an economic system that fosters an individual's right to rise, those who reap the rewards of that system should rightly be expected to pay back a fair tax to the government. That income, in turn, would be used to perpetuate the overall system and keep it vigorous. We're all in this together.

A Balanced Budget and the National Debt

Because of the ongoing recession caused by the Financial Panic of 1857, Lincoln came to power when there was virtually no money in the United States Treasury. That's one reason his administration raised taxes, created the first IRS, established a national currency backed and secured by the government, and implemented federal regulations to control banking practices. When Lincoln officially took office in 1861, the national debt was about $65 million. At the end of 1864, the last full year of his presidency, it was slightly less than $2 billion. Obviously, the federal government had to go into debt to fund and win the Civil War. And by the way, in 1860, the annual budget deficit was $29 million, but in 1864, it had zoomed to $781 million, 89 percent of which was allocated to defense.

Today, the current annual federal budget deficit is approximately $2.5 billion (2016 statistics). It reached a high of nearly $10 billion in 2009 due to the Great Recession. The national debt (federal only) is approximately $18 trillion (the highest on record). This number (47 percent of which is foreign-held) is the amount of money owed by the federal government. The monthly interest paid on it is approximately $20 billion (2016), with an average interest rate of 2.43

percent. There has been significant controversy over both of these inordinately high numbers. Most argue that interest paid on the national debt benefits only those who hold the notes and puts the American taxpayer in a bind. The same argument is made regarding annual budget deficits, because the money that has to make up for the shortfall cannot merely be printed at the Treasury Department, but also has to be borrowed. A minority of individuals, however, seem relatively unconcerned with the national debt and also believe that budget deficits don't matter.

It is my opinion that if Lincoln were president today, he would say that only in time of war or serious financial crises should the national debt and the budget deficit be allowed to rise precipitously. In normal times, the federal government should balance its budget every year, and the national debt should be kept as low as possible. He would certainly understand that a yearly balanced budget fosters a lower debt, which reduces interest payments, and that, in turn, provides much-needed public funds that can be used elsewhere. Lincoln might also go so far to say that to carry major budget deficits year after year in times of peace and prosperity is simply irresponsible. And so is having a national debt that will clearly plague future generations. Simply dealing with deficits by taking out new bonds only leads to a downward-spiraling cycle of debt, which will eventually lead to financial despair. Abraham Lincoln, like any responsible national leader, would feel compelled to implement a long-term plan to reduce the nation's staggering national debt. He would also strive to balance the federal budget as fast as possible and work toward a sustained surplus, which would provide the long-term revenue necessary to ensure the survivability of important social programs like Social Security and Medicare.

Veterans Affairs

A federal department related to taking care of America's veterans did not exist before the Civil War. Abraham Lincoln created one on July 14, 1862, and made its services retroactive to the first day of his presidency (March 4, 1861). Run out of a small office in the War

Department, it provided funds for disability payments and benefits for widows and dependents, and covered all health care costs for diseases incurred while in the service.

Today, the Department of Veterans Affairs has an annual budget of approximately $80 million, employs about 300,000 people, and serves more than 21 million American veterans. I am relatively certain that if Abraham Lincoln were here today, he would accord this cabinet-level agency the very highest priority and make certain it was well funded and exceptionally led. He would say that we must never forget the brave men and women, living and dead, who have fought so that "government of the people, by the people, for the people, shall not perish from the earth." Specifically, today's Lincoln would increase the budget for the Department of Veterans Affairs and ensure that all veterans receive the finest health care possible. He would also pay particular attention to see that all hospitals and clinics associated with the Veterans Health Administration are run with the highest efficiency and sense of urgency.

In the very last paragraph of Abraham Lincoln's second inaugural address, he did not forget America's men and women in uniform. "Let us strive on," he said, ". . . *to care for him who shall have borne the battle, and for his widow, and his orphan.*"

I hope I am a Christian.

— Lincoln, after emerging from personal
despair over his son's death on
February 20, 1862

| ISSUES
Religion and Politics
Politics and the Military
Congressional Investigative Committees
Torture and the Geneva Conventions

11

The Fiery Trial

★ ★ ★

L INCOLN ENTERED WILLIE'S ROOM. He walked slowly
to the bed, lifted the cover from his son's face, and began to
weep. "My poor boy," he said softly, "he was too good for this
earth. God has called him home. I know that he is much better off
in heaven, but then we loved him so. It is hard, hard to have him
die." Then Lincoln buried his face in his hands. His entire body
trembled as he sobbed in grief.

It was early evening on February 20, 1862. Eleven-year-old Willie
had taken sick a few weeks earlier with what was probably typhoid fever (caused by salmonella poisoning from contaminated
food or water), and had finally succumbed around 5:00 p.m.
Eight-year-old Tad had contracted a milder case of the disease
but would soon recover. Devastated by the loss, Mary Lincoln

went into a deep depression, wept inconsolably, and mourned for more than a year. The president also isolated himself, cried for days, and after the funeral went back to busy 18-hour days. The work kept him going, but his fight to hold the nation together was now joined by another, much more personal battle. Lincoln began to struggle seriously with his faith. Why had God allowed his son to die?

Abraham Lincoln's spirituality was grounded early in life by his mother, Nancy Hanks Lincoln, a devout woman who regularly read the Bible to him. As he got older, though, the unusually intelligent young man was put off by organized religious dogma. "I have found difficulty in giving my assent, without mental reservation, to the long complicated statements of Christian doctrine," he once said. Lincoln had a problem, for instance, with the concept of eternal damnation preached by so many authoritarian ministers — preferring to believe that all wrongdoers could be forgiven and redeemed. It was for such reasons that, as an adult, he never formally joined a church. And, of course, in the rural communities of Illinois, Lincoln was attacked politically for that decision, especially when he ran for U.S. Congress against a well-known Methodist missionary named Peter Cartwright. But he responded straightforwardly and in writing. "[It is true] that I am not a member of any Christian Church," he said, "but I have never denied the truth of the Scriptures, and I have never spoken with intentional disrespect of religion in general, or any denomination of Christians in particular." Eventually, it became clear to most voters that Abraham Lincoln could be trusted, and he was elected to Congress.

Over the course of his career, Lincoln's views on religion and politics remained clear. While he believed in the Jeffersonian doctrine relating to separation of church and state, he also said, "I do not think I could myself be brought to support a man for office, whom I knew to be an open enemy of, and scoffer at, religion." And although Lincoln frequently used quotes from biblical scripture in both his speeches and writings, he did not preach conversion to one denomination or another, leaving, as he said, "the higher matter of eternal consequences, between [a person] and his Maker."

As president, Lincoln and his family attended the New York Avenue Presbyterian Church, and when Willie died, the pastor there, Reverend Phineas D. Gurley, presided over the funeral. He described the boy as "a child of bright intelligence and of peculiar promise," who was "inquisitive and conscientious . . . , amiable and affectionate . . . , kind and generous . . . [and] gentle." Many people had described Lincoln, himself, as having these very same qualities. Even Mary once said of her husband that there was a "kind of poetry in his nature." Young Willie, too, was a budding poet. On a trip to Chicago in 1859 with his father, the eight-year-old had written to a friend of their hotel accommodations:

> Me and father have a nice room to ourselves.
> We have two little pitchers on a washstand.
> The smallest one for me, the largest one for father.
> We have two little towels on top of both pitchers.
> The smallest one for me, the largest one for father.
> We have two little beds in the room.
> The smallest one for me, the largest one for father.
> We have two little wash basins.
> The smallest one for me, the largest one for father.

The loss of a son who was so much like him struck Lincoln particularly hard. All his friends and those with whom he worked attended Willie's funeral. "Senators, ambassadors, and soldiers, all struggling with their tears," one witness recalled, "[were] sorrowing with the president as a stricken man and a brother." Even General George B. McClellan was present "with a moist eye when he bowed in prayer." Although he and the president had feuded about how to conduct the war, McClellan had taken the time not only to attend the funeral, but to write a touching letter of condolence to Lincoln. "I have not felt authorized to intrude upon you personally," the general wrote. "Yet I cannot refrain from expressing to you the sincere and deep sympathy I feel for you."

★ ★ ★

Many modern presidents have faced a hostile military whose members were affiliated with the opposing political party. In Lincoln's time, the majority of high-ranking Union officers were Democrats — and that included George B. McClellan. Young and impetuous, McClellan had referred to President Lincoln as "an idiot" and "a well-meaning baboon." That sentiment also seemed to permeate his staff, which, according to General John Pope, had discussed "Lincoln's weakness and the necessity of replacing him by some stronger man."

Less than a month after Willie Lincoln died, the president removed McClellan as general-in-chief of all the Union armies and left him in command of only the Army of the Potomac. Then, following a failed campaign along the Virginia Peninsula, McClellan led Union forces to a draw at the Battle of Antietam in Maryland. Despite not using two divisions that were larger than Confederate general Robert E. Lee's entire army, McClellan managed to push the rebels back into Virginia, but did not pursue the enemy as the president had wished. *[With more than nearly 23,000 soldiers killed, wounded, or missing, the Battle of Antietam (on September 17, 1862) produced the bloodiest single day of the Civil War.]*

Shortly after Antietam, it was reported to Lincoln that Major John J. Key, when asked why McClellan hadn't pursued Robert E. Lee's forces, replied: "That is not the game. . . . The object is that neither shall get much advantage of the other [and] that both shall be kept in the field until they are exhausted, when we will make a compromise and save slavery."

Major Key, a member of General Henry Halleck's staff in Washington (and the brother of McClellan's judge advocate), was immediately summoned to the White House. When Lincoln confirmed that Key had, indeed, made the statement, the president "forthwith dismissed [him] from the military service of the United States." To Key, Lincoln wrote that it was "wholly inadmissible for any gentleman holding a military commission from the United States to utter such sentiments." Explaining his action later to John Hay, the president stated that "it was his object to break up that game" and that he had "dismissed Major Key for his silly treasonable talk because [he] feared it was staff talk and [he] wanted [to make] an example [of Key]."

Also concerned about the political ramifications of too many Democrats in the American military, the Republican majority in Congress had previously created the Joint Committee on the Conduct of the War and had initially summoned witnesses to testify against General McClellan. Further investigations led to the discovery of fraud in War Department contracting, which eventually led to Lincoln's removal of Simon Cameron. Additional investigative committees formed by Congress included the House Select Committee on Government Contracts and a judiciary committee to examine the administration's censorship of the press. As president, Lincoln would have to endure continual interference and oversight by Congress, but he handled it deftly by treating members with respect, by telling the truth, and by openly providing relevant information. However, he always kept in mind that his own party was in the majority, and as a result, no truly devastating political problems would befall his administration, especially since he was fighting a war to save the Union. That did not prevent the opposition party from increasing political rhetoric leading up to the November 1862 midterm elections. Both War Democrats and Peace Democrats attacked Lincoln relentlessly for suspending *habeas corpus,* for not winning any major military victories, for raising taxes, and for dramatically expanding the federal government. Lincoln, too, noted that "our newspapers [are] vilifying and disparaging the administration," and he soon became exceedingly worried that the Republicans might, indeed, lose control of Congress.

★ ★ ★

For the rest of 1862, one of the ways Lincoln dealt with the loss of his son was to keep busy. As soon as the weather got warm enough, he headed out into the field to mix and mingle with the troops. Traveling and being around people was good therapy for him. On one occasion, he ventured over to the Washington Navy Yard to watch a demonstration of a couple of new weapons. While there, he caught sight of an axe, picked it up, and performed his trick of holding it out at arm's length by the tip of the handle. Lincoln only smiled when none of the other men standing around could duplicate the feat. On another trip, accompanied by Secretary of War Stanton, the president visited the logistical supply point at Aquia Creek, about 50 miles down the Potomac River in Virginia. When an officer pointed out a trestle bridge being built over a ravine about a hundred feet above the water, Lincoln looked at the single wood plank traversing the span, said, "C'mon, let's walk over," and quickly took off. About halfway across, Secretary Stanton got dizzy and had to be helped. But the president bounded across with ease and waited on the other side, probably delighted at his boyish romp.

When he was stuck in the White House, Lincoln also liked to sneak out and walk across the lawn to the telegraph office at the War Department. "I come here to escape my persecutors," he explained to one telegraph operator. Upon arriving, Lincoln would usually go to the drawer where dispatches were filed in order of receipt. Then he would read them from the top down until he came to one he had seen at his last visit. "Well, boys, I've got down to the raisins," he'd say to the operators present. After hearing the expression several times, someone finally asked him what it meant, and Lincoln responded:

Well, it's like this. There was once a little girl who ate some raisins before going to a birthday party. Once there, she took part in the festivities by stuffing herself with cake, candy, and other goodies. At home, though, she got sick and started to throw up. Up came the goodies and up came the candy, and up came the cake. Finally, up came the raisins. Then the little girl looked up at her mother and said: "I'll be all right now, Ma, for I have got down to the raisins."

One afternoon during the late summer of 1862, President Lincoln asked Major Thomas Eckert, head of the telegraph office, if he could borrow some paper and use Eckert's desk to write "something special." Lincoln then sat down, wrote out a few lines, and began staring out the window. After a while, he jotted down another couple of lines, looked up, and stared out the window again. This routine continued until the president was ready to leave, at which point he asked Eckert to hold on to the draft and not let anyone read it. The next day, when Lincoln showed up, Eckert unlocked his desk and handed the papers to the president, who read what he had written, revised it, and then wrote some more. This went on for nearly two weeks until, finally, one day, he took all the papers back with him to the White House. "Well, boys," he'd often say, "I will go home now. I had no business here, but as the lawyer said, I had none anywhere else."

★ ★ ★

The results of the 1862 midterm elections were bad, but not as bad as Lincoln had feared. The Democratic Party gained legislative control of the Pennsylvania and Indiana legislatures and the governor's offices in New York and New Jersey. In the U.S. Congress, Democrats picked up 28 seats in the House of Representatives, but actually lost 1 seat in the Senate. So at the end of the day, Republicans retained a majority in both houses of Congress, but their political strength was seriously weakened. The president was particularly disturbed to learn that his friend Illinois senator Orville Browning had been defeated, and that his home congressional district had gone Democratic. When asked how he felt about the losses, Lincoln responded, "I feel somewhat like that boy in Kentucky, who stubbed his toe while running to see his sweetheart. The boy said he was too big to cry, and too badly hurt to laugh."

Major newspapers described the election results as a serious rebuke to the Lincoln administration. The *New York Times* wrote that the elections represented "a want of confidence" in the president, himself, and the *New York Herald* hailed them as the beginning of a "Conservative Revolution." And most political pundits still did not believe Abraham Lincoln had the wherewithal to handle the presidency during such a crisis. He was just a nice guy with "a sort of boyish cheerfulness," said one. He was "an honest old codger," who was obviously "unequal to his place," said another.

Lincoln, however, brushed off the criticism, put the bad news behind him, and quickly returned to his forceful handling of the war effort. On November 5, 1862 (the day after the elections), he relieved George B. McClellan of command of the Army of the Potomac and sent him to Trenton, New Jersey, to await new orders (which never arrived). Lincoln had been fed up with McClellan ever since the Battle of Antietam but purposely waited until after the elections to fire him, telling Secretary Chase that it would be "inexpedient" to do so sooner. In McClellan's place, the president appointed the politically neutral General Ambrose E. Burnside.

Knowing that the president had fired McClellan in part because he'd refused to move toward Richmond, Burnside quickly put together a plan to do just that, which Lincoln immediately approved. The first step in Burnside's strategy was to take Fredericksburg, Virginia—located on the Rappahannock River halfway between Washington and the Confederate capital. But by the time the Army of the Potomac's 120,000 troops arrived, Robert E. Lee had already taken the high ground outside Fredericksburg with the Army of Northern Virginia (85,000 men strong). Over several days of fighting, Lee and his top general, Stonewall Jackson, outmaneuvered Burnside and his senior officers (who included Joe Hooker and George Meade) in what was another terrible Union defeat. *[Union casualties were 12,653 killed or wounded versus 5,377 for the Confederates.]*

President Lincoln was immediately blasted by the Democrats, who blamed the loss in part on his replacement of their man McClellan with Burnside. So they called for a peace agreement with the Confederacy that might allow slavery. Radical Republicans in the Senate also issued a resolution demanding "a change in and partial reconstruction of the Cabinet." In discussing the event with a friend, Lincoln said, "[These men] wish to get rid of me, and I am sometimes half disposed to gratify them. . . . We are now on the brink of destruction . . . and I can hardly see a ray of hope." Lincoln's despair over the repercussions caused by the loss at Fredericksburg became starkly clear when he told another friend, "If there is a place worse than hell, I'm in it!"

Almost immediately, however, the president sat down and wrote a public letter praising the Union troops, which read, in part: "The courage with which you, in an open field, maintained the contest against an entrenched foe . . . [shows] that you possess all the qualities of a great army, which will yet give victory to the cause of the country and of popular government." He also rode down to the Potomac River and visited the troops as they returned from the front.

The Battle of Fredericksburg was representative of the horrors of war. Thousands of bodies littered the battlefield, one section of which became known as the Slaughter Pen. The town also was virtually destroyed, as private homes and businesses were burned or looted. And as the Civil War raged on, things only got worse. In the first two years (1861–1862) alone, at least four major battles were fought in Virginia (Bull Run, Fredericksburg, Seven Days, and Second Bull Run), three in Tennessee (Fort Donelson, Shiloh, and Stones River), and one in Maryland (Antietam). There were also countless smaller battles fought in 15 states or territories (Arkansas, Florida, Georgia, Kentucky, Louisiana, Minnesota, Mississippi, Missouri, New Mexico, North Carolina, Oklahoma, South Carolina, Texas, Virginia, and West Virginia). In all, casualties amounted to previously unimagined heights — nearly a quarter of a million killed or wounded (Union and Confederacy combined). And as passions and intensities ramped up, so did related war atrocities, such as starvation and torture of prisoners, hostage-taking, and wanton executions and massacres.

Although disturbed and humbled by all the gore and bloodletting, Abraham Lincoln did not let up on his forceful prosecution of the Union war effort. He did, however, attempt to mitigate cruelty whenever possible. For example, after a series of Indian raids in Minnesota killed hundreds, 303 Sioux were scheduled for a mass execution in December 1862. But the president had all trial records sent to him, and after reviewing each personally, he commuted the sentences of 265 of the condemned Sioux. When a Minnesota senator suggested that more political capital could have been gained had he let all the executions go on as scheduled, Lincoln responded: "I [can] not afford to hang men for votes."

Less than six months later, the Lincoln administration issued General War Order No. 100, which contained the first United States code regulating military conduct in times of war. Better known as the Lieber Code (named after its author, Columbia University professor Franz Lieber), it enumerated a series of laws designed to regulate behavior and prohibit abuses. Specifically mentioned, for instance, were the rights of prisoners of war (food, clothing, housing, etc.), along with the prohibited use of torture as a method to extract confessions or other information. Distinctions between combatants and civilians were also made explicit, and whenever possible, the lives, property, and honor of local residents had to be spared. Initiated under the direction of the Army's chief of staff, General Henry Halleck, the Lieber

Code provided the basis for future military codes, including the Geneva Conventions. *[General Order No. 100 was signed by President Lincoln on April 24, 1863. Five thousand copies of an associated pamphlet were distributed to the Union military under the title* Instructions for the Government of the Armies of the United States in the Field.*]*

* * *

"Where's the fire — what's burning?" asked the president, bursting through the White House doors late one night in 1864.

"It seems to be around the vicinity of the stable," replied the security guard.

With that, Lincoln bolted down the steps and ran around to the east side of the building, where he saw the stables engulfed in flames. "[He] jumped over the boxwood hedge," recalled one witness, "[and] threw open the stable doors to try to get the horses out." But the soldiers restrained him from going inside. All the animals "were lost in the fire," he was later told. That night, Lincoln was seen standing at an east window of the White House, weeping. Willie Lincoln's pony had been in that stable.

Two years had passed since his son had died, but Lincoln's heartache was fresh, the pain still palpable. He had gone through a rough period of personal despair, struggled with his faith, and earnestly tried to find answers. As part of that process, Lincoln spoke a number of times with Reverend Phineas D. Gurley, continued to read the Bible every morning (only now with more intensity), and prayed often. After some time, Lincoln crystallized his thoughts in regard to his spiritual beliefs and arrived at several conclusions.

First, Lincoln believed that, ultimately, it was God's will that his son had been taken. Second, as he told a friend, "I think I can say with sincerity, that I hope I am a Christian." He had lived, he said, "until my boy Willie died, without fully realizing these things. That blow overwhelmed me [and] showed me my weakness as I had never felt it before." To another friend, Lincoln confessed, "I am very sure that if I do not go away from here a wiser man, I shall go away a better man for having learned here what a very poor sort of man I am."

John H. Littlefield, who studied law with Lincoln for two years, confirmed that he was "a man who had arrived at a point in Christianity without going to church that others struggle to attain, but do not reach, by going. . . . I never associated with a man who seemed so ready to serve another." And Francis B. Carpenter, an artist who stayed at the White House for six months, said of Lincoln that "no man had a more abiding sense of his dependence upon God . . . and in the power and ultimate triumph of Truth and Right in the world."

President Lincoln also concluded that the Civil War, too, was in God's hands. But because he personally had experienced no divine revelations, he had to act on his own best judgment. "These are not the days of miracles," said Lincoln. "[So] I must study the plain physical facts of the case, ascertain what is possible, and learn what appears to be wise and right." To Mrs. Eliza Gurney in October 1862, Lincoln wrote: "We are indeed going through a great trial — *a fiery trial*. In the very responsible position in which I happen to be placed . . . , I have desired that all my works and acts may be according to His will . . . but if after endeavoring to do my best in *the light* which He affords me, I find my efforts fail, I must believe that for some purpose unknown to me, He wills it otherwise." [Italics added.]

In reality, over the last several years of his life, Abraham Lincoln experienced two fiery trials — a very public one as the nation engaged in a civil war, and another very private struggle in dealing with the loss of his son. That he deeply felt the pressure of both is patently obvious in the closing to his second annual message to Congress (delivered on December 1, 1862). In leading up to the issuance of the Emancipation Proclamation exactly one month later, these are the eloquent words President Lincoln used to inspire his countrymen to continue striving toward the light:

Fellow citizens, *we* cannot escape history. We of this Congress and this administration, will be remembered in spite of ourselves. *No personal significance, or insignificance, can spare one or another of us.* The *fiery trial* through which we pass, will *light* us down, in honor or dishonor, to the latest generation. . . . We — even we here — hold the power, and bear the responsibility. In giving freedom to the slave, we assure freedom to the free — honorable alike in what we give, and what we preserve. We shall nobly save, or meanly lose, the last best hope of earth. Other means may succeed; this could not fail. The way is plain, peaceful, generous, just — a way which, if followed, the world will forever applaud, and God must forever bless. [Italics added.]

LINCOLN ON LEADERSHIP FOR TODAY

Religion and Politics

Abraham Lincoln read the Bible every morning, attended church, and purchased a family pew. Yet he was not a member of any particular Protestant sect, nor did he ever formally join a church. He lived by teachings and principles of the Old and New Testaments, yet he rejected hard-core dogma preached by many leaders. In other words, Lincoln was spiritual without being overly religious. He understood and believed that the Founders intended that the U.S. government not impose any restrictions on religious freedom.

Today, religion and politics in America are seen as extensions of each other, and there is a never-ending debate on the role of religion in public life—and the separation of church and state, which is a doctrine not mentioned in the Constitution. In addition, a solid base of one of the two major political parties identifies with conservative religious fundamentalism and believes that the party platform should mirror their beliefs and aims. As a result, the issue of a person's faith often takes center stage during political debates.

If Abraham Lincoln were to survey what is happening today, I'm sure he would reaffirm that the United States of America guarantees freedom of religion to all people and prohibits discrimination based on religious preference. In my opinion, he would also support a separation of church and state, where the government does not involve itself in church doctrine, and where no religious organization influences government to any significant degree, most especially in legislation.

Lincoln today would still read the Bible every morning. He would still live his life according to the principles of the Old and New Testaments, and he would continue to shy away from religious dogma. Lincoln would reject the notion that any one religion is superior to any other. He would accord all religions equal respect—and he would respect every human being, regardless of religious affiliation.

Politics and the Military

When Abraham Lincoln was president, a majority of officers in the American military were members of the opposition party. Many resented his involvement in military planning, denigrated him behind his back, and didn't necessarily want to advance his political goals. As a matter of fact, when Lincoln learned that a member of General Halleck's staff had stated that the Army did not pursue Lee's forces after the Battle of Antietam because "that is not the game," and that their object was to force a compromise to save slavery, Lincoln fired the officer "to break up that game" and to make an example of him.

Today, as back then, most of the officers of the armed forces of the United States (which report to the president as commander in chief) are members of one particular political party, which is often not that of the president. And there is controversy when a high-ranking member of the military speaks out publicly against the policies of the executive branch.

Given Lincoln's actions during the Civil War, I don't think there would be much doubt about his position on this issue. He would clearly understand that, in the United States, politics and the military are ill-fitting bedfellows. America's Founding Fathers were trying to get away from the concept of one person, one monarch, or one dictator ruling with absolute power — and the Constitution reflects that desire in terms of the relationship between civilian and military leadership. I believe Lincoln would say that members of the military who disagree with executive policies should not express their personal beliefs in public, because doing so might negatively affect military discipline or performance. In such a case, Lincoln would review each such instance, and if he found it to be a particularly grievous breach, he would most likely dismiss the offending officer.

Congressional Investigative Committees

As president, Lincoln had to endure continual interference and oversight from Congress. Among the more well-known investigations were the House Judiciary Committee's look at the administration's censorship of the press, and the Joint Committee on the Conduct of the War, which discovered fraud in the War Department and led to the dismissal of Lincoln's first secretary of war, Simon Cameron.

Today, Congress still has the responsibility to make sure members of the executive branch of government do not abuse their positions or shirk their responsibilities. Congressional investigative committees serve an important role in fulfilling that charge. However, far too often, such committees are formed for purely partisan political reasons (to cast suspicion on the presidential administration or to influence the next national election, etc.).

If Lincoln were alive today, he might use a homespun metaphor to describe congressional investigative committees as something like "chiggers on the body politic." They are small, ever-present annoyances that cause itching and a rash, and can only be seen when clustered in groups on the skin. Their life cycle usually lasts only 2 to 12 months, but they can have a large impact. Chiggers cannot be dismissed out of hand, because they won't go away, nor can congressional committees, because they are part of the government.

I do not believe Lincoln would condone investigative committees being formed for purely partisan political reasons. He would say that they bring dishonor to members of Congress, are a waste of valuable time and public funds, and are disrespectful to the vast majority of the American public. Still, Lincoln would respect them as being representative of congressional authority — and he would see value in legitimate investigations that uncover wrongdoing. Overall, I think he would smother committees by providing all relevant information, answering all questions, and letting the chips fall where they may.

Torture and the Geneva Conventions

Abraham Lincoln recognized the irony that he could never bring himself to shoot a deer but found himself in the middle of the bloodiest of all wars. Yet he strove on to fight for a larger principle. He chose not to avoid the battlefield, but, rather, witnessed the brutality and saw the blood for himself. After receiving reports of torture and inhumane conditions in prisoner of war camps, Lincoln encouraged General Henry Halleck to develop the first United States code regulating military conduct in time of war. Among other things, it defined the rights of prisoners of war and prohibited the use of torture. The Lieber Code, as it was known, became the basis for future military codes, including the Geneva Conventions.

In the wake of the 9/11 terrorist attacks, major controversy erupted when (1) President George W. Bush signed an executive order suspending the Geneva Conventions in relation to al-Qaeda and the Taliban, and (2) his administration approved the use of "enhanced interrogation techniques," which was widely viewed as a euphemism for torture. President Barack Obama, on his second day in office, issued a new executive order essentially rescinding Bush's previous directive.

In my opinion, if Abraham Lincoln were here today, he would take the position that any form of torture is morally wrong and should not be allowed under any circumstances. He would recognize that the Geneva Conventions were established by international consensus for the express purpose of ensuring some degree of basic humanity during times of major conflict — and that any signatory nation is bound, both legally and morally, to uphold them. The Geneva Conventions are part of the belt and suspenders of moral law that prevent human beings from engaging in depravity and animalistic instincts. I don't believe Abraham Lincoln would subscribe to the doctrine of "an eye for an eye." And he might ask us if anyone who approved of or practiced torture on other human beings could possibly be on God's side.

The powder in this bombshell will keep dry, and when the fuse is lit, I intend to have them touch it off themselves.

> — Lincoln, to clergyman C. Edwards Lester,
> shortly after revoking General John Frémont's
> edict freeing slaves in Missouri
> September 11, 1861

All persons held as slaves within any State or designated part of a State, the people whereof shall then be in rebellion against the United States, shall be then, thenceforward, and forever free. . . . And upon this act, sincerely believed to be an act of justice, warranted by the Constitution, upon military necessity, I invoke the considerate judgment of mankind, and the gracious favor of Almighty God.

> — Abraham Lincoln
> Emancipation Proclamation
> January 1, 1863

ISSUES
Public Opinion Polls
Political Idealism Versus Political Reality

12

The Thunderbolt

★ ★ ★

ABRAHAM LINCOLN HAD BEEN sitting at Major Thomas Eckert's desk in the telegraph office on and off nearly every day for a couple of weeks. Curious, but remaining respectfully quiet, Eckert had guessed that the president was writing "something of great importance," but he had no idea exactly what. After the document was finished, Eckert recalled that the president "for the first time told me that he had been writing an order giving freedom to the slaves of the South, for the purpose of hastening the end of the war." Major Eckert may have been the first person to know that Lincoln had completed a draft of the Emancipation Proclamation. Not only had the president not told anyone he was writing it, he hadn't even told anyone he was *contemplating* writing it.

The next people told were a group of congressmen and senators from the border states. Inviting them to the White House on July 12, 1862 (shortly before Congress adjourned), Lincoln asked them "to consider and discuss [possible emancipation] among yourselves" before leaving Washington and, once back home, to "commend it to the consideration of your states and people." The president was also very explicit as to why he had elected to tell them of his plans first. "Believing that you of the border states hold more power for good than any other equal number of members [of Congress], I feel it a duty . . . to make this appeal to you." He also made it clear that he did not "speak of emancipation *at once,* but of a *decision* at once to emancipate *gradually.*" And finally, Lincoln both justified his proposal and tried to inspire the legislators by saying: "Our common country is in great peril, demanding the loftiest views, and boldest action to bring it speedy relief."

The very next day (Sunday, July 13, 1862), Lincoln brought up the idea for the first time to Secretary of State Seward and Secretary of the Navy Welles on a carriage ride. "[The president] dwelt earnestly on the gravity [and] importance . . . of emancipating the slaves by proclamation," recalled Welles. "He said he had given it much thought and had about come to the conclusion that it was a military necessity absolutely essential for the salvation of the Union." After Lincoln asked them to "frankly state how the proposition struck us," both Seward and Welles said they needed more time to think about it before answering. "[This] was a new departure for the President," recalled Welles, because whenever the subject of emancipation had come up previously, "he had been prompt and emphatic in denouncing the subject." Actually, within the past year, Lincoln had revoked similar proclamations from his commanders in the Department of the West (John C. Frémont, September 11, 1861) and the Department of the South (David Hunter, May 10, 1862), and from his first secretary of war (Simon Cameron, December 1, 1861). Each time, the president had objected to his subordinates taking action "on a question which belongs exclusively to me."

At first blush, it might seem that Lincoln was only reacting to someone else infringing on his decision-making territory, but that was not the main reason he reacted the way he did. Lincoln *had* to reserve the right to make any decision on the future of slavery exclusively for himself because too much was riding on it. He understood that the right move at the wrong time could prove fatal — to the Union, to the president, himself, and to the 4 million people in bondage. He could, for instance, lose the border states to the Confederacy, which was the main reason he told their congressional representatives about his idea before the members of his own cabinet. On this issue, Lincoln realized that timing and approach were everything. An executive order abolishing slavery could not simply be issued with an expectation that everybody would obey it unconditionally. It was too radical a move. Lincoln had to bring forth the entire concept cautiously, or "gradually," as he repeatedly phrased it. He had to give people time to get used to the idea so a majority would eventually support, accept, and even call for it. To Lincoln, political idealism was one thing, but political reality was another. "To act differently at this moment, would . . . weaken our cause," he told Reverend C. Edwards Lester shortly after revoking Frémont's proclamation. "We must wait until every other means has been exhausted. The powder in this bombshell will keep dry, and when the fuse is lit, *I intend to have them touch it off themselves.* This thunderbolt will keep." [Italics added.]

And Lincoln did try a number of "other means" to achieve his ultimate goal to end slavery. The truth is that he was feeling his way — searching for a solution that would be acceptable to the American public. One of his first efforts (in November 1861) was a bill drafted with his friend Massachusetts senator Charles Sumner for gradual emancipation in the small slave state of Delaware. *[Recall that Sumner was nearly beaten to death on the Senate floor in 1856.]* Basically, the plan was for the federal government to purchase all of Delaware's slaves over an extended period of time. If the plan worked, it might provide a model for the rest of the nation. But neither Lincoln nor Sumner could gain much support for the idea, so it was not introduced as legislation. Undaunted, however, in March 1862, Lincoln proposed that Congress adopt a joint resolution that the government "cooperate with any state which may adopt gradual abolishment of slavery, giving . . . pecuniary aid . . . to compensate [the state] for the inconveniences produced by such change of system." Although Lincoln stressed that the plan should be voluntary, no border state representatives would support the idea — and that proposal, too, died on the vine. *[This Lincoln proposal, however, did result in the Compensated Emancipation Act, which freed slaves in Washington, D.C., on April 16, 1862.]*

Another major proposal pushed by Lincoln was to send freed slaves outside the United States to either Africa or Central America. The idea was based on a common belief that blacks and whites would never be able to live together peaceably. Politically, colonization was more palatable to border state representatives, and also to Northerners who feared that freed slaves would take jobs away from whites. In June 1862, Congress designated $500,000 for colonization expenses, and in July 1862, Lincoln recommended an additional appropriation of $20 million for the same purpose. Then, hoping to gain support from blacks, themselves, the president invited a group of African American residents of Washington, D.C., to the White House. He presented his idea for colonization, earnestly tried to persuade them of its merits, and asked for support. But the men said no. America was their home, too, they protested. Here they were born, and here they wanted to stay. After speaking privately with his friend African American abolitionist Frederick Douglass, Lincoln came to the conclusion that the majority of blacks, free or slave, felt the same way. And to him, their opinion mattered, because they were Americans, too. So when Lincoln combined this reality with the fact that it was logistically impossible to repatriate 4 million people out of the country, he eventually changed his mind about colonization.

Many leaders do not take the time to actually speak with or ask the opinions of citizens who are directly impacted by their proposed initiatives. Although Lincoln, at first, did not like what he heard, he was at least willing to listen to what his constituents thought. And it is a mark of great leadership that this president was personally secure enough to alter his position when it became clear in his own mind that sending black Americans out of the country was morally wrong. Furthermore, by "floating" the ideas of compensated emancipation and colonization to the public, Lincoln was actually practicing the more modern political tactic of launching "trial balloons." As far back as the Civil War, then, Abraham Lincoln realized it was wiser to gauge public opinion before hurriedly implementing controversial programs.

By mid-July 1862, Lincoln sensed that the timing was right to move forward with an emancipation proclamation. The Union had lost most of the major battles with the Confederacy, Northern support for the war effort was beginning to fracture, the Peace Democrats and War Democrats were dividing Congress, and Lincoln was worried about internal splits within his own party. Taking a forceful step toward abolition might mend some of the developing cracks in his fragile coalition. Also, "ending slavery" would add a morally based reason to his cause (in addition to "preserving the Union"). More practically, a formal decree freeing the slaves would strengthen the Republican Party, cut off European aid to the Confederacy (because it would be viewed as favoring slavery), and weaken the South by taking away its slave workforce (both in the military and on the cotton plantations). Equally important in Lincoln's mind was the very real possibility that former slaves heading north could enlist in the Union military and fight for their own freedom — and *that military necessity* would provide the president's justification for what he knew would be a constitutionally ambiguous executive order.

On July 22, 1862, Lincoln read the draft of his preliminary Emancipation Proclamation to the entire cabinet, saying he was determined to issue it. "As Commander-in-Chief of the Army and Navy of the United States," he would declare that, as of January 1, 1863, all persons held as slaves in any rebellious state would be freed. The draft did not include slaves in Kentucky, Missouri, Maryland, or Delaware, although it did specifically mention that "in due time" the president would recommend that citizens be compensated for "all losses by acts of the United States, including the loss of slaves." In discussing the matter, Lincoln's cabinet was divided, with some strongly in favor, some strongly opposed, and some taking no stance at all. Secretary of State Seward, however, advised the president to wait for a military victory. If done at the present time, with the recent string of military defeats, "it would be considered our last shriek, on the retreat." After thinking about it for a day or so, Lincoln realized that Seward was right. "The wisdom of the Secretary of State," he said, "was an aspect of the case that, in all my thought upon the subject, I had entirely overlooked." So Lincoln put the document aside for the time being. There was more work to be done in shaping public opinion. People had to be more optimistic on the whole — more willing to accept such a bold stroke. And a military victory or two would certainly help fill the need.

★ ★ ★

"Our government rests in public opinion," said Abraham Lincoln. "A majority . . . always changing easily with deliberate changes of public [sentiment] is the only true sovereign of the people." Lincoln understood that leaders, in general, must pay attention to public opinion for three key reasons: (1) to understand what people want and how they feel, (2) to know whether the leaders will meet resistance when implementing change, and (3) to know whether or not public opinion needs to be molded in another direction. "Whoever can change public opinion can change the government," said Lincoln. "He who molds public sentiment . . . makes statutes and decisions possible or impossible to be executed."

Changing public opinion, however, is easier said than done. In order to do so, a leader has to understand people. That's why Lincoln seriously studied and often reflected on human nature. Take, for example, his thoughts on how people react to change. First and foremost, he observed that they don't like it: *"It is not much in the nature of man to be driven to anything,"* he said. Second, if proposed change gets too close to them, they are even more resistant: *"[They are even less likely] to be driven about that which is exclusively [their] own business."* And third, resistance is greatest if money is involved: *"And [they will be] least of all [to change] where such driving is to be submitted to at the expense of pecuniary interest."*

If people do not change easily or quickly, then a leader has to plan for the long term. But that can be a problem, too. "What an ignorance of human nature . . . to expect a whole community to rise up and labor for the happiness of others . . . [especially] after we shall be dead and gone," Lincoln once said. "Great distance, in either time or space, has a wonderful power to lull and render quiescent the human mind." Lincoln even had a joke to illustrate this point:

An honest man once saw a fellow named Paddy getting ready to steal a shovel. "Better lay that down, Paddy," he said. "If you don't, you'll have to pay for it at judgment day."

Paddy thought for a moment and then responded: "Well, if

the powers that be won't get around to coming after me until then, I think I'll take another shovel!"

So if people are unwilling to change, especially when they have money invested, if people think in the here and now, and if they think short term rather than long term — then how in the world does a leader go about changing things? Well, Abraham Lincoln offered some advice about that, too:

> If you would win a man to your cause, *first* convince him that you are his sincere friend. Therein is a drop of honey that catches his heart, which, say what he will, is the great high road to his reason and which, when once gained, you will find but little trouble in convincing his judgment of the justice of your cause, if indeed, that cause really be a just one.

If, as Lincoln said, "a man's heart is the high road to his *reason*," then he might also advise leaders to approach major change by trying to persuade through reason *over an extended period of time*. But he might also caution us to prepare for the natural resistance to change, and to be both persistent and resilient. Of course, that also takes time and hard work, and can lead to false impressions. For instance, many people thought Lincoln, as president, was slow to make a decision regarding what to do about slavery. That perception, however, was false. As a matter of fact, Lincoln had already made three key decisions on this issue: (1) he made the decision to issue an Emancipation Proclamation; (2) he made the decision to wait for a military victory before issuance; and (3) he made the decision to work on public opinion. The mere fact that Lincoln had not yet *acted* on abolishing slavery led those who were less patient to *perceive* that he was an indecisive leader. But the truth is that this president was acting with care and thought for the future. In other words, Lincoln was being prudent in his decision-making.

Because leadership is about people, what they *think* is of paramount importance. Therefore, a true leader must *keep tabs on, respect,* and *influence* public opinion. Abraham Lincoln *kept tabs on* it by carving time out of his day to meet with the general public. "I call these receptions my public opinion baths," he said. "[They] are renovating and invigorating to my perceptions of responsibility and duty." Lincoln *respected* public opinion by viewing it as part of his "responsibility and duty" to act for the wants and needs of the people he represented. And a great example of how and why Lincoln *influenced* public opinion can be seen in his actions between July 22, 1862 (when Secretary of State Seward advised him to wait on emancipation), and January 1, 1863 (when the Emancipation Proclamation was issued).

★ ★ ★

Just as he had done while riding the circuit and running for the U.S. Senate in Illinois, *President* Lincoln courted and coddled the press. After reading too many negative articles in the *New York Times* about the administration's conduct of the war, he invited its publisher, Henry J. Raymond, to the White House for some schmoozing. At one point, Lincoln tried to tell Raymond what he was going through. "I feel like a man renting out rooms at one end of the house while the other end is on fire," he said. After the meeting, Lincoln made sure that all *Times* reporters had access to the cabinet secretaries, and he even wrote to a new congressman that "Raymond is my Lieutenant General in politics," a statement that was sure to get back to the publisher.

The president, moreover, maintained friendships with other newspaper publishers he'd known for years, such as John W. Forney of the *Philadelphia Press.* Such liaisons began to pay off when in July 1862, the *New York Times* editorialized: "It seems not improbable that the President considers the time near at hand when slavery must go to the wall." And on July 30, the *Press* urgently called for the president to take forceful action in ending slavery.

Perhaps Lincoln's most effective action during this period of time was the passionate letter he wrote in response to criticism from the *New York Tribune's* Horace Greeley. On August 20, 1862, the outspoken newspaperman published an editorial entitled "The Prayer of Twenty Millions," which blasted the president for "the policy you seem to be pursuing with regard to the slaves of rebels." Greeley charged that Lincoln was "strangely and disastrously remiss in the discharge of his official [duties]," and that he was "unduly influenced by the representatives of certain fossil politicians hailing from the Border Slave States."

Lincoln immediately dashed off a letter in response to Greeley:

> My paramount object in this struggle is to save the Union, and is not either to save or to destroy slavery. If I could save the Union without freeing any slave I would do it, and if I could save it by freeing all the slaves I would do it; and if I could save it by freeing some and leaving others alone I would also do that. . . . I have here stated my purpose according to my view of official duty; and I intend no modification of my oft-expressed personal wish that all men everywhere could be free.

Rather than sending his response directly to Greeley, Lincoln gave it to his friend James Welling at the *Washington National Intelligencer,* who published it on Saturday, August 23, 1862. The next day, it was picked up by other newspapers and published widely across the country — but not in the *New York Tribune,* because Greeley refused to work on the Sabbath. He finally put Lincoln's response in the *Tribune* on Monday, August 25, after being scooped by every other major media outlet in the nation. "I can't trust your 'Honest Old Abe,'" griped Greeley to a friend. "He is too smart for me."

By this time, the combined actions of Union newspapers had created such a push for the president to move on emancipation that the *New York World* labeled it "Proclamation Mania." *[This intentional escalation of public sentiment is what Lincoln meant when he said he intended to "have them touch (off the powder in this bombshell) themselves."]* Not even a disastrous Union loss at

Second Bull Run on August 30, 1862, could derail the momentum. So when George McClellan pulled out his victorious draw with Robert E. Lee at Antietam, Lincoln quickly called his cabinet together. After reading a chapter from humorist Artemus Ward's new book, which most seemed to enjoy, the president turned to his purpose for the meeting. "Gentlemen, I have, as you are aware, thought a great deal about the relation of this war to slavery," he said. "The time for acting on it [is now]." Lincoln then told his team that he was not there to ask advice, because he already knew where they stood on the matter. But before reading the proclamation, he made this stern statement:

> Though I believe that I have not so much of the confidence of the people as I had some time since, I do not know that, all things considered, any other person has more. There is no way in which I can have any other man put where I am. I am here. I must do the best I can, and bear the responsibility of taking the course which I feel I ought to take.

Abraham Lincoln issued the preliminary Emancipation Proclamation on September 22, 1862, explicitly writing that it would take effect on January 1, 1863. In doing so, he was strategically giving the entire nation three months' notice — to react, to discuss, and to get used to the coming change. And as Lincoln, himself, had predicted, it did indeed prove to be a "thunderbolt."

All factions of the Democratic Party, as usual, attacked the president. The proclamation, they said, would "render eternal hatred" between North and South. Confederate newspapers claimed it would incite a slave insurrection. General George McClellan called it "an accursed doctrine." The stock market plummeted. All the negativity and vitriol simply added to the already-inflamed campaign season and definitely contributed to Republican losses in the November 1862 midterm elections.

On the other hand, abolitionists everywhere were euphoric and flocked to Lincoln's defense. Outdoor rallies were held all across the Northern states. And members of the Republican

Party united in their praise for the president. Free blacks couldn't believe that such a great thing had happened in their own life-times. "We shout for joy that we live to record this righteous decree," wrote Frederick Douglass. "Abraham Lincoln may be slow . . . , [but] he has taught us to . . . confide in his word."

★ ★ ★

On Thursday afternoon, January 1, 1863, Secretary of State Wil-liam Seward brought the Emancipation Proclamation to Abra-ham Lincoln's office and laid it on his desk for the signing cere-mony. The magnitude of the document in front of the president was unprecedented in American history. It was purely an execu-tive order, written by Lincoln, himself, without the approval of Congress. And although it declared all slaves free in only those states in rebellion, that number still amounted to 3.5 million hu-man beings. "All persons held as slaves within any State or des-ignated part of a State, the people whereof shall then be in rebel-lion against the United States, shall be then, thenceforward, and forever free," read the document. And to the preliminary Eman-cipation Proclamation's previous wording, Lincoln had added a clause that allowed "such [slaves] of suitable condition will be re-ceived into the armed service of the United States." Finally, Lin-coln closed the document with "And upon this act, sincerely be-lieved to be an act of justice, warranted by the Constitution, upon military necessity, I invoke the considerate judgment of man-kind, and the gracious favor of Almighty God."

Lincoln picked up and set down his pen a couple of times. He had spent much of the previous three hours shaking hands with New Year's Day visitors, and his arm was aching. "I never in my life felt more certain that I was doing right than I do in signing this paper," he said. "If my name ever goes into history, it will be for this act, and my whole soul is in it. [But] if my hand trembles when I sign the Proclamation, all who examine the document hereafter will say, 'He hesitated.'"

Finally, the president picked up the pen one more time and "slowly, firmly" signed his full name, Abraham Lincoln. "Then," as Francis Carpenter wrote, "he looked up, smiled, and said: 'That will do.'"

Several months after the Emancipation Proclamation was signed, a reporter for the Chicago Tribune *dropped by the president's office and found him at his desk counting out greenbacks. "This is something out of my usual line," explained Lincoln. "The money belongs to a [black] porter in the Treasury Department. He's currently very sick in the hospital and cannot draw his pay. . . . I have been at considerable trouble to overcome the difficulty and get it to him, and have succeeded in cutting red tape."*

Public Opinion Polls

Clearly, Lincoln paid particular attention to public opinion. He spent a lot of time in the field and let people into the White House so he could take "public opinion baths." He also floated new ideas and launched trial balloons about how to solve the problem of slavery. Early in his term, he realized that the timing was not right to forcefully address the issue and that more work needed to be done in shaping public opinion. Back then, newspapers had the most influence on the political thoughts of people. So Lincoln wrote public letters on the subject, which publishers were only too happy to print. He also strategically courted and coddled editors and reporters. He invited them to the White House for chats and schmoozing. He maintained close friendships with several key publishers. And by mid-1862, newspapers across the Union were urging the president to take forceful action against slavery. And that's when Lincoln realized the time had arrived to issue the preliminary Emancipation Proclamation.

These days, there are many media outlets that influence thinking on political issues, and, of course, there is a surplus of organizations that conduct public opinion polls. Although the results of some polls can be manipulated, reliable ones may provide valuable insights for a leader. Controversy does exist, however, within some political factions who argue that the use of polls and gauging public opinion is "pandering" to the general populace. Strong leadership, they argue, is staying in the White House and taking decisive action only on one's own initiative. I believe Abraham Lincoln would disagree with that position.

"Our government rests in public opinion," he said in 1856. "A majority . . . always changing easily with deliberate changes of public [sentiment] is the only true sovereign of the people." In other words, the true mission of good leaders is to represent the wants and needs and hopes of the majority of people they represent. That's why keeping tabs on, respecting, and influencing public opinion is so important in leadership. So if Lincoln were here today, I'm sure he would still go to the field as much as possible in an effort to mingle with citizens to find out what they were thinking. And he would constantly monitor what he would believe to be reliable public opinion polls. He would certainly not introduce a major initiative unless he believed he had broad-ranging support for it. "With public sentiment, nothing can fail," said Lincoln; "without it, nothing can succeed."

Political Idealism Versus Political Reality

Abraham Lincoln's entire political career was dedicated, in part, to fighting slavery — holding it in check, restricting it, and abolishing it. When he became president, he faced constant pressure to take some sort of dramatic action along those lines. Lincoln, however, would not be hurried, because he knew the timing had to be just right or he might lose forever his chance to hit slavery hard. And predictably, because he did not act immediately, he was attacked as being weak.

The same sort of phenomenon still happens today. Presidents are elected to office based on all kinds of promises to enact new legislation, much of which is based on political ideology. And if they do not take forceful steps right away, they are often branded as "weak" or "wishy-washy" or "indecisive." Yet I'm sure Lincoln would agree that trying to force a major political ideal on the public before they are ready to receive it harms everyone, and may very well doom the idea to failure before it begins.

There is a difference between acting on principle and the tactics used to achieve that principle. Some tactics might involve waiting a longer period of time, because change is difficult — and the more difficult the change, the longer it takes to achieve. Good leaders, then, do not act precipitously on their own idealism (except, possibly, in a crisis). Rather, if they really want to get their idea through and make it law, they must be thoughtful, patient, disciplined, and persistent. Recall that it was more than a decade from the time Abraham Lincoln started fighting slavery in 1854 to the time he actually ended it (with passage of the 13th Amendment in 1865).

If Lincoln were here today, he would advise our leaders to set out a long-range plan to achieve their major goals; focus on achieving each individual step along the way; wait for the timing to be right —and then seize the moment when it is. He might also point to a verse in the Bible: *"There is a time for everything, and a season for every activity under the heavens" [Ecclesiastes 3:1].*

In this time of national peril I would have preferred to meet you upon a level one step higher than any party platform; because I am sure that from [a] more elevated position, we could do better battle for the country we all love, than we possibly can from those lower ones, where from the force of habit, the prejudices of the past, and selfish hopes of the future, we are sure to expend much of our ingenuity and strength, in finding fault with, and aiming blows at each other.

— Lincoln, in response to a partisan
attack from New York Democrats
June 12, 1863

ISSUES
The Draft
Partisan Political Attacks

13

A More Elevated Position

★ ★ ★

MY GOD! MY GOD!" said Lincoln, walking up and down the room, his hands clasped behind his back. "What will the country say? What will the country say?"

It was three o'clock in the afternoon on May 6, 1863. The president had just been informed that Joe Hooker and the Army of the Potomac had been routed at the Battle of Chancellorsville by Robert E. Lee and the Army of Northern Virginia, despite the fact that Union forces outnumbered the Confederates by more than two to one. A witness present said that when Lincoln received the news, he was "broken, dispirited, and ghostlike." Rumors quickly spread around the capital that Hooker had been cut to pieces and that Lee was marching his army straight to Washington. The president quickly straightened up, and at 4:00 p.m. he boarded a boat at the Washington Navy Yard with General Henry Halleck and steamed down the Potomac to find out what the situation was for himself.

Hooker's clash with Lee at Chancellorsville was part of a spring military offensive put together by Lincoln and his generals during the early winter months of 1863. While Hooker was going to make a move toward Richmond to try and flush Lee into the open, General Ulysses S. Grant was planning a move south along the Mississippi River toward Vicksburg. General William Rosecrans was directed to move toward Chattanooga and southeastern Tennessee, and Admiral Samuel Du Pont was going to assault Confederate defenses at Charleston Harbor in South Carolina. As operations got under way, Lincoln told a friend, "I expect the best, but I am prepared for the worst."

On April 7, 1863, Du Pont's nine battleships (including two ironclads) attacked Fort Sumter, but were forcefully repulsed by Confederate defenses. Grant had taken Port Gibson, Mississippi (on May 1, 1863), but then stalled on his way south. Rosecrans was making no progress in Tennessee, and after a week of maneuvering and fighting, Hooker had been completely outgeneraled by Lee. When the two armies met at the small outpost of Chancellorsville (only 10 miles west of Fredericksburg on the south bank of the Rappahannock River), the Army of the Potomac (130,000 men strong) was reorganized, well supplied, and well rested after several months off. Lee was aggressive and repeatedly divided his 60,000 soldiers into smaller fighting units. Hooker, on the other hand, lost his nerve, went on the defensive, and eventually retreated back across the river. Union casualties numbered 17,000, while the Confederates suffered 14,000, including the death of

General Stonewall Jackson, mistakenly fired upon by his own men.

When President Lincoln arrived at the front, he found a shaken and surprised Hooker. After being briefed about the battle and the current condition of the army, Lincoln expressed confidence in the officer corps and men, and then quickly headed back to Washington. All in all, he and Halleck spent only a couple of hours at the front, and when back at the Executive Mansion, the two immediately conferred with Secretary of War Stanton to review the situation and kick around options. Stanton and Halleck departed about 9:00 p.m., and Lincoln was left alone on the second floor of the White House except for his clerk, William O. Stoddard. [*Stoddard was the young editor of the* Central Illinois Gazette *whom Lincoln had met years before in West Urbana.*]

As Stoddard handled the mail in his office across the hall, the only sound he heard was "the tread of the President's feet as he strode slowly back and forth across the chamber" (probably with his hands clasped behind his back). "Ten o'clock came, without a break in the steady march, excepting now and then a pause in turning at either wall," recalled Stoddard. "Eleven o'clock came, and then another hour of ceaseless march. . . . A little after twelve, there was a break of several minutes, and the tramp began again. . . . Two [a.m.] and he was walking yet." A little after 3:00 a.m., Stoddard left to get some sleep, and the last sound he heard was the president still pacing in his office. When the young clerk returned just before 8:00 a.m., he saw the president's door open and went inside. "There sat Mr. Lincoln eating breakfast alone," recalled Stoddard. "He had not been out of his room. Beside his cup of coffee lay the written draft of his [letter] to General Hooker."

It was now May 7, 1863, and with little or no sleep the night before, Lincoln boarded a special train at 10:00 a.m. with General Halleck and traveled down to Hooker's headquarters at Falmouth, Virginia. The president stayed a little longer this time, but not much. He conferred with Hooker in person and may also have handed him the letter he had written the night before. "What next?" asked Lincoln. ". . . I [do not] wish anything done in desperation or rashness. An early movement would . . . help to supersede the bad moral effects of the recent one, which is said to be considerably injurious." After walking among the soldiers and offering them his thanks, the president once again expressed confidence in General Hooker. Then he went back on the train by himself, leaving Halleck in the field.

A short time later, Hooker proposed a new plan, but the president didn't like it. Noting that Robert E. Lee had actually crossed the Rappahannock and was headed north, "Fighting Joe" suggested moving toward Richmond in full force. Lincoln wrote back and reminded Hooker that "Lee's army, and not Richmond, is your true objective point." Meanwhile, progress was being made in returning the Mississippi River to complete Union control. Less than a week after Chancellorsville, General Grant's army began an impressive movement through Mississippi. From May 12 to May 17, 1863, it won four major battles (Raymond, Jackson, Champion Hill, and Big Black River) and finally laid siege to Vicksburg on May 18. Grant's victories pulled Lincoln out of his post-Chancellorsville funk, and just like after the previous devastating losses at Bull Run and Fredericksburg, his energy returned, with even more determination and strength.

★ ★ ★

One day, as the president bounded up the stairs to the second-floor telegraph office in the War Department, he paused on the landing between floors, where a military guard was standing. Lincoln smiled and pointed to a pair of axes hanging on the wall. "What are these for?" he asked the guard.

"They are to be used in case of fire, Mr. President."

"Well now," said Lincoln, "I wonder if I could lift one of those axes up by the end of the handle?" And then, as the guard later recounted, the president took one down, gripped it with only the thumb and forefinger, and "laying the heavy end on the floor, commenced raising it till he held it out at arm's length, and kept it there several seconds."

"I thought I could do it," said Lincoln. "Here, you try it."

The guard did try and failed. The president grinned and said, "When I used to split rails thirty years ago in Illinois, I could lift two axes that way — and I believe I could do it now, [but] I will try it some other time."

★ ★ ★

While Abraham Lincoln was fighting to hold the Union together on battlefields across the country, members of the Democratic Party were waging *political* warfare against his administration. And the Union's loss at Chancellorsville added fuel to this "fire in the rear," as Lincoln called it. Democrats attacked him for incompetent management at the War Department and for personal ineptness as commander in chief, and they further demanded that he begin peace negotiations with the Confederacy. For Lincoln, however, it was par for the course, because Democrats had been flexing their muscle ever since gaining strength in the previous midterm elections. Launching a broad assault on the Lincoln administration, they attacked the issuance of the Emancipation Proclamation, charged that Lincoln was now making the war a crusade to free slaves, and resurrected condemnations of the administration's suspensions of *habeas corpus*.

On April 13, 1863, Ambrose Burnside issued General War Order No. 38, which prohibited "acts for the benefit of the enemies of our country" and "the habit of declaring sympathies for the enemy." Outraged at the new edict, former Ohio Democratic congressman Clement Vallandigham gave a fiery public speech in which he, among other things, called the president "King Lincoln," stated that the war was being waged "for the purpose of crushing out liberty and erecting a despotism," and said that "the sooner the people . . . not submit to such restrictions upon their liberties, the better." Without telling the president, Burnside had Vallandigham arrested and tried in a military court, where he was found guilty and given a two-year prison sentence. But sensing disaster, Lincoln quickly commuted the former congressman's sentence and banished him to the Confederacy. Vallandigham then made his way to Canada, where he remained for the rest of the war.

Compounding Lincoln's problems in the early months of 1863 was a dramatic drop in the number of army volunteers. Terms of enlistment were expiring, soldiers were wary of the high casualty rates, and thousands of them did, in fact, go AWOL (absent without leave). Although the president offered amnesty to the deserters if they returned to their regiments, it had little impact on the Army's declining numbers. So on March 3, 1863, Abraham Lincoln signed the Enrollment Act, which put into place the first military draft in United States history. It called for every male citizen between the ages of 20 and 45 (including immigrants who had filed for citizenship) to register for military duty. Quotas were set by congressional districts and enforced by federal marshals. Exemptions from the draft could be made by finding a substitute or by paying $300 to the government. *[The Confederate States of America also passed a conscription law that drafted men between the ages of 18 and 35 — later expanded to ages 17 to 50.]*

Needless to say, the new draft became another major political issue objected to by Democrats, especially the clause that allowed the wealthy to avoid service. Undaunted by the continuing attacks, Lincoln pushed for an even more controversial initiative, one he had already provided for in the Emancipation Proclamation: the recruitment of blacks into the Union army. "I suppose the time has come," he told Andrew Johnson (then governor of Tennessee). Lincoln realized that recruitment was "progressing too slowly . . . in some quarters" because of resistance to the proclamation, so "we must also take some benefit from it." He further wrote to Johnson that the black population "is the great *available* and yet *unavailed* of, force for restoring the Union. The bare sight of fifty thousand armed and drilled black soldiers on the banks of the Mississippi would end the rebellion at once. And who doubts that we can present that sight, if we but take hold in earnest?"

Recruitment of blacks proceeded at a rapid pace, with training provided by young white officers who volunteered specifically for the duty. And African Americans soon demonstrated their courage in several major battles, including Port Hudson, Louisiana (May 27, 1863), Milliken's Bend, Louisiana (June 7, 1863), and Fort Wagner, South Carolina (July 18, 1863). Lincoln recognized the irony that white men in the South were fighting to destroy the Union, while black men in the North were fighting to preserve it. He was also particularly moved by reports of heroism after the Battle of Fort Wagner, in which a black sergeant carried the American flag despite suffering multiple gunshot wounds. *[Sergeant William H. Carney, a former slave and member of the 54th Massachusetts Regiment, was later awarded the Congressional Medal of Honor.]* By the end of the war, more than 180,000 African Americans were serving in the United States armed forces. The Union's most "important successes could not have been achieved," Lincoln said, "but for the aid of black soldiers."

Continually frustrated that their assaults on Lincoln did not seem to deter the president, on May 19, 1863, a group of New York Democrats met in Albany and passed three resolutions specifically addressed "To His Excellency the President of the United States." The first resolution demanded that "the Administration be true to the Constitution [and] exert all its powers to maintain the supremacy of civil over military law." The second denounced the arrest and trial of Clement Vallandigham "for no other reasons than words . . . in criticism of . . . the Administration." And the third attacked the policy of military tribunals as abrogating "the right of the people to assemble," the freedom "of speech and the press," "trial by jury," the "privilege of *habeas corpus*," and "the authority of the State and Federal Constitutions."

At this point, Lincoln was fed up with the ongoing attacks, so he sat down and wrote another one of his "public letters." Dated

June 12, 1863, it was addressed to Erastus Corning, leader of the New York Democrats (also president of the New York Central Railroad). After thanking Corning for passing along the Albany resolutions, Lincoln wrote that he would not have replied on anything "personal to myself," but he was concerned "that more injurious consequences might follow the censures systematically cast upon me for doing what, in my view of duty, I could not forbear." And then, in the body of this nearly 4,000-word letter, Lincoln meticulously and skillfully defended the actions of his administration as being constitutional in times of rebellion. He also pointed out that "under cover of 'Liberty of speech' 'Liberty of the Press' and '*Habeas corpus,*'" the rebels were attempting to employ the rights of the Constitution they wanted to destroy, that they knew exactly what they were doing, and that he, Abraham Lincoln, was not going to let them get away with it. Referring to the Vallandigham arrest, Lincoln stated that "he who dissuades one man from volunteering, or induces one soldier to desert, weakens the Union cause as much as he who kills a Union soldier in battle. . . . Must I shoot a simple-minded soldier boy who deserts, while I must not touch a hair of a wily agitator who induces him to desert?" Then Lincoln chastised the Democrats for playing by lower ethical standards than the occasion called for:

> In this time of national peril I would have preferred to meet you upon a level one step higher than any party platform; because I am sure that from [a] more elevated position, we could do better battle for the country we all love, than we possibly can from those lower ones, where from the force of habit, the prejudices of the past, and selfish hopes of the future, we are sure to expend much of our ingenuity and strength, in finding fault with, and aiming blows at each other.

Lincoln subsequently released this letter to the *New York Times* and had copies sent out to leading Republicans.

★ ★ ★

After Chancellorsville, an emboldened Robert E. Lee decided to take the war to Northern territory, where he hoped to eventually threaten Philadelphia. Such a military campaign (where Yankees experienced the war firsthand) might sway public opinion toward the growing movement for peace negotiations. In preparing for the invasion, shortly after the Army of Northern Virginia crossed into Pennsylvania, Lincoln relieved Joe Hooker from command of the Army of the Potomac and replaced him with George Gordon Meade, a Pennsylvania native who Lincoln said would "fight well on his own dunghill." Ultimately, the two armies clashed at Gettysburg in what proved to be a turning point in the Civil War. After three days of fighting (July 1–3, 1863), combined casualties amounted to a stunning 46,000 killed or wounded (evenly divided among both sides). But when Robert E. Lee finally made an error by ordering 12,500 of his men to attack the center of the Union line, the resulting disaster (Pickett's Charge) effectively ended the battle. As the Confederates beat a hasty retreat back to Virginia, Meade had an opportunity to close out the war by attacking the badly wounded rebel army. But much to Lincoln's chagrin (and against his encouragement to mount an assault), Meade only followed the rebels until they crossed the Potomac River to safety.

The day after fighting concluded at Gettysburg (July 4, 1863), the 47-day siege of Vicksburg ended when Confederate general John C. Pemberton surrendered his 30,000-man army to Ulysses S. Grant. The entire Mississippi River (lifeblood of the nation's commerce and trade) was now in Union hands — and Louisiana, Arkansas, and Texas had been cut off from the other eight Confederate states. Two days later, on July 6, 1863, the U.S. Navy, under the command of Admiral John A. Dahlgren, commenced a bombardment of South Carolina's Charleston Harbor, which would result in a 51-day siege.

After such a string of good news on the military front, President Lincoln might have expected the Democrats to lessen their attacks and the American people to give him some credit. But he would have been wrong. The victories at Gettysburg and Vicksburg only increased calls for a negotiated peace, in part because now that the Confederacy was on the ropes, its leaders would be more likely to agree to Democratic Party terms, which included the continuation of slavery and the possibility of two nations. Moreover, resistance to the draft reached a fevered pitch in Indiana, Massachusetts, Ohio, Pennsylvania, and Wisconsin. But it was worse in New York City, where full-scale riots began on July 13, 1863, and lasted four days. Poor Irish American immigrants protested the fact that conscription favored the wealthy, and mobs roamed the streets looting stores, burning homes, and killing policemen. Blacks, targeted for being the cause of the war, were shot, beaten, tortured, lynched, and set on fire. By the time the number of casualties reached about 2,000, Union troops arrived from Gettysburg and finally ended the violence.

Pressure on President Lincoln now grew more severe. He was urged to suspend the draft indefinitely, but refused. He was advised to appoint a special prosecutor to investigate and determine responsibility for the riots, but wouldn't do that, either. Whatever the findings revealed, he said, would "have simply touched a match to a barrel of gunpowder. One rebellion at a time is about as much as we can conveniently handle."

The draft, blacks serving in the military, the constitutionality of the Emancipation Proclamation, and peace negotiations to end the war were all issues put forward by the Democrats leading up to the 1863 fall elections. [*President Lincoln had to deal with national elections every year, which might impact the makeup of Congress and the governorships of states.*] And a great deal was at stake, because if the Democratic Party continued to make gains, the 1864 presidential election could very well be affected. To draw attention to the suspension of *habeas corpus,* Democrats even nominated Clement Vallandigham for governor of Ohio. Running his campaign from Canada on a "peace at any price"

platform, Vallandigham constantly attacked the president, saying, among other things, that Lincoln had made the United States
"one of the worst despotisms on earth."

The politically shrewd Lincoln had decided to continue his
public opinion campaign against the Democrats, so when he was
invited to speak at a Republican rally in Springfield, Illinois, he
seized the opportunity. But rather than attending personally, Lincoln composed another message to be read in front of the crowd.
On September 3, 1863, the president's friend James C. Conkling
had the letter read to a crowd in excess of 50,000. In it, every major issue was addressed directly to the Democrats, as such:

Ending the War

"You [say] you desire peace; and you blame me that we do not
have it. But how can we attain it? If you are not for *force*, nor for
dissolution, there only remains some imaginable *compromise*. I
do not believe any compromise, embracing the maintenance of
the Union, is now possible."

The Emancipation Proclamation

"You say it is unconstitutional. I think differently. I think the constitution invests its commander-in-chief with the law of war, in
time of war. . . . The proclamation . . . can not be retracted any
more than the dead can be brought to life."

Blacks in the Military

"You say you will not fight to free negroes. Some of them seem
willing to fight for you. But no matter. Fight you, then, exclusively
to save the Union. . . . I issued the proclamation on purpose to
aid you in saving the Union. . . . But negroes, like other people,
act upon motives. Why should they do anything for us, if we will
do nothing for them? If they stake their lives for us, they must be
prompted by the strongest motive — even the promise of freedom. And the promise being made, must be kept."

Finally, Lincoln ended his letter by praising African Americans fighting for the nation, and admonishing Democrats for their political shenanigans:

> Peace does not appear so distant as it did. I hope it will come soon, and come to stay; and so come as to be worth the keeping in all future time. It will then have been proved that, among free men, there can be no successful appeal from the ballot to the bullet; and that they who take such appeal are sure to lose their case, and pay the cost. And then, there will be some black men who can remember that, with silent tongue, and clenched teeth, and steady eye, and well-poised bayonet, they have helped mankind . . . ; while, I fear, there will be some white ones, unable to forget that, with malignant heart, and deceitful speech, they strove to hinder it.

Lincoln also simply stated, "I freely acknowledge myself the servant of the people, according to the bond of service — the United States Constitution — and that, as such I am responsible to them." This presidential communiqué was soon published in nearly every major newspaper in the North. It was also included in a Republican campaign pamphlet entitled *The Letters of President Lincoln on Questions of National Policy,* which sold for eight cents a copy. Five hundred thousand copies were printed, and, overall, the Conkling letter was estimated to have been read by an astonishing 10 million people.

In the end, the November 1863 elections went very well for Lincoln and the Republican Party. Military success at Gettysburg and Vicksburg bolstered support for the administration, as did progress by Grant in Tennessee and the fall of Charleston Harbor (on September 7, 1863), which placed Fort Sumter back in Union hands. Republicans gained key political victories in Iowa, New York, and Pennsylvania — and Clement Vallandigham was soundly defeated for the governorship of Ohio.

★ ★ ★

In early November, President Lincoln was invited to give "a few appropriate remarks" at the dedication of a new Soldiers' National Cemetery at Gettysburg on November 19, 1863. Believing it was time to renew purpose, just as he had done in his year-end speeches to Congress in 1861 and 1862, Lincoln decided to accept the invitation and, in his speech, endeavor to lift the meaning of the war to "a more elevated position."

President Lincoln's brief remarks in front of a crowd of 10,000 contained only 272 words and took barely two minutes to deliver. He made no distinction between North and South, Union or Confederacy. In fact, he did not even use those words. And he began by referring to a common bond shared by not only all the soldiers who fought at Gettysburg, but by all the people involved in the Civil War:

> Four score and seven years ago, our fathers brought forth on this continent a new nation, conceived in liberty and dedicated to the proposition that all men are created equal.

Lincoln went on to use the word "nation" four more times — not "country," because that implied territory or land, and not "Union," because that referred to the Northern states only. Rather, Abraham Lincoln understood that the word "nation" refers exclusively to a large group of *people* who are conscious of their unity and possess a government uniquely their own. And in this case, he left no doubt that he believed a nation like the United States of America was worth fighting for:

> We here highly resolve that these dead shall not have died in vain — that this nation, under God, shall have a new birth of freedom — and that government of the people, by the people, for the people, shall not perish from the earth.

At one stop on Lincoln's train ride to Gettysburg, a little girl appeared on the platform near an open car window. She lifted a bouquet of rosebuds up and said, with a lisp, "Flowerth for the President." Hearing her, Lincoln may have been reminded of his son Tad, who also had a lisp. Stepping to the window, the president bent his long frame down, accepted the flowers, and kissed the little girl on the cheek. "Thank you," he said. "You are a sweet little rosebud yourself. I hope your life will open into perpetual beauty and goodness."

LINCOLN ON LEADERSHIP FOR TODAY

The Draft

The Lincoln administration implemented the first military draft in United States history by calling for the registration of every male citizen between the ages of 20 and 45 (including immigrants who had filed for citizenship). There were major protests in many of the Union states, with New York City seeing full-scale riots that lasted four days. Poor Irish American immigrants were especially upset that conscription favored the wealthy. A century later, major resistance to the draft took place all across the country in protest of the Vietnam War, which was not widely supported by the American people and, in fact, spawned the expression "rich man's war, poor man's fight."

Today, the United States has an all-volunteer army of approximately 500,000 soldiers on active duty. However, unpopular wars in the Middle East have caused a reduction in enlistments, and increasingly more money has to be budgeted for recruitment costs. Some have even suggested that the United States, similar to Israel, should implement a mandatory military service of two years for all citizens when they reach the age of 18.

In my opinion, Lincoln would support an all-volunteer army in times of peace and prosperity, but he would most certainly not rule out conscription if a major armed conflict had to be fought. Before taking the country to war, however, Lincoln would carefully consider whether it was a cause worth sending American troops into harm's way. Clearly, if it was not, implementing a draft would face major resistance. If the cause was justified, he would next determine if current military numbers (including those in the reserve forces) were adequate to proceed. If forces were deemed insufficient, I believe Lincoln wouldn't hesitate to enact conscription. But first he would make his case to the American people that it was a necessary and worthy thing to do, and he would keep everyone fully apprised of the time frame and steps involved.

It's my sense that Abraham Lincoln did not have an elitist bone in his body. Rather, he had a common man's heart. There's an old saying that it's the elite who usually start the wars, and the common man is the one who fights them. So I believe the issue of whether or not a draft was necessary would weigh heavily on Lincoln.

Partisan Political Attacks

During the Lincoln-Douglas debates of 1858, people attacked Lincoln because of his stance on slavery. But he would say nothing retaliatory about slave owners, preferring, rather, to speak out only against the institution itself. And when he ran for president in 1860, Lincoln was called just about every name in the book, including a baboon, a coarse vulgar joker, dishonest, a third-rate country lawyer, and a disgrace. In every campaign, Lincoln usually did not respond in any substantive way, and certainly did not lower himself to the name-calling tactics of his opponents. He just kept moving forward, focusing on the issues and trying to persuade the public that his views were just.

Partisan political attacks are nothing new in American politics. They have been going on since the dawn of the Republic. Today, however, the volume and intensity of personal attacks has increased and been amplified because of television, the Internet, and the 24-hour news cycle. Most Americans express personal frustration with national candidates who act more like whining, name-calling children than serious statesmen and potential presidents.

If Lincoln were here today, he might say something like "When you put fresh pine on a fire, the closer you are to it, the more likely you'll get singed by flying embers." In other words, personal attacks come with the territory. I believe Lincoln would size up the landscape and recognize that most of the partisan criticisms are done for effect. The more outrageous, the more entertaining, and, as a result, the more viewers will be attracted. And that translates into more money and higher profits for the television networks. Moreover, extreme factions must use political attack ads to lure voters from the majority. In truth, it's one of the few ways they can increase their numbers.

So how would Abraham Lincoln handle an ongoing 24-7 news cycle where cable news networks constantly loop attack videos all day, every day? My sense is that he would have his staff monitor the political attacks with instructions to let all the small stuff go. But when something arose that seriously misrepresented his character in a way that could affect the electorate, he would fire back immediately. That does not mean he would respond in kind by calling names or attacking the opposition personally. Rather, I believe Lincoln would simply counter, refute, and maintain the high moral and ethical ground. He would also be entertaining in his own right by applying humor or telling stories that would place partisan attacks in a slightly different light. He would get people to laugh about it — and when people laugh, you know they're with you. Lincoln knew that, and had a real knack for getting voters to respond to his humorous yarns.

In the end, leaders simply cannot spend all their time refuting accusations made by the opposing political party. If they did, they wouldn't have time to get anything done. Lincoln, I believe, would keep moving ahead, focus on the issues, and strive to achieve the task at hand. And he would never, ever lower himself to the dark side of political campaigning. He would rather lose an election by holding the high moral and ethical ground than win it in any other way.

Let us discard all this quibbling about this man and the other man, this race and that race, and the other race being inferior, and therefore they must be placed in an inferior position. . . . Let us discard all these things, and unite as one people throughout this land until we shall once more stand up declaring that all men are created equal.

> — Lincoln, in debate with Stephen A. Douglas
> Quincy, Illinois
> October 13, 1858

ISSUES
The Death Penalty
Immigration
Race Relations

14

A Fair Chance in the Race of Life

★ ★ ★

"Y OU SHOULD NOT have that rebel in your house!" said General Daniel Sickles to the president.

"Excuse me, General Sickles, my wife and I are in the habit of choosing our own guests," replied Lincoln. "We do not need from our friends either advice or assistance in the matter."

Emilie Todd Helm was Mary Todd Lincoln's half sister, and her husband, Confederate general Benjamin Hardin Helm, had been killed at the Battle of Chickamauga in Tennessee. Lincoln invited her to come to Washington to be with family, and she had arrived on December 13, 1863, with her daughter, Katherine. Despite negativity from the unfriendly press and people like Sickles, Lincoln had welcomed his sister-in-law with kindness and open arms — hugging her and weeping with her over the loss of her husband. He also did not hesitate to have her present in the receiving line at a White House holiday reception, where General Sickles met her.

Whether it was a holiday gathering, a formal reception, or a walk through the first-floor hallway each morning, there always seemed to be a lot of people in the White House. Although the selfish side of human nature disturbed him, Lincoln was a man who really liked being around people. So he had to take the good with the bad. Speaking of selfish people, Lincoln once said to journalist Noah Brooks: "Sitting here, where all the avenues to public patronage seem to come together in a knot, it does seem to me that our people are fast approaching the point where it can be said that seven-eighths of them are trying to find how to live at the expense of the other eighth." But Lincoln surely wasn't afraid to turn down people who wasted his time with self-seeking requests. When a farmer came in and wanted compensation for a horse commandeered by Union soldiers, Lincoln turned him away with the story about the captain on the Illinois River who was steering his vessel through dangerous rapids when a young boy pulled on his coat. "Say, Mister Captain," said the boy. "I wish you would stop your boat a minute — I've lost my apple overboard." Another time, a congressman asked the president to intervene on behalf of a woman in Mississippi whose slaves were freed by the Union army passing through. When Lincoln was told that she wanted the president to give her an equal number of black laborers to work her farm, he replied: "I'd rather take a rope and hang myself!" And then there was the story of an officer who was drummed out of the service and had twice been turned down for reinstatement by the president. When he showed up a third time and said, "Well, sir, I see you are fully determined not to do me justice!" — Lincoln grabbed him by the coat collar, threw him out into the hall, and told him never to show his face in the White House again.

On the flip side of the coin, Lincoln almost never turned down a legitimate request for help, especially if it came from the mother or wife of a young soldier. "My son is wounded badly and in the hospital," one woman told the president. "I have been trying to get him out, but couldn't, so they said I had better come to see you. If you will let me take him home I will nurse him up, and just as soon as he gets well enough, he shall go right back and help put down the rebellion. He is a good boy and does not shrink from the service." With tears gathering in his eyes and his lips slightly quivering, the president wrote out a note and handed it to the woman. "Here," he said, "you will have your son."

The fact that the doctor or hospital administrator in this case sent the woman to see the president of the United States was not unusual during the Civil War. First, nearly everybody knew she would likely get in to see him if she was patient and persistent. And second, they knew Lincoln would likely help her, because his compassion for people, especially young soldiers, had become legend. The president received hundreds of requests to pardon boys who were sentenced to be shot for falling asleep on guard duty, or fleeing in battle, or deserting their regiments. "It breaks my heart to have these poor boys shot," Lincoln said to a friend. "I think [they] can do us more good above ground than underground." And presidential assistant John Hay noted in his diary "the eagerness with which the president caught any fact [that] would justify him saving the life of a condemned soldier." Hay also recorded the many times he had reviewed such cases with Lincoln. On July 18, 1863 (in the wake of Gettysburg and Vicksburg), "one hundred court martials [in] six hours"; on January 7, 1864, "63 court martials"; on February 9, 1864, 46 court-martials; and on April 1864, "four long sessions with court martial cases." In the spring of 1863, President Lincoln even received in one envelope the files of 55 soldiers who had been sentenced to be shot for desertion. He simply wrote on the envelope: "Pardoned — A. Lincoln."

Secretary of War Stanton and Secretary of the Treasury Chase, along with most of the high-ranking officers in the Army, did not like Lincoln's penchant for pardoning soldiers found guilty by court-martial. They felt it undermined the military's authority and destroyed discipline. The rank-and-file soldiers, on the other hand, loved Lincoln for it — and they outnumbered the officers by a factor of nine to one. As John Hay also noted, however, the president could be "merciless where meanness or cruelty were shown." He refused to pardon, for example, American slave trader Nathaniel Gordon, who had been tried, convicted, and sentenced to death for abducting and transporting by ship nearly 900 Africans (mostly children) from the Congo. "I believe I am kindly enough in nature," said Lincoln, "but any man who, for paltry gain and stimulated only by avarice, can rob Africa of her children to sell into . . . bondage, I never will pardon, and he may stay and rot in jail before he will ever get relief from me." *[Gordon was hanged on February 21, 1862.]* Nor did the president show any mercy for Dr. David M. Wright, a physician from Norfolk, Virginia, who was sentenced to death by a military court for shooting and killing a young Army lieutenant who was marching his regiment of black troops through town shortly after Norfolk fell. Dr. Wright, a fervent segregationist, had pleaded temporary insanity, but Lincoln didn't buy it. *[Dr. Wright was hanged on October 23, 1863.]* Compare that with the case of West Bogan, a black man who, in early 1864, was sentenced to death in Arkansas for murdering his particularly cruel plantation master with an axe. On Bogan's appeal for commutation, Lincoln wrote that the deceased, "when he met his death, was in violation of law and right holding the prisoner in absolute slavery [and] imposing upon him ceaseless toil and cruel punishments." The president's decision, as written, was "sentence disapproved."

★ ★ ★

It was pouring down rain around midnight when Henry W. Knight, a guard at the War Department, saw President Lincoln come through the door headed to the telegraph office. After spending about an hour reading the latest dispatches, Lincoln was ready to go back to the White House, so Private Knight met him at the entrance with several other guards. "The President," Knight recalled, was "wrapped in an old gray shawl, wearing a shockingly bad hat, and carrying a worse umbrella."

"Don't come out in this storm with me tonight, boys," said Lincoln, "I have my umbrella and can get home safely without you."

"But Mr. President, we have positive orders from Mr. Stanton not to allow you to return alone — and you know we dare not disobey his orders."

Lincoln paused for a moment and relented. "No, I suppose not. If Stanton should learn that you had let me return alone, he would have you court-martialed and shot inside of twenty-four hours."

★ ★ ★

Not long after the victories at Gettysburg and Vicksburg in the summer of 1863, many members of Congress, now confident that they would win the war, began discussing the conditions upon which rebellious states might be readmitted to the Union. Part of the debate centered on Louisiana, most of which was then in Union hands, and Arkansas, which was moving in that direction. Certain lawmakers, including radicals in the Republican Party, wanted very much to exact revenge on the South and began suggesting such punitive measures as allowing Congress to rename the individual Confederate states and reverting them to territorial status, which would have precluded representatives from being seated in the House or Senate. President Lincoln, however, wanted reconstruction to be more lenient and forgiving. And although he knew the war was a long way from being won, he decided to get out in front of the turbulent discussions and be first to propose formal procedures.

Lincoln used his annual message to Congress on December 8, 1863, to commence action. "Looking to the . . . future," he wrote, "I have thought fit to issue a proclamation . . . in the hope that it may do good without danger or harm [and] will save labor and avoid great confusion." In taking this step now, Lincoln was using the power of his position as president of the United States to issue another executive order in what was essentially a mass pardon with conditions. If the people of the South agreed to terms, Lincoln was going to "let 'em up easy."

The president's Proclamation of Amnesty and Reconstruction (also issued on December 8, 1863) had three main provisions. First, Lincoln stated that according to the Constitution, as president, he had the "power to grant reprieves and pardons for offenses against the United States." Therefore, he declared that "a full pardon is granted to [the many persons who have committed . . . treason] with restoration of all . . . property (except slaves) . . . upon the condition that every such person take . . . an oath [and maintain it]." Second, a new state government could be formed when 10 percent of eligible voters had taken that oath of allegiance to the United States. And third, in order to be admitted back into the Union, a state government had to accept emancipation *and* enact specific plans to provide for freed slaves.

Reaction by Congress to Lincoln's new proclamation was predictable: they didn't like it. And they particularly didn't like the fact that the president beat them to the punch in setting policy on future reconstruction. Within a few months, Senator Benjamin Wade (Ohio) and Representative Henry Winter Davis (Maryland), both Radical Republicans, had joined together to introduce much tougher legislation. Their bill demanded that 50 percent (a majority) rather than only 10 percent of eligible voters take a more onerous oath than Lincoln had proposed. They further stated that every Southern state be required to allow former slaves the right to vote. The Wade-Davis bill passed both houses of Congress on July 2, 1864, and was sent to the White House. When Senator Zachariah Chandler (Michigan) asked the president if he was going to sign it, Lincoln responded, "Mr. Chandler, this bill was placed before me a few minutes before Congress adjourned. It is a matter of too much importance to be swallowed in that way." This particular clash with Congress ended quietly, because Lincoln pocket-vetoed the Wade-Davis bill. *[A pocket veto is a maneuver where the president does not sign a bill, and because Congress is not in session, it cannot be returned there for an override vote within 10 days. Therefore, the bill simply dies on the vine.]*

In 1864, President Lincoln made a lesser-known attempt to make reconstruction more palatable to the Confederate states. With slavery ended, he realized that Southerners would lose their greatest business engine and would need some sort of promising commercial enterprise in order to thrive. So the president prepared an economic incentive plan designed to persuade the South to accept peace more readily. On his own, Lincoln suggested allowing Southern planters to sell cotton to the United States government. He tried to push the idea on his cabinet and members of Congress by promoting it as having a positive impact on inflation, gold reserves, and reduction of the national debt. Even though the idea failed to materialize, it is noteworthy, because in one creative initiative, Lincoln attempted to be kind to the South while, at the same time, appealing to its own self-interest. "If pecuniary greed can be made to aid us . . . ," he said, "let us be thankful that so much good can be got out of [it]." In other words, Lincoln was trying to make the selfishness of others work in his favor. And giving the South some hope of viable commerce after the war was his way of doing it.

Another idea Lincoln dreamed up to promote commerce and fuel the economy after the war involved the divisive issue of immigration. Years before, he had seen the Illinois Central Railroad (chartered by the state) recruit large numbers of foreign-born laborers (mostly Irish, German, and Scandinavian) to successfully build its infrastructure in Illinois, so he thought it would be a good idea to do something similar on a national basis. Of course, Lincoln was well aware of the backlash that had occurred in the 1850s from the mass influx of immigrants. So many Americans voiced opposition to such a large number of foreigners entering the country that they even formed a new organization, the Native American Party, to stop the practice. Nicknamed the "Know-Nothings" (because its members always responded "I know nothing" when asked about their movement), the organization argued that the lower-paid immigrants took jobs away from hardworking Americans, and that if allowed to vote, they would swing the balance of power away from the status quo. The Know-Nothings also alleged a conspiracy by the Catholic Church (because so many immigrants were Irish Catholic), which in their minds did not represent American values. So they not only sought an end to liberal immigration practices but also proposed government sanctions against the church.

From the very beginning, Abraham Lincoln vehemently rejected the anti-immigration movement. "As a nation, we began by declaring that 'all men are created equal,'" he wrote to a friend in 1855. "We now practically read it 'all men are created equal, *except negroes.*' When the Know-Nothings get control, it will read 'all men are created equal, except negroes, *and foreigners, and Catholics.*'" He also forcefully spoke out against almost everything they proposed, including overt attempts to suppress immigrant minority votes through government legislation.

After becoming president, Lincoln did not change his mind. Moreover, he was particularly disturbed that one of the effects of the Civil War was to greatly *reduce* immigration to the United States. And that left no one to fill the labor shortages in industry and agriculture resulting from so many men moving into military service. Lincoln's strategy, therefore, was to both increase and speed up immigration, in order to create more workers and ensure that Union war production needs were met. "I regard our immigrants as one of the principal of replenishing streams," he told Congress. In addition to aiding the war effort, these new immigrants would remain in the country once peace was secured. And similar to what occurred in Illinois, they would then help build infrastructure, provide more population for growth, and fuel economic development. So at the recommendation and prodding of President Lincoln, Congress passed a law entitled "An Act to Encourage Immigration" on July 4, 1864. *[The Republican Party also placed in its 1864 election year platform an endorsement stating "that foreign immigration . . . should be fostered and encouraged by a liberal and just policy."]* As the first major federal immigration law in American history, it established the U.S. Immigration Bureau and the Office of the Commissioner of Immigration. "This great national policy," said Lincoln, "is manifested by most of the European States, and ought to be reciprocated on our part by giving the immigrants effective national protection." Abraham Lincoln's immigration plan was bold, creative, and ahead of its time. In fact, the roots of America's Industrial Revolution rest in our 16th president's vision of a future national workforce that was diverse and multicultural.

There was more to the president's immigration policy than met the eye, however. In anticipating the end of the Civil War, Lincoln told Congress that "the nation is beginning a new life." But the many immigrants he foresaw wanting to come to America would also be "beginning a new life." And therein lies the higher level of morality Lincoln had in mind with his new immigration act. It was all about the people who were hoping not just for a *new* life, but for a *better* life. "When they look through [the] Declaration of Independence they find . . . 'We hold these truths to be self-evident, that all men are created equal.'" And *that,* said Lincoln, "is the father of all moral principle. . . . [It] links the hearts of patriotic and liberty-loving men together . . . as long as the love of freedom exists in the minds of men."

★ ★ ★

Regarding his plans for reconstruction, Lincoln gave an analogy to Maine representative James G. Blaine: "The pilots on our Western Rivers steer from point to point, as they call it — setting the course of the boat no farther than they can see," he explained. "And that is all I propose to [do] myself in this great problem." On first blush, we might take this comment to mean that Lincoln was shortsighted. In reality, however, his anticipation of what was going to happen in the future (i.e., his leadership vision) was remarkable in that he could see much farther down the road than others.

In addition to everything else on his mind, Abraham Lincoln gave considerable thought to race relations after the Civil War ended. With slavery gone, he knew there would not only be "a total revolution of labor," but also a more dramatic cultural shift nationwide, especially in the former Confederate states. In an 1863 letter to General Nathaniel Banks (commander of the Department of the Gulf, based in New Orleans), Lincoln suggested not only that Louisiana "make a new Constitution recognizing the emancipation proclamation," but that it also "adopt some practical system by which the two races could gradually live themselves out of their old [relationship] to each other, and both come out better prepared for the [coming] new [relationship]." By proposing a gradual transformation, Lincoln was leaning on his strategy of long-term planning and his understanding that the more difficult the change, the longer it takes to achieve. "Whites and blacks alike will have to look out for themselves," he told a colleague, "and I have an abiding faith that they will go about it . . . in a very agreeable way." In this particular instance, Abraham Lincoln, although well-intentioned, might have been wrong. No matter how you cut it, the part of reconstruction that applied to a social mingling of the races was not going to go smoothly. After a couple of centuries of precedent, social structures and racist tendencies were simply too embedded in people's DNA to transform even gradually.

Lincoln, of course, had never even heard of DNA, because it wasn't discovered until 1869. But he certainly understood the inherited natural human tendency to fight with one another, and he frequently cautioned against the passion or violence that often accompanies racial tensions. "I am opposed to encouraging that lawless and mobocratic spirit," he said early in his political career. "It is much better not to be led from the region of reason into that of hot blood," he said later. And it is certain that Abraham Lincoln did not like the constant rhetoric from racists that one race was better than another. "Let us discard all this quibbling about this man and the other man, this race and that race, and the other race being inferior," he said during the Lincoln-Douglas debates. "Let us discard all these things, and unite as one people throughout this land until we shall once more stand up declaring that all men are created equal." Nor did he approve of casting aside those who are different from the majority. "If it was like two wrecked seamen on a narrow plank, when each must push the other off or drown himself, I would [neither] push the [black man] or the white man off," he said in 1860. "The plank is large enough for both. This good earth is plenty broad enough for white and [black] both."

Whether it was for his sister-in-law Emilie Todd Helm, or young boys falling asleep on guard duty, or Southerners who were going to have to recover from the ravages of civil war, or immigrants from another country, or slaves who were soon to be freed, or a new child born anywhere in the world, Abraham Lincoln had one abiding belief that no one could take away from him, because he made a point of repeating it in some form or fashion over and over and over again throughout the war. And he said it best in his first major address to Congress on July 4, 1861:

This . . . is a struggle . . . to elevate the condition of men — to afford all . . . a fair chance in the race of life.

A poor woman from Philadelphia was sitting in the White House hallway with a baby in her arms, hoping for a chance to see President Lincoln. Her young soldier husband had gotten drunk and deserted his regiment, was put on trial, and was convicted and sentenced to be shot. She had waited for three days in hopes of securing a pardon, but presidential assistants had been unable to squeeze her in. Late in the afternoon of the third day, Lincoln walked into a private room to get a cup of tea when he heard a baby cry.

"Is there a woman with a baby in the anteroom?" Lincoln asked the assistant on duty.

"Yes, Mr. President. And if you would allow me to say, it is a case you should hear, because it's a matter of life and death."

"Send her to me at once," said the president.

A few minutes later, the woman, clutching her child and crying with joy, walked out of Lincoln's office with a pardon for her husband. The presidential assistant quickly walked up to her and whispered, "Madam, it was the baby that did it."

The Death Penalty

During the Civil War, Abraham Lincoln pardoned hundreds and hundreds of soldiers who were sentenced to be shot for falling asleep on guard duty, or fleeing in battle, or deserting their regiments. "I think [they] can do us more good above ground than underground," he said. Yet there were several well-known examples of Lincoln letting men go to the gallows. He refused to pardon, for example, an American slave trader who had abducted and transported by ship hundreds of children to America. Nor would he show any mercy to a Virginia physician who killed a Union army lieutenant who was marching his black regiment through Norfolk.

Back then, there was no major debate about eliminating the death penalty, which was simply a normal punishment for murder and treason, etc. Actually, Lincoln went against the grain for not wanting to have people hanged or shot. Today, however, there is much controversy over the death penalty, and it has become a political issue. Many state governors, for instance, refuse to pardon people on death row for fear of voter backlash. Others have placed a moratorium on the death penalty, because it has been shown that a flawed judicial process has led to the conviction and execution of innocent people — the vast majority of whom tend to be poor or members of a minority. As a result, many progressives want to do away with capital punishment altogether. And some drug manufacturers refuse to let their products be used for executions by lethal injection.

In my opinion, Lincoln today would probably not abolish the death penalty, but would still believe firmly that the government must not be motivated by revenge or "punish merely for punishment's sake." And I believe he would agree that any individual who takes the life of another in a heinous, immoral manner must be removed from society. Whether or not such an individual pays the ultimate penalty should be left to the states. But I envision Lincoln personally seeing to it that every state has a proper judicial process in place. And if he were president today, I believe he would err on the side of humanity when asked to use his executive authority to pardon the condemned. In fact, if he had any inkling that a petitioner may be innocent, he might immediately commute the death sentence and then ask for an additional investigation.

Immigration

Abraham Lincoln guided through Congress the first major federal immigration law in American history (creating the U.S. Immigration Bureau and the Office of the Commissioner of Immigration). He entitled it "An Act to Encourage Immigration," termed it a great policy, and said it would give America's immigrants "effective national protection." Lincoln often referred to immigrants as "one of the principal of replenishing streams." America, he said, has a system that allows people to prosper, to rise, and to get rich. But when that system is successful, it creates a shortage of affordable labor. New immigrants fill that void. In Lincoln's day, it was filled primarily by Irish and Chinese immigrants. Today, it is filled largely by people from Latin America, particularly Mexico.

Unfortunately, the once-mighty U.S. immigration system has been degraded to a point where it is no longer effective, as witnessed by the estimated 11 million undocumented immigrants living in the country today. An ongoing argument pits conservatives — who say that undocumented workers take jobs away from Americans, don't pay taxes, and are a drain on local and state resources — against progressives, who say that opposition to immigration is rooted in racism. Some propose building a wall along the entire 1,954-mile border between Mexico and the United States. Others want to deport the entire undocumented population, as well as 300,000 so-called anchor babies (children born in the U.S. to undocumented immigrants).

My sense is that if Abraham Lincoln were surveying all of this today, he would remind us that the United States was built on immigration, and that, except for Native Americans, we are all descended from immigrants who journeyed to America looking for a new and better life. In my opinion, he would clearly agree that our immigration system is broken. But he would also say that closing the borders is not the answer, that building a multibillion-dollar wall along the border is ill-advised, and that forcibly deporting 11 million people is unfeasible. He would ask us to consider who provides most of the affordable labor in this country. Lincoln's view of immigrants as "one of the principal of replenishing streams" is still as valid now as it was in his day.

A leader like Lincoln, however, would definitely take action on such a broken system. He might propose change in two steps. First, he might implement a plan to legitimize those undocumented immigrants who are already here through a onetime offer of amnesty. Concurrent with that program, he would probably create a more effective and comprehensive immigration system more like what the United States had at the turn of the 20th century, when most European immigrants came through Ellis Island. With our technological capabilities today, there is no excuse for not being able to keep track of everybody who goes through the system. And once a new national immigration structure is reset, it must be strictly enforced.

Abraham Lincoln knew that all people everywhere desire freedom and opportunity. So let us all remember that for millions of oppressed people the world over, America is still the "last best, hope of earth."

Race Relations

Human nature is such that there will always be conflict between people of different races. What has exacerbated tensions more recently is, in part, the growing gap between haves and have-nots, which inordinately affects poor and ethnic minorities. Income inequality, combined with showings of overt racism, pushes poor people to their absolute limits of tolerance and often results in violent protests.

During the summer of 2014, for example, two weeks of major unrest took place in Ferguson, Missouri, after a black man was fatally shot by a white police officer. Charges of racism in the police department and corruption in the local judicial system drew national attention and sparked emotional debates about the relationship between black citizens and police departments across the country. Two years later, in 2016, protests erupted across the United States after similar incidents occurred in Minnesota and Louisiana. At one demonstration in Dallas, Texas, five white police officers were shot and killed (seven were wounded) by a lone black gunman.

I believe Abraham Lincoln would be very proud of the responses from Dallas mayor Mike Rawlings and Dallas chief of police David Brown in the immediate aftermath of their city's tragedy. "We've been through several protests in the last five or six years [and] these *were* peaceful protests until this incident happened," said Mayor Rawlings. "We were blocking streets to protect people's right to protest . . . and [ensure] everyone's freedom of speech."

"Police officers are guardians of this great democracy," added Chief Brown. "The freedom to protest, the freedom of speech, the freedom of expression — all [are] freedoms we fight for *with our lives.* It's what makes us who we are as Americans. . . . And we are not going to let a coward [who would ambush police officers] change our democracy! We're not going to do it! Our city, our country, is better than that!"

It's my sense that today's Lincoln would say that although violence is unacceptable, it may be understandable in some circumstances — especially when it is in reaction to a situation that has become intolerable. Clearly, there is a wide disparity between rich and poor when it comes to education, employment, and wages, among many other things. And this fact is what Lincoln might label the root cause of today's racial tensions. People who are out of work or disenfranchised do not feel like they have access to the American dream. And when people lose hope, they often become desperate.

Certainly, Lincoln would still believe that the federal government has a responsibility to provide equal access to opportunity *and* a level playing field for all its citizens. He might set up a cabinet department or a major agency to address this seemingly never-ending problem of race relations. Its charge would be to come up with a long-term plan that combines a broad national strategy with a grassroots application. Emotional fears, stereotypes, and prejudices are best overcome through personal human contact, communication, and cooperation. So a wise plan would include local communities, states, and the federal government bringing people together to talk, discuss, and get to know one another — so they can see the humanity of both sides. We must gradually live ourselves out of our poor relationships with one another into new relationships of harmony and understanding.

I am struggling to maintain government, not to overthrow it!

— Lincoln, two weeks before the
presidential election of 1864
October 19, 1864

We cannot have free government without elections; and if the rebellion could force us to forego or postpone a national election, it might fairly claim to have already conquered and ruined us.

— Lincoln, to a crowd of well-wishers after
being elected to a second term
November 10, 1864

ISSUES
The National Election Process
Influence of the Press in National Affairs

15

This Terrible, Bloody War

★ ★ ★

SITTING AT HIS DESK on the morning of August 23, 1864, Abraham Lincoln took a sheet of paper and wrote out the following short statement:

This morning, as for some days past, it seems exceedingly probable that this Administration will not be reelected. Then it will be my duty to so cooperate with the President-elect, as to save the Union between the election and the inauguration; as he will have secured his election on such ground that he cannot possibly save it afterwards.

He folded the paper several times over, pasted it shut, and then took it to his cabinet meeting later that day, where he asked each secretary to sign his name on the outside. The president did not divulge its contents, nor is there any record that his team asked what was in this "blind memorandum," as it later came to be known.

Just two and a half months before the presidential election, Lincoln's friends and advisers all told him that his reelection was "an impossibility," that "the tide is strongly against us," and that there was not "the slightest hope of success." At one point, he replied solemnly, "You think I don't know I am going to be beaten? But I do and unless some great change takes place, badly beaten."

In and around Washington, most of 1864 was consumed with election-year politics. Eight presidents had come and gone since Andrew Jackson had managed to secure two terms. Each had served only one, and there was still a strong popular sentiment for rotation in office. Democrats and Republicans knew that Lincoln was vulnerable, so both attacked him. Even Secretary of the Treasury Salmon P. Chase made a play for his boss's job. As early as February, Chase's backers had issued an anonymous pamphlet entitled *The Next Presidential Election,* which labeled Lincoln as vacillating, indecisive, feeble, and possessing a "want of intellectual grasp." Chase falsely denied having anything to do with the offensive publication and offered his resignation. But the president knew the score. "I suppose he will, like the bluebottle fly, lay his eggs in every rotten spot he can find," Lincoln told John Hay. Still, he refused to either accept Chase's resignation or fire him. "I am entirely indifferent as to his success or failure in these schemes, so long as he does his duty as the head of the Treasury Department," said Lincoln. "I will be responsible for that [decision]."

The truth is that up until Chase's pamphlet hit the streets, Lincoln had been so consumed with doing his job that he hadn't really given much thought to running for reelection. But he quickly woke up and committed himself to securing a second term. "I want to finish this job of putting down the rebellion and restoring peace and prosperity to the country," he told a friend. To secure that end, however, Lincoln had his work cut out for him, especially since things weren't going all that well on the military front.

After Gettysburg and Vicksburg, Union progress had slowed considerably. So on March 10, 1864, Lincoln promoted Ulysses S. Grant to command of all the Union armies. A short time later, the ever-aggressive general presented a broad summer military plan that included sending William Tecumseh Sherman's army into Georgia and other commanders into Alabama and eastern Virginia. Grant, himself, would ride with the Army of the Potomac into central Virginia to challenge Robert E. Lee head-on.

From May 5 to 7, 1864, more than 100,000 Union troops fought about 60,000 Confederates in dense forests near Spotsylvania (better known as the Battle of the Wilderness). In what Grant, himself, would later say was "as desperate fighting as the world has ever witnessed," the two armies suffered a staggering 28,000 casualties (17,000 Union, 11,000 Confederate) before Grant withdrew. Shortly after receiving news of the battle, Lincoln was observed "pacing back and forth along a narrow passage . . . , his hands behind him, great black rings under his eyes [and] his head bent forward." Even Speaker of the House Schuyler Colfax, who had dropped by for a conference, witnessed the president's gloomy mood. "Why do we suffer reverses after reverses!" he heard Lincoln say. "Could we have avoided this terrible, bloody war! . . . Is it ever to end!"

Rather than withdraw and regroup, however, Grant immediately gave the word that the Army of the Potomac was going to pursue Lee as he headed south toward Richmond. This order not only heartened the president, but also thrilled Grant's soldiers, who were weary of their previous commanders' tendencies to give up after setbacks. Less than a month later, after a 65-mile pursuit, Grant caught up to the Army of Northern Virginia at Cold Harbor (about 15 miles northeast of the Confederate capital). After nearly two weeks of fighting (from May 31 to June 12), Lee beat Grant again, despite being outnumbered two to one in troop strength. Union forces suffered 12,000 casualties, compared with 5,000 for the Confederates. Still undeterred, General Grant gave an order for his entire army to move south another 25 miles and attempt to take Petersburg.

During and after the Battle of Cold Harbor, thousands of wounded Union soldiers were transported up the Potomac River to field hospitals in and around Washington, D.C. President Lincoln, who often rode out to greet the long lines of ambulances, always thanked the troops for their sacrifices and made sure the doctors and nurses had everything they needed. On his way back one evening, he ran into a congressman and stopped for a minute. "Look yonder at those poor fellows," Lincoln said, pointing toward the line. "I cannot bear it. This suffering, this loss of life, is dreadful." Another time, he reflected to a senator on his situation with some irony: "Doesn't it seem strange to you that I should be here? . . . That I, who couldn't cut the head off a chicken, and who was sick at the sight of blood, should be cast into the middle of a great war, with blood flowing all around me?"

★ ★ ★

As if Abraham Lincoln didn't already have enough to worry about, during the middle of the Battle of Cold Harbor, the Republican National Convention of 1864 was held in Baltimore, strategically chosen for its border state location. The Republicans had renamed themselves the National Union Party, in part to attract more War Democrats to their ranks, but also to send a subtle message that reunification of the nation was paramount to its platform. Overall, the Republican Party seemed to be unraveling at the seams and splitting apart. Radicals outraged at Lincoln's veto of the Wade-Davis bill convened a separate convention in

Cleveland and nominated John C. Frémont for president. And although conservatives attended the main event in Baltimore, they were still fuming about the Emancipation Proclamation, believing that Lincoln had changed the reason for fighting the war away from preservation of the Union to freeing the slaves. Fortunately for the president, his supporters controlled the convention, and he was easily nominated.

Even though Lincoln did not travel to Baltimore, he quietly had a lot more to do with what happened at the convention than he let on. Through back-channel talks and intermediaries, the president made his wishes known as to what was written into the platform. He also okayed the choice of Andrew Johnson, a Democrat, to replace Hannibal Hamlin as his vice presidential running mate. Lincoln appreciated the fact that Johnson, who had stayed in the Senate after Tennessee seceded, had endorsed his 10 percent reconstruction plan and was serving loyally as military governor of his state. So when the nomination process was all said and done, Abraham Lincoln was set to run for reelection on the Union ticket with a Democrat as his running mate — a Southerner, no less, from one of the Confederate states. The symbolism couldn't have been more obvious. Reuniting the nation was Lincoln's paramount objective. He was going to bring people together rather than divide them.

The presidential election of 1864 was going to be one of the most important in American history, and Lincoln knew it. Everything was riding on the outcome — whether the war would end before final victory was secure, whether the United States would be held together or become two countries, whether reconstruction would be harsh or forgiving, and whether slavery in America would end or continue. With so much at stake, Lincoln decided to break precedent and actively campaign for his own reelection. So one week after his renomination, for example, the president showed up in Philadelphia to speak at the Great Central Fair (a fund-raiser for the U.S. Sanitary Commission, which supported sick and wounded soldiers). Lincoln personally donated 48 autographed copies of the Emancipation Proclamation to the event. Each sold for $10, and that, in turn, helped the fair raise more than a million dollars. When it came time for him to speak at the large banquet hall, he did not make a typical political speech. He complimented and praised the members of the commission for their "voluntary contributions, given freely, zealously, and earnestly" as "proof that the national spirit of patriotism is even [firmer and] stronger than at the commencement of the [war]." But then Lincoln made a point to mention not only the harsh realities of the Civil War, but his unshakable determination to continue the effort until final victory:

> War, at best, is terrible — and this war of ours, in its magnitude and in its duration, is one of the most terrible. It has deranged business. . . . It has destroyed property and ruined homes. It has carried mourning to almost every home, until it can almost be said that the "heavens are hung in black." Yet it continues. . . .
>
> This war has taken three years. . . . We accepted [it] for an object, a worthy object, and the war will end when that object is attained. . . . And for the American people, as far as my knowledge enables me to speak, I say we are going through on this line if it takes three [more] years.

Of course, it was the Army that had to carry on the fighting, and in this speech, Lincoln stated that the most credit "is due to the soldier, who takes his life in his hands and goes to fight the battles of his country." He also mentioned that Grant and "the brave officers and soldiers" of the Army of the Potomac were "in a position [at Petersburg]" from where [they] "will never be dislodged until Richmond is taken." So it is not surprising that President Lincoln's next stop after Philadelphia was to make an unannounced visit to Grant's headquarters at City Point, Virginia, which was only eight miles behind the Union lines near Petersburg. In addition to conferring with his generals, Lincoln spent two days among the troops. And as always, he reminded them *what* they were fighting for, *why* they were fighting, and *how im-*

portant their efforts were to the nation, to the American people, and to history, itself. This consistent message took on even more importance in an election year, because there were now more than 850,000 men in the armed forces, all of whom were going to be able to vote. But whom would they support? The presumptive nominee of the Democratic Party was retired general George B. McClellan, who was already talking about ending the war with "peace at any price." One would think that an end to the fighting and bloodshed would appeal to the average soldier. But, then again, what about all the sacrifices that had already been made? And what about all their friends who had given their lives for the cause? Whichever way it went, Lincoln let it be known that he was going to make it as easy as possible for the troops to vote. "I would rather be defeated with the soldier vote behind me than to be elected without it," he said.

In addition to making key speeches and spending as much time with the troops as he could, Lincoln and his political associates tended to more pragmatic tasks involved in winning a major election. Three weeks after securing his nomination, for instance, the constant political thorn in the president's side, Salmon P. Chase, again offered his resignation over a minor matter. This time, Lincoln accepted the resignation, stating: "You and I have reached a point of mutual embarrassment in our official relation which it seems cannot be overcome, or longer sustained, consistently with the public service." *[Lincoln appointed Senator William P. Fessenden to replace Chase as secretary of the Treasury.]* Additionally, *New York Times* publisher Henry J. Raymond authored a campaign book that included speeches, letters, and proclamations. The volume, titled *History of the Administration of Abraham Lincoln,* was approved by the president and put together with White House assistance. Raymond closed out his best seller by writing:

If the measures which President Lincoln has inaugurated for quelling the rebellion and restoring the Union are permitted to work out their natural results, unchecked by popular impatience and sustained by public confidence, we believe they will end in reestablishing the authority of the Constitution, in restoring the integrity of the Union, in abolishing every vestige of slavery, and in perpetuating the principles of democratic government upon this continent and throughout the world.

Of particular note in this most important election year is that Lincoln made few, if any, compromise decisions that might lead Americans to vote his way. Many politicians advised him to drop freeing the slaves as a condition of reconstruction, for example. He was even asked to rescind the Emancipation Proclamation. Again and again, both before and *after* the election, Lincoln consistently refused to do so. He was most resolute in his final annual message to Congress:

> I repeat the declaration made a year ago, that "while I remain in my present position I shall not attempt to retract or modify the emancipation proclamation, nor shall I return to slavery any person who is free by the terms of that proclamation, or by any Acts of Congress." If the people should, by whatever mode or means, make it an Executive duty to re-enslave such persons, another, and not I, must be their instrument to perform it.

In other words, if that was what the American people wanted done, they were going to have to get somebody else to do it.

And when the prospects looked bleakest for his reelection, President Lincoln was even asked to cancel the November elections so he could remain in office. "I am struggling to maintain government, not to overthrow it!" he responded. The election would go forward as scheduled.

★ ★ ★

There were really two campaigns in 1864 — one political, one military — and by late summer, the military one was not going well. Grant was stalled outside Petersburg as the Confederates waged a furious defense. So, too, had Sherman stalled at Atlanta, which was under siege. During six weeks of virtually nonstop fighting that summer of 1864, the Union army had suffered almost 100,000 casualties (killed or wounded). To compound the situation, on July 11, 1864, word reached Lincoln that Confederate general Jubal Early and his 16,000 troops had come up the Shenandoah Valley, crossed the Potomac, and were approaching Washington from the north at Maryland Heights. That afternoon, Lincoln rode out to Fort Stevens (barely six miles from the White House) and was standing on the parapet when the Confederates attacked. Union forces eventually repelled the assault and forced General Early's retreat. But the president, extremely alarmed, met with General Grant at Fort Monroe in Virginia to discuss why Jubal Early had been able to so easily invade Maryland and threaten the nation's capital. Lincoln pushed the general to be more aggressive and also reminded him that it was an election year. Almost immediately, Grant ordered Phil Sheridan to chase Early's troops as they retreated into the Shenandoah Valley. Additionally, Lincoln put out a draft call for an additional 500,000 men from "every town, township, ward of a city, precinct or election district" to serve a one-year term beginning on September 5, 1864. Because this politically dangerous order was to take effect only two months before the November elections, Republican leaders begged Lincoln to postpone it. But he refused, stating: "What good is the presidency to me if I have no country?"

Any leader who takes bold action will face some blowback. That's both part of human nature and the reality of being a good leader. As such, Lincoln was well aware that he was going to suffer political consequences from his draft order and from the mere fact that current military operations had stalled. When the national press took him to task and began calling for peace negotiations with the South, Lincoln first counseled forbearance. "We must be patient and all will come out all right," he said. "I did not expect Sherman to take Atlanta in a day, nor Grant to walk right into Richmond. We will have them both in time." But when the media's impatience went too far, Lincoln's political acumen came to the forefront. Take, for instance, the case of Horace Greeley and the so-called Niagara Falls peace conference of August 6, 1864. The publisher of the *New York Tribune* had already written a blistering letter to the president saying: "I venture to remind you that our bleeding, bankrupt, almost dying country . . . longs for peace, shudders at the prospect of fresh conscriptions, of further wholesale devastations, and of new rivers of human blood."

The meddling Greeley, who seemed to think of himself as a pseudo-president, also wrote that he feared Lincoln did not "realize how intently the people desire peace," and further suggested that "a frank offer by you to the insurgents . . . may save us from a northern insurrection." But when Greeley next told the president he had received word that "two Ambassadors" from Jefferson Davis were in Niagara Falls, Canada, and asking to negotiate peace, Lincoln smelled a rat. "[Greeley] intends to influence the peace sentiment of the North, to embarrass the administration, and to demoralize the army," he told a colleague.

The president then cleverly authorized Greeley to go to Niagara Falls and negotiate on the nation's behalf, sending his aide John Hay along with a personal handwritten note that read:

> To whom it may concern: Any proposition which embraces the restoration of peace, the integrity of the whole Union, and the abandonment of slavery . . . will be received and considered by the Executive government of the United States.

When Greeley arrived in Canada, he and Hay learned that the "two Ambassadors" had no credentials whatsoever from Confederate leaders. Returning to New York with his tail between his legs, Greeley was mortified to learn that the press not only blamed him for the failed peace negotiations, but also ridiculed

him for the entire episode. "Lincoln skewered me!" Greeley told
his staff at the *Tribune.* "Why would he want to do this to me?
Will somebody tell me, please?"

The answer to that question might be what the president said
to his cabinet afterward:

> Greeley is like an old shoe — good for nothing now, whatever
> he has been.... In early life ... we used to make our shoes
> last a great while with much mending, and sometimes, when
> far gone, we found the leather so rotten the stitches would not
> hold. Greeley is so rotten that nothing can be done with him.
> He is not truthful; the stitches all tear out.

Three weeks after Lincoln "skewered" Horace Greeley, the
Democratic Party held its national convention in Chicago and
nominated George B. McClellan to run for president. The media labeled the event the "Chicago Surrender," because Democrats roundly condemned the war and called for immediate
peace negotiations. If McClellan won the election, the survival
of both the Confederacy and slavery probably would be ensured.
But over the next few months, the Union military made several
breakthroughs. Admiral David *"Damn the Torpedoes, Full Speed
Ahead"* Farragut captured Mobile Bay, Alabama, the last major
Gulf port still controlled by the Confederacy. The siege of Atlanta finally ended as William Tecumseh Sherman successfully
secured the city. And Phil Sheridan, after a series of hard-fought
battles, took control of the entire Shenandoah Valley in Virginia.
These victories shifted the tide of public opinion and turned the
election in Lincoln's favor.

On November 8, 1864, the Union ticket won 55 percent of the
popular vote (2.2 million to 1.8 million). Of particular note was
that Lincoln, not McClellan, won 80 percent of the soldiers' vote,
which may very well have made the difference. He also won every state except Delaware, Kentucky, and New Jersey (McClellan's
home state), leading to a rout of 212–21 in the Electoral College.
[None of the Confederate states participated in the election, with

*the exception of Union military districts in Louisiana and Tennes-
see, where no electoral votes were counted.]*

After receiving the final tally, Lincoln addressed a group of
well-wishers at the White House. "It has long been a grave question whether any government, not *too* strong for the liberties of
its people, can be strong *enough* to maintain its own existence
in great emergencies. . . . The election was a necessity. We cannot have free government without elections; and if the rebellion
could force us to forego, or postpone a national election, it might
fairly claim to have already conquered and ruined us."

★ ★ ★

On November 11, 1864, the newly elected President Lincoln called
his cabinet together. "Gentlemen, do you remember last summer
I asked you all to sign your names to the back of a paper of which
I did not show you the inside?" he said, holding up the document. "This is it."

After asking John Hay to open it, Lincoln read the contents:

> This morning, as for some days past, it seems exceedingly prob-
> able that this Administration will not be reelected. Then it will
> be my duty to so cooperate with the President-elect, as to save
> the Union between the election and the inauguration; as he will
> have secured his election on such ground that he cannot possi-
> bly save it afterwards.

"I resolved, in the case of the election of General McClellan,"
Lincoln continued, "that I would see him and talk matters over
with him. I would say, 'General, the election has demonstrated
that you are stronger, have more influence with the American
people than I. Now let us together, you with your influence and
I with all the executive power of the Government, try to save the
country. You raise as many troops as you possibly can for this final trial, and I will devote all my energies to assisting and finishing the war."

"And the General would answer 'Yes, yes,'" replied Secretary of State Seward, "and would have done nothing at all."

"At least I should have done my duty and have stood clear before my own conscience," said the president.

So exactly what was this "blind memorandum" really all about? Back on August 23, 1864, when he wrote it, Lincoln was depressed that all his advisers were telling him that his reelection chances were hopeless. Clearly, he was anticipating the possibility that he would lose and that his goals of saving the Union and ending slavery forever would be in real jeopardy. Should that happen, Lincoln resolved, then and there, to try like the devil to win the war during the final four months of his presidency. But such action from a lame-duck president would have been unprecedented in American history. And besides, if he had any hope of success, his cabinet members were going to have to help make it happen. So Lincoln wrote out his memorandum, folded it, and asked his team to sign it without knowing the contents. He did not want them to know he was seriously contemplating losing the election, because it might dispirit them. But after the fact (if he lost), he also wanted them to know that he was not driving forward for political reasons or from personal anger at having lost the election.

Abraham Lincoln had thought things through. He was going to do everything in his power to save the Union even if it killed him — politically or physically. Now, *that* was commitment to his cause!

At one o'clock in the afternoon on June 21, 1864, a "long, gaunt bony-looking man," dressed in black and looking like "a professional undertaker," passed through a hedge and scrambled up to General Grant's tent at City Point, Virginia. A guard stopped him and told him to "keep out of here."

"I think General Grant will allow me inside," said the man in black.

"No sanitary folks allowed inside!" said the guard sternly.

"Well, I am Abraham Lincoln, President of the United States, seeking an interview with General Grant."

With that, the guard saluted and motioned for him to pass. Upon seeing Grant, Lincoln said: "I just thought I would jump aboard a boat and come down and see you."

LINCOLN ON LEADERSHIP FOR TODAY

The National Election Process

In Abraham Lincoln's time, national candidates were chosen by political party insiders, 80 percent of all eligible voters participated in national elections, and Election Day was always on a Tuesday so that farmers (who rested on the Sabbath) could travel a full day to their county seats in order to vote. Today, each major political party has a different system of choosing its nominee via primaries and delegates, elections are still held on Tuesdays, and voter participation averages about 53 percent (putting the United States in the bottom 20 percent of global voter participation by nation). My sense is that Lincoln would definitely address two issues of modern elections that have become much more controversial in recent years: (1) the Electoral College and (2) gerrymandering.

Many people want to do away with the Electoral College process that is used in presidential elections. Each state is assigned a certain number of electoral votes based on population, and *that number* is assigned to the candidate who wins the popular vote. The candidate who garners a majority of electoral votes nationwide then wins the presidency. Detractors argue, among other things, that the true will of the people is not carried out if a candidate wins the overall popular vote, but doesn't win a majority of the Electoral College. My sense is that today's Lincoln would probably not change a thing. He knew that the Founding Fathers wanted a buffer between the general population and the selection of a president, with some assurance that only a qualified person would become president. The Electoral College, they felt, would make it less likely that one candidate, or one party, could manipulate the citizenry. It also protects and empowers minorities, and provides smaller states a more equal voice against larger states.

Every 10 years, the number of seats in the U.S. House of Representatives is reapportioned among the states (based on the new United States Census). In turn, the states are tasked to revise their

240

district boundaries according to population changes. In some states, legislators of the majority party then redraw districts to give their own party a numeric advantage over the minority party. This process, commonly termed "gerrymandering," results in the unfair protection of incumbents and a clear misrepresentation of the public in Congress. In my opinion, today's Lincoln would encourage and support national legislation (and a constitutional amendment) to take state redistricting out of the hands of party-controlled state legislators and give it to an independent national commission comprised of unbiased citizens who are not members of any political party. Its charge would be to redraw districts based on the geographic distribution of population alone, without any regard to likely party affiliation. Then Congress could better represent the overall will of the people.

Influence of the Press in National Affairs

During Abraham Lincoln's presidency, there were many attempts by major newspapers to have him change his policies or commence some sort of action he was not inclined to take. For instance, when it was suggested that the United States intervene in Mexico to counter Napoleon III's creation of a puppet government there, Lincoln brushed it off by saying that one rebellion at a time was about all he could handle. And when Horace Greeley attempted to maneuver him into untimely peace negotiations with the Confederacy, the president both outsmarted and "skewered" him (as Greeley, himself, later said). Generally, Lincoln did not let the press influence his direction, but, rather, he held back, made his own decisions, and stood on principle. Nor did he give the press much to work with, especially in the content of his public speeches. Rarely did Lincoln speak extemporaneously, because he knew he would be more likely to make a mistake. Rather, he was extremely careful about what he said, invariably writing out every word ahead of time.

But if Lincoln were here today, I believe he would be more vocal with the press. Today's media is so widespread and so diverse that it reaches virtually every American citizen in some form or another

—and almost instantaneously. Also, rather than simply reporting the news in an unbiased manner, many media outlets become very involved in attempting to sway, influence, and manipulate national affairs. Because of that reality, I think Lincoln would recognize that a national leader simply has to become more involved in both presenting administration policy and countering ill-advised proposals. For example, if the press is advocating sending troops into a foreign country, or proposing some special interest–sponsored solution to immigration control, a modern-day President Lincoln might deal with it straight on. He'd perhaps call out whoever suggested such a proposal and, not necessarily in an antagonistic way, simply say, "Okay, give me your reasoning, and let's discuss it publicly." The president could then explain the administration's policy and provide pertinent facts that the general public might not know about.

Americans are always looking for strong leadership in both the White House and the halls of Congress. In the absence of such leadership, a void will be created that elevates the power of the media to directly influence the direction of government. In truth, this is already happening to some degree now. And I'm sure Abraham Lincoln would agree that the United States always needs a president who will deal with the national media from a position of strength and authority.

Section 1. Neither slavery or involuntary servitude, except as a punishment for crime whereof the party shall have been duly convicted, shall exist within the United States, or any place subject to its jurisdiction.

Section 2. Congress shall have power to enforce this article by appropriate legislation.

— Thirteenth Amendment to the United States Constitution
Passed by Congress: January 31, 1865
Ratified by the states: December 6, 1865

ISSUES
Voting Rights for Minorities
Abortion
Women's Rights

16

With Malice Toward None

★ ★ ★

ON APRIL 14, 1876, 11 years to the day after Abraham Lincoln was shot at Ford's Theatre, former slave and abolitionist Frederick Douglass publicly noted the 16th president's "wonderful success in organizing the loyal American people for the tremendous conflict before them, and bringing them safely through that conflict." At that moment, Douglass also insightfully noted something that neither he nor anybody else had fully understood while Lincoln was alive. "We are compelled to admit," said Douglass, "that his great mission was to accomplish two things: first, to save his country from dismemberment and ruin, and second, to free his country from the great crime of slavery. Had he put the abolition of slavery before salvation of the Union, he would have inevitably driven from him a powerful class of the American people and rendered resistance to rebellion impossible."

Although, as Lincoln said in 1862, his "paramount object [was] to save the Union," he did, indeed, have an unstated goal to end slavery. The president couldn't advocate such action, however, because to do so would have further weakened the Union's already-fragile political coalition. There is certainly no doubt that Lincoln detested slavery from the time he first saw a slave auction in New Orleans as a young man. And later, as a politician, he specifically noted that he hated the institution for its "monstrous injustice," because "it deprives our republican example of its just influence in the world," and because it "enables the enemies of free institutions . . . to taunt us as hypocrites." "If slavery is not wrong," he wrote in 1864, "nothing is wrong." The truth is that Lincoln had been steadily speaking out against slavery over the course of his political career, and after winning the presidency, he used his executive power to chip away at it. Here are some of the major steps Lincoln took toward permanent abolition:

January 10, 1849	Proposed legislation (as a U.S. congressman) to end slavery in Washington, D.C.
October 16, 1854	Spoke out against the Kansas-Nebraska Act (Peoria, Ill.)
June 26, 1857	Spoke out against the *Dred Scott* decision (Springfield, Ill.)
August–October, 1858	Raised slavery to national dialogue in Senate campaign debates with Stephen A. Douglas
January 16, 1861	Rejected the Crittenden Compromise (as president-elect)
April 16, 1862	Compensated Emancipation Act ending slavery in Washington, D.C.

September 22, 1862   Preliminary Emancipation Proclamation

January 1, 1863   Emancipation Proclamation

June 7, 1864   Insisted that the Republican/National Union Party platform include a resolution to support a constitutional amendment abolishing slavery

Lincoln understood that in order to dismantle something like slavery, an economic institution so ingrained in everyday culture across the country, a leader must think long term and try to change it *gradually,* removing key pieces of the foundation as public sentiment allows. "A man watches his pear tree day after day, impatient for the ripening of the fruit," Lincoln once explained to an abolitionist. "Let him attempt to *force* the process, and he may spoil both fruit and tree. But let him patiently *wait,* and the ripe pear at length falls into his lap."

By mid-1864, in Lincoln's mind, there was only one thing left to do in regard to slavery. If circumstances permitted, he would seize the opportunity to push a constitutional amendment through Congress and send it to the states for ratification. But timing was everything. He was going to have to do it *before* the Civil War formally ended, so that the states in rebellion could not vote against the amendment. Lincoln sensed his opportunity had arrived in November after being elected to a second term. He had solidified his power nationally by winning a commanding mandate, the military situation was going the Union's way, and people were optimistic that the war would soon be over. In short, public opinion was now on his side. The pear was ready to fall.

Despite the fact that the next Congress (to be seated on March 5, 1865) would have a much larger Republican majority thanks to the November election victories, Lincoln did not want to wait. He was well aware that this seated Congress had failed to completely pass such an amendment back in June 1864. *[On April*

8, 1864, the U.S. Senate passed the 13th Amendment, 38–6. However, on June 15, 1864, the U.S. House of Representatives voted 93–65 (with 23 abstentions) in favor — 13 votes short of the necessary two-thirds majority needed to pass.] But acting with a great leader's sense of urgency, Lincoln wanted the lame-duck House to vote again. "[I] recommend reconsideration and passage of the measure," he wrote in his December 6, 1864, annual message. "The next Congress will [almost certainly] pass the measure. . . . It is only a question of *time.* . . . [So] may we not agree that the sooner the better?" The president then went on to point out that "the most reliable indication of public purpose in this country is derived through our popular elections." And as the election had gone his way, "some deference [must] be paid to the will of the majority, [which] has most dearly declared in favor of such [a] constitutional amendment."

Lincoln's request in this instance was remarkable not only because he was asking Democrats in the House to compromise on their idealistic view of states' rights for a cause they had already voted down, but also because the vote had gone almost entirely along party lines. *[Only four Democrats broke ranks to vote for the amendment.]* And that meant that Lincoln was going to have to break congressional gridlock — an undertaking that nearly every politician, political pundit, and even members of Lincoln's own cabinet thought impossible. Get lame ducks, angry after having been voted out of office, to change their minds? Get House Democrats to overcome intense political pressure from friends and colleagues? Who did Lincoln think he was kidding? Well, Lincoln wasn't kidding, and here are the tactics he used to break gridlock.

Step 1: Force action.

Lincoln had Massachusetts representative John B. Alley formally reintroduce the 13th Amendment to the House.

Step 2: Involve the team.

Lincoln dispatched his cabinet members to help. For instance, he gave broad leeway to Secretary of State William Seward to lead the effort. In response, Seward formed a team of lobbyists, put pressure on congressmen, and even came up with a slush fund for bribes.

Step 3: Personally lobby key members of Congress.

The president met personally with legislators, either going to them or inviting them to his office in the White House. Lincoln employed his personal powers of persuasion, just as he used to do as a lawyer trying to convince a jury to vote his way. He said the amendment would not only kill the institution of slavery, but would help end the war: "The passage of this amendment will clinch the whole subject." He begged for help: "It is going to be very close, a few votes one way or the other will decide it." And he used stories and metaphors: "We are like whalers who have been long on a chase. We have at last got the harpoon into the monster, but we must now look how we steer, or with one 'flop' of his tail, he will send us all into eternity."

Step 4: Use the power of the presidency.

Lincoln and his representatives promised federal jobs and key appointments to outgoing congressmen, doled out government contracts and campaign funds for future political runs, offered to delay legislation, and twisted arms to secure every possible vote.

Step 5: Flex muscle and use the power of your personality.

At one point near the end of the monthlong debates, two Republican congressmen were summoned to the White House and told that they had to procure two more votes. When one asked how it could be done, Lincoln exploded in a rare display of force-ful intimidation. "I am President of the United States, clothed with immense power!" he shouted. "The abolition of slavery by constitutional provision settles the fate, for all coming time, not only of the millions now in bondage, but of unborn millions to come — a measure of such importance that *those two votes must be procured.*" Settling down a bit, Lincoln sent the congressmen on their way, saying, "I leave it to you to determine how it shall be done — but remember that I . . . expect you to procure those votes."

Step 6: If necessary, employ political subterfuge.

Several weeks earlier, Lincoln had allowed Francis P. Blair Sr. (one of the founders of the Republican Party) to travel to Richmond and meet with Confederate president Jefferson Davis to explore a possible avenue toward peace. Davis authorized three representatives to travel to Washington for negotiations. That Confederate delegation left Richmond on January 29, 1864, and passed through Union lines at Petersburg, before Lincoln ordered General Grant to hold them at Fort Monroe, near Hampton Roads, Virginia. Rumors of impending peace negotiations soon reached the raging amendment debate in Congress and threatened to upset all previous bargains. On the morning of January 31, 1864 (a final vote was scheduled for that afternoon), a frantic John Alley sent the president a note from the floor of the House.

> The report is in circulation that peace Commissioners are on their way or are in the city, and is being used against us. If it is true, I fear we shall lose the bill. Please authorize me to contradict it, if not true.

Lincoln, who was preparing to send Seward down to Fort Monroe to meet with the Confederates, calmly wrote out and sent back the following message:

So far as I know, there are no peace commissioners in the city, or likely to be in it. *[Signed]* A. Lincoln.

The president's response was a crafty lawyer's answer that, while misleading, was technically true. But when his note was read on the floor of the House, everything calmed down and the vote proceeded as scheduled. And on the afternoon of January 31, 1865, to wild cheering from both legislators and people in the gallery, the U.S. House of Representatives passed the 13th Amendment to the U.S. Constitution by a vote of 119–56, which secured the necessary two-thirds majority by only two votes. *[All Republicans voted in favor. Sixteen Democrats, 14 of whom were lame ducks, crossed over to vote yes. There were 8 abstentions.]* The final bill read simply:

> Section 1. Neither slavery or involuntary servitude, except as a punishment for crime whereof the party shall have been duly convicted, shall exist within the United States, or any place subject to its jurisdiction.
> Section 2. Congress shall have power to enforce this article by appropriate legislation.

The next day, February 1, 1865, President Lincoln signed the amendment and then sent it to the states for ratification. Immediately afterward, he addressed a crowd that had gathered on the White House lawn. "I believe all will bear witness that *I never shrank from doing all that I could to eradicate slavery,*" said Lincoln. "This amendment is a King's cure for all the evils. It winds the whole thing up. . . . I congratulate all present, the country, and the whole world upon *this great moral victory.*" [Italics added.]

Two days later, President Lincoln steamed down to Hampton Roads to meet with Seward and the three Confederate commissioners, which included Lincoln's old friend Alexander Stephens (vice president of the Confederacy), former U.S. Speaker of the House Robert M. T. Hunter, and former Supreme Court justice

John A. Campbell. On board the *River Queen,* Lincoln told them that he would not allow the nation to be divided into two countries, that there would be no compromise on slavery, and that he would not negotiate until the rebels laid down their arms (which essentially meant unconditional military surrender). When Hunter pointed out that even Charles I negotiated with people in rebellion against him, Lincoln adroitly responded, "I do not profess to be posted in history, [but] I distinctly recollect . . . that Charles I lost his head in the end."

Secretary Seward also told the commissioners that the 13th Amendment had just been passed in Congress and was being sent to the states for ratification. Lincoln then leaned toward Stephens, his former "Young Indian" congressional colleague, and said: "I'll tell you what I would do if I were in your place. I would go home and get the Governor of the State [of Georgia] to call the legislature together . . . and ratify this [amendment], so as to take effect, say, in five years. Such a ratification would be valid in my opinion."

The Hampton Roads Peace Conference ended without agreement on anything — and Lincoln knew that was the way it was going to turn out, because he possessed all the leverage. After so many years of fighting, and so many lives lost, Lincoln was not about to give ground on anything. His sense of urgency in securing passage of the 13th Amendment to end slavery was now paying off. And as he told his wife, Mary, "It is best when you undertake a job, to finish it."

* * *

In the middle of the House debate on the 13th Amendment, a group of workingwomen from Philadelphia visited President Lincoln at the White House (on January 26, 1865). Six months earlier, he had received a petition from the larger group they represented ("Twenty thousand Working Women of Philadelphia") requesting that the government "increase the price of female labor," that they receive "an equitable price for their labor," and that "four times the number of women" be added to the workforce. Lincoln forwarded the petition to Secretary of War Edwin Stanton with an endorsement that these requests seemed "just and reasonable."

During the Civil War, women from both North and South stepped forward to help out while men were serving in the military. In the Union, thousands of ladies aid societies were organized to supply food, work with sanitary commissions, work in hospitals, sew clothes, and do virtually everything else a woman could think of to provide assistance. They also flocked to government factories that manufactured munitions, uniforms, tents, blankets, and other war-related materials. Not treated as equals of men, these women had to fight for their rights. They asked for fair treatment, equal pay, comparable work hours, and even federal pensions. When these requests made it to Lincoln's desk, he tried to have them fulfilled "within the legal power of the government."

It's not surprising that, as president, Lincoln made every effort to both listen to and help women. He had been doing so ever since entering politics. During his 1836 run for reelection to the Illinois legislature, for example, he had written: "I go for all sharing the privileges of the government, who assist in bearing its burdens. Consequently I go for admitting all whites to the right of suffrage, who pay taxes or bear arms (by no means excluding females)." And as a lawyer riding on the Eighth Judicial Circuit in Illinois, he represented hundreds of women who needed help to secure their legal rights to inheritance and property. His law partner William Herndon confirmed that Lincoln viewed women as equals. "Seeing that Woman was denied in free America her right to the elective franchise," he wrote, "being the equal but the other side . . . , he always advocated her rights." In 1837, Lincoln said, "I want in all cases to do right, and most particularly so, in all cases with women." And 20 years later, Lincoln stated that a black woman "in her natural right to eat the bread she earns with her own hands . . . is my equal and the equal of all others. . . . If a white man wants to marry a [black] woman, let him do it — if the [black] woman can stand it." Regarding the American people openly advocating for women's rights, however, Lincoln said: "This question is one simply of time."

Even though most Union workingwomen lost their jobs once the Civil War was over, Lincoln's early support helped change the U.S. government's view of women's rights. His actions paved the way for significant advancements that began in following years. In 1869, for instance, both the American Woman Suffrage Association and the National Woman Suffrage Association were formed. And on December 10 of that year, the Wyoming Territory's legislature granted women the right to vote, the first act of its kind in U.S. history.

★ ★ ★

On March 4, 1865, Abraham Lincoln stepped to the podium at the east front of the United States Capitol to be sworn in for his second term. He took seven minutes to deliver one of the briefest inaugural addresses in U.S. history (barely 700 words in length). "With high hope for the future," Lincoln began — and then he recalled the situation four years previous. "Both parties deprecated war," he said, "but one of them would *make* war rather than let the nation survive; and the other would *accept* war rather than let it perish." And Lincoln stated once again (as he had in his first inaugural) that slavery "was, somehow, the cause of the war."

"Both read the same Bible, and pray to the same God," he continued, "and each invokes His aid against the other. It may seem strange that any men should dare to ask a just God's assistance in wringing their bread from the sweat of other men's faces; but let us judge not that we be not judged." Lincoln insisted several times that "the Almighty has his purposes." "Fondly do we hope — fervently do we pray — that this mighty scourge of war may speedily pass away," he said. "Yet if God wills that it continue . . . ,

[then] the judgments of the Lord, are true and righteous altogether."

And finally, Lincoln closed with a remarkably poetic paragraph that let everyone on both sides of the conflict know that he intended to move forward with forgiveness and compassion:

> With malice toward none; with charity for all; with firmness in the right, as God gives us to see the right, let us strive on to finish the work we are in; to bind up the nation's wounds; to care for him who shall have borne the battle, and for his widow, and his orphan — to do all which may achieve and cherish a just, and a lasting peace, among ourselves, and with all nations.

The oath of office was then administered by the new chief justice of the United States, Salmon P. Chase, whom the president had nominated for the position upon the death of Roger B. Taney. The scene was a visual symbol of the message Lincoln had just delivered. After all, it was Chase who had worked behind his back in a failed attempt to secure the 1864 Republican Party nomination for himself. "I know meaner things about Chase than [anyone] can tell me," Lincoln said in explaining his decision. "[But] we have stood together in the time of trial, and I should despise myself if I allowed personal differences to affect my judgment of his fitness for the office."

At the end of the month, Lincoln was back in the field again meeting with Grant, and this time, also with General Sherman and Admiral David Porter, aboard the *River Queen* near City Point, Virginia. The three confirmed to the president that one more major offensive was needed to defeat the rebels. Now anticipating that the war would soon end, President Lincoln spoke to his commanders about how to treat the defeated Confederates. He knew full well that the South was in serious trouble economically and that its population was suffering broadly from a lack of food, clothing, and other bare necessities. "Let them all go," Admiral Porter recalled Lincoln saying. "Let them have their horses to plow with, and, if you like, their guns to shoot crows with. . . .

I want no more bloodshed . . . , no one punished. Give them the most liberal and honorable terms." Sherman confirmed that all the president wanted was "[for us] to defeat the opposing armies . . . and get the Confederate armies back to their homes, at work on their farms, and in their shops."

On March 29, 1865, the day after meeting with Lincoln, General Grant launched a Union offensive that succeeded in breaking Confederate supply lines to both Petersburg and Richmond. Robert E. Lee was able to avoid capture by ordering his troops to move west toward Virginia's interior. The next day, April 3, 1865, both cities came under Union military control. President Lincoln went to Petersburg that very day to thank the troops and again confer with Grant. Dead bodies still littered the battlefield as he rode by on horseback, his head bowed and tears streaming down his cheeks. The next day, Lincoln went to Richmond to visit and thank the troops there. As he walked along the streets holding his son Tad's hand (April 4, 1865, was Tad's twelfth birthday), "the Great Emancipator" was cheered by throngs of former slaves.

The president lingered for a while at the front before finally heading back to Washington. Upon his arrival on April 9, 1865, he learned that Grant had finally caught Lee at Appomattox and forced a surrender. The Union commander had, as instructed, given the Confederates generous and fair terms. While rifles and cannons were turned over, all were allowed to keep their pistols, horses, and mules. The hungry soldiers were also provided food and allowed to return home immediately. In effect, the Civil War was over.

★ ★ ★

In his final days, Abraham Lincoln was looking toward the future. He told the Speaker of the House, Schuyler Colfax, that he believed "the mineral wealth of our Nation . . . [was] practically inexhaustible," and that he was going to "encourage [such development] in every possible way." Lincoln was going to continue his support of immigration and advise potential new citizens to head west and work in the mines. He also saw the development of mining as a source of employment for Civil War veterans — Union and Confederate alike. In that vein, Lincoln was perpetually focused on helping veterans regain their lives after the fighting came to an end. He sent a note of encouragement, for instance, to General Winfield Scott, who was working to find jobs for disabled veterans, stating that he would always be ready "to recognize the paramount claims of the soldiers of the nation." He also issued a new proclamation (with the approval of Congress) stating that "all deserters [who] return to their posts . . . within sixty days . . . shall be pardoned." And even in the days after Appomattox, Lincoln continued to pardon young soldiers who had been court-martialed and sentenced to be shot. "Let the Prisoner be pardoned and returned to his Regiment," he wrote in the case of a New York private on April 12, 1865.

In his very last public speech, given to a crowd of citizens who had gathered outside the White House two days after the surrender at Appomattox, President Lincoln took no personal credit for victory. "No part of the honor, for plan or execution, is mine," he said. "To Gen. Grant, his skillful officers and brave men, all belongs." And then, after complimenting the Louisiana legislature for ratifying the 13th Amendment, Lincoln suggested that voting rights be given to blacks, especially "those who serve our cause as soldiers." This comment harkened back to his 1836 statement, "I go for admitting all whites to the right of suffrage, who pay taxes *or bear arms* (by no means excluding females)." [Italics added.] So Abraham Lincoln was now openly suggesting that in addition to allowing women to vote, the nation should also extend the right to vote to black soldiers who had fought for the Union.

In making this audacious and unprecedented proposal, Lincoln was taking the first step in enacting major change. Just as he had done before issuing the Emancipation Proclamation to end slavery, he was, for the first time, floating the idea of black suffrage — so the people could think about it, get used to it, and then later accept it. Of course, Lincoln knew it would be some time before this pear was ripe and ready to fall. But he also was confident that blacks would eventually be granted the right to vote, and with that right, they would receive full U.S. citizenship.

By April 14, 1865, when Abraham Lincoln met with his cabinet for the last time, 14 of the 27 states needed had already ratified the 13th Amendment. *[Official ratification took place on December 6, 1865.]* During that meeting, the president told his team that "there [are] men in Congress who, if their motives [are] good, [are] nevertheless impracticable, and who [possess] feelings of hate and vindictiveness in which [I can not] sympathize and [can] not participate." According to Edwin Stanton, he "spoke very kindly of General Lee and others of the Confederacy." Gideon Welles also quoted Lincoln as saying, "We must extinguish our resentments if we expect harmony and union." So by that time, Lincoln had not only led the effort to win the Civil War and reunify the nation, he had also successfully set up the institution of slavery to be forever wiped from the map of the United States. At the same time, he had made it clear that he wanted no malice or retribution directed toward anybody and that he cared about all American citizens, Southerners included. And therein lies one of Abraham Lincoln's greatest legacies. The ability to combine a drive to achieve with a capacity to care is part of the foundation upon which all leaders stand. And because leaders deal primarily with people, *respect for others* is the cement that keeps that foundation strong.

★ ★ ★

As the president left for Ford's Theatre that evening, White House guards snapped to attention and stood at "present arms," which is a military sign of respect. One of those guards noted that Lincoln, as he always did, bowed and touched his hat in response. "It always seemed to me as much a compliment to the devotion of the soldiers on his part," recalled the guard, "as it was a sign of duty and deference on the part of the guard."

Abraham Lincoln had earned the trust and respect of his troops, and he returned it in kind.

Viewed from the genuine abolition ground, Mr. Lincoln seemed tardy, cold, dull, and indifferent; but measuring him by the sentiment of his country, a sentiment he was bound as a statesman to consult, he was swift, zealous, radical, and determined.

He was assailed by abolitionists; he was assailed by slave-holders; he was assailed by the men who were for peace at any price; he was assailed by those who were for a more vigorous prosecution of the war; he was assailed for not making the war an abolition war; and he was bitterly assailed for making the war an abolition war.

But now behold the change.

Frederick Douglass
April 14, 1876

LINCOLN ON LEADERSHIP FOR TODAY

Voting Rights for Minorities

After securing passage of the 13th Amendment (abolishing slavery) and receiving news of Lee's surrender to Grant at Appomattox, Abraham Lincoln made his last public speech. During those brief remarks, he suggested that voting rights be given to blacks, especially "those who serve our cause as soldiers." He was the first American president to ever advance such an idea.

Today, we have three constitutional amendments guaranteeing the right to vote to every American citizen, explicitly stating: "The right of citizens of the United States to vote shall not be denied or abridged . . . on account of race [or] color" (15th Amendment), "on account of sex" (19th Amendment), or "on account of age" [18 or older] (26th Amendment). And yet, as minorities, the poor, and the elderly increase in our population, there has been a growing movement among some states to curb their rights to vote. For example, state laws passed to require photo IDs at polling places unduly affect the poor, people of color, and elderly voters, who are less likely to have a driver's license or other form of photo identification.

In my opinion, Abraham Lincoln today would agree that there must be some way to verify that people who want to vote are, in fact, American citizens. But requiring picture identification cards may not be the answer. The goal is to verify a potential voter's citizenship, and that can be done way ahead of Election Day and without negatively affecting minorities, the poor, or the elderly. I believe Lincoln would propose legislation to implement the latest technology, which would allow all registered voters' names to be loaded into a computer database that could be accessed at polling places, where a signature, a Social Security card, or a health insurance/Medicare card could be used to verify citizenship. Better yet, the United States could allow all citizens to vote online (from home or anywhere else), which is now done in a number of large countries around the world.

Overall, I believe Lincoln would say that no state or municipal law should be passed in which an American citizen is prohibited from voting on a technicality or for a reason that affects one group more than another. And he would probably use the full power of the federal government to stop such practices. As he said in 1859: "We the people of these United States are the rightful masters of both congresses and courts not to overthrow the Constitution, but to overthrow [those] who pervert the Constitution."

Abortion

Abraham Lincoln appears to have made no specific statements on this issue even though it is estimated that 20 percent of pregnancies during the 19th century were purposely terminated and anti-abortion laws began showing up in the 1820s. Today, of course, it is one of the most divisive of all issues, with arguments being waged by honest and passionate people who call themselves either "pro-life" or "pro-choice."

It is my sense that Lincoln might first try to calm the fiery debate by asking us if we have paused long enough to listen to the anguish of those who hold the opposite view. I believe he would then look at the issue from both a moral and ethical perspective, seek input from both the religious and scientific communities, and then attempt to come down on the side of humanity — the humanity of the woman and the humanity of the unborn. If he found tension there, I believe he would search for some middle ground in an attempt to resolve the conflict.

In my opinion, Lincoln would ask us if we might be able to knit together an approach that works for all. If a fetus can survive outside the womb, I see him saying, "Well, we can't allow the life to be taken at that point." But he might also determine that it would be a woman's decision up to that point. And that decision should be between the woman and her maker, rather than between the woman and the government. Abraham Lincoln was always searching for the middle ground. That's what I see him doing with this issue.

Women's Rights

William Herndon stated that his law partner Abraham Lincoln viewed women as equals to men, deserving of the right to vote, and quoted him as saying the issue "is one simply of time." In January 1865, President Lincoln was visited in the White House by a group of women from Philadelphia who presented him with a petition representing their organization (20,000 in number), which requested the federal government to "increase the price of female labor," provide "an equitable price for their labor," and add "four times the number of women" to the workforce. Lincoln endorsed these requests as "just and reasonable" and forwarded the petition to the secretary of war.

Women received the right to vote in the United States on August 18, 1920, when the 19th Amendment to the Constitution was ratified. In 1963, Congress passed the Equal Pay Act, requiring that men and women in the same workplace be accorded equal pay for equal work. And in 1972, the Equal Rights Amendment (first introduced in 1923) was reintroduced and passed by both houses of Congress. *[Section 1 simply stated, "Equality of rights under the law shall not be denied or abridged by the United States or by any State on account of sex."]* However, it failed to receive ratification by the necessary 38 states and did not become part of the U.S. Constitution. And a more recent law (2009) and an executive order (2014) have been implemented to strengthen enforcement of equal pay laws for women. Despite all this progress, a gender pay gap still exists. As of 2014, women earned $0.79 for every $1.00 earned by men. And the gap is even wider for African American and Latina women.

Any country that values human rights must provide equal rights to women. In my opinion, that is what Abraham Lincoln would say if he were here today. And he would act to ensure that women have all the rights accorded to men — in government, in the workplace, and in everyday life. I believe he would issue additional executive orders directing equal pay for women in all federal jobs and for those employed by companies that contract with the federal government.

He would submit new legislation guaranteeing equal pay for women in all aspects of American business and industry. And he would resurrect the Equal Rights Amendment and push for ratification.

There is no reason in the world that can justify a women not receiving the same compensation as a man for doing the same work. Abraham Lincoln once suggested that it was just a matter of time before every woman secured full and equal rights under the Constitution of the United States. Well, the time has come.

Human nature will not change. In any future great national trial, compared with the men of this, we shall have as weak, and as strong; as silly and as wise; as bad and [as] good. Let us, therefore, study the incidents of this, as philosophy to learn wisdom from, and [not] as wrongs to be [avenged].

— Abraham Lincoln
November 10, 1864

17

Peace with All Nations

★ ★ ★

O N FIRST SIGHT, most people didn't think much of Abraham Lincoln. He was described as an "ill-favored man with little grace of manner or polish of appearance," "uncouth," and "grotesque," with "a face furrowed, wrinkled, and indented, as though it had been scarred by vitriol." A reporter at his Cooper Institute speech in 1860 took one look at him as he approached the podium and said, "Old fellow, you won't do." At first, most members of his own cabinet didn't like him, respect him, or think him qualified to be president. And yet almost everybody who ever got to know Lincoln put aside their negative first impressions and came to "respect [his] personal character." He was then described as "earnest" and "full of good sense," with "a logical intellect." He had a "kindly nature" with "an unselfish heart." He was "a genial, quiet, essentially peaceful man," who had a "deep . . . sympathy [for] people." He combined "greatness with goodness," and he was "the very impersonation of good humor and fellowship."

Such qualities are valued, appreciated, and admired by people. As a matter of fact, Secretary of State William Seward prized them so highly that he called Lincoln "the best and wisest man he [had] ever known." Attorney General Edward Bates said Lincoln was "very near being a perfect man." And Ulysses S. Grant simply said, "He was . . . the greatest man I ever knew."

But wait! Seward, Bates, and Grant all *worked* for Abraham Lincoln. How could they have liked him so much if he was their boss? Well, it turns out that these very same attributes recognized in Lincoln are also qualities that people universally approve of in their leaders. So here we have a revealing connection between Abraham Lincoln, people, and leadership. And if we agree with historians that Lincoln was one of history's greatest leaders, then we can logically conclude that there is a major connection between people and the principles of leadership.

Abraham Lincoln was a born leader. How else can we explain him, as a boy, mounting a tree stump and giving speeches to the other kids? He had an innate sense of optimism, of hope, of empathy and cooperativeness. He also possessed a certain street-smart intuitiveness, an abundance of common sense, and an agreeable sense of humor. Lincoln was fortunate to have been born into a family that grounded him in morality and human decency. His parents taught him the values of hard work, honesty, integrity, and trustworthiness, and to always treat others with kindness and respect. His mother and stepmother, through their positive reinforcement and biblical teachings, cultivated in him a sense of security and a moral self-confidence that enabled him to stand fearless in the face of adversity. But one of Lincoln's most valuable assets was his natural desire and ability to learn and improve. And one of the subjects he was most interested in was human nature.

"[Man] *must* be understood by those who would lead him,"

Lincoln said in 1842 (at the age of 33). And 22 years later, after being reelected to a second term as president, he said: "Human nature will not change. In any future great national trial, compared with the men of this, we shall have as weak, and as strong; as silly and as wise; as bad and [as] good." So it's clear that, over most of his adult life, Lincoln thought deeply about people and what made them tick. He seemed particularly interested in the root elements of human nature. For instance, in his speeches, writings, and documented conversations, there are frequent references to the "selfish" and the "unselfish." "Slavery is founded in the *selfishness* of man's nature," he said. [Italics added.] Lincoln praised his hero, Henry Clay, for being "unselfish." He accounted for "General George B. McClellan's attitude" as being rooted "in the very selfishness of his nature." And as for himself, Lincoln claimed "no greater exemption from selfishness than is common."

Today, more than a century and a half after his death, Lincoln's insight has been shown to have a basis in scientific fact. Noted American biologist Edward O. Wilson observed that there are two sides to the human condition: *Selfish,* which furthers the interest of the individual, and *Altruistic* (or *Selfless*), which furthers the interest of the group. The two sides, Wilson found, are perpetually in conflict with each other.

Abraham Lincoln also observed this conflict. He called it "the eternal struggle between . . . right and wrong, throughout the world. They are the two principles that have stood face to face from the beginning of time, and will ever continue to struggle." Further, it is probably what Lincoln meant when he said the Civil War was "a people's contest." "On the side of the Union," he said, "it is a struggle for maintaining in the world that form and substance of government whose leading object is to elevate the condition of men." On the other side was the Confederacy, which wanted to propagate an institution (slavery) with "an immense pecuniary [self] interest." These two basic sides of human nature have given rise to people dividing human actions into "good and evil," "sin and virtue," "right and wrong." "Individual selection is responsible for much of what we call sin," wrote Wilson, "while group selection is responsible for the greater part of virtue. Together, they have created the conflict between *the poorer* and *the better angels of our nature*." [Italics added.]

"A free people, in times of peace and quiet — when pressed by no common danger — naturally divide into parties," said Lincoln in 1852. Of course, he was referring to the two very different political parties of his day. The "Selfish" party was anti-immigration, anti–public education, and anti-tax, and believed in nongovernment intervention in almost everything. It attracted right-wing extremists and conservatives, whom Lincoln described as good people forced "into an open war with the very fundamental principles of civil liberty." On the flip side of the coin, the "Altruistic" party was pro-immigration, pro–public education, and pro-tax, and believed in government involvement to help people. It attracted progressives, liberals, and left-wing extremists. Both parties, in various ways, attempted to recruit moderates and independents into their ranks.

E. O. Wilson convincingly demonstrated that throughout the evolutionary history of life, "Selfish" individuals win over "Altruistic" individuals if they are in the same group. However, groups of "Altruists" always beat groups of "Selfish" individuals — and they do so by forming what Wilson called a "superorganism." Superorganisms approach "the highest level of social intelligence" and are characterized by "an extraordinary capacity to conquer their competing environment." They are "able to mobilize the entire" group to "act together in achieving a common goal." Unity and empathy characterize every individual in the "superorganism." A family-like culture of cooperation, collaboration, and communication is created — with abundant diversity and a proper balance of workers and supervisors. Now, that sounds like a solid organization with effective leadership. And truth be told, through great leadership, that's exactly what Abraham Lincoln created for the Union during the Civil War — a "superorganism." In the long run, the Confederacy could never have won the Civil War — not with a leader like Lincoln in charge. _E. O. Wilson: "The opposition has no chance against the superorganism. No chance."_

There are other direct parallels between E. O. Wilson's observations about success in human nature and Lincoln's leadership. Here are just a few examples:

Lincoln Looked Long Term

As most great leaders do, Lincoln crafted a vision, set goals, and involved as many people as possible to achieve them. He planned for difficult change by chipping away at each issue in steps. This strategy had the effect of overcoming the emotional and natural resistance to change. In effect, once people bought into the vision and goals, they were no longer worried about having to change. They were simply working to achieve goals. _E. O. Wilson: "By long-range planning we defeat the urging of our emotions."_

Lincoln Practiced Teamwork

For his presidential cabinet, Lincoln pulled together a group of highly competent, ego-centered individuals and got them to work together to achieve a single mission: to preserve the United States of America. Although there was a lot of internal squabbling, Lincoln managed to hold his cabinet together, in part by respecting each secretary, letting them run their own departments, and usually deferring to their judgment. As in any true team, Lincoln's cabinet put the needs of their country first and realized that they would jointly win or lose the Civil War. _E. O. Wilson: "[Group leaders say,] 'We will all stand together . . . or we will fall together.'"_

Lincoln Created a Family-Like Culture

The president spent as much time as possible with the troops. He listened to them, let them know he cared about them, tried to meet their needs, and praised them for their dedication. In return, they respected and cared about him, too. Lincoln also maximized his skills in communication (personal conversations, speeches, writings, stories and anecdotes, etc.) to connect with soldiers and inspire them to collaborate with him to achieve the overriding mission. *E. O. Wilson: "Communication gives us the amazing capacity to cooperate."*

Lincoln Delegated

Once the president found the right general, he put him in charge and let him go. It took almost three years before Lincoln promoted Ulysses S. Grant to the Union's top military position. By then, Lincoln believed that his new commander would do exactly what he would do if he were in the field himself. It was Grant who took the Union across the threshold to final victory. *E. O. Wilson: "When [a superorganism] is firmly established, extensions of the [leader] . . . are created in [his or her] image."*

Lincoln Anticipated

Lincoln's understanding of human nature contributed immensely to his outstanding political intuitiveness. He thought deeply about how people would behave in any given situation, how they might react to his public opinion letters, for instance, or how a general might act in a tense situation. Then, based on that knowledge, Lincoln would plan out his own actions. *E. O. Wilson: "The ability to read each other's intentions . . . gives an advantage over those who do not [have] the ability."*

★ ★ ★

During the Civil War, although castigated and relentlessly disparaged, Abraham Lincoln was still recognized for his leadership qualities. The *Chicago Tribune* noted his "avoidance of extremes," and that he had "a mental constitution that is never off its balance." Even the rabidly Confederate *Charleston Mercury* admitted, although grudgingly, that Lincoln was a skilled leader:

> In the Cabinet and the field he has consistently and fearlessly carried out the search for men who could advance his cause and has as unhesitatingly cut off all those who clogged it with weakness, timidity, imbecility, or failure. Blackguard and buffoon as he is, he has pursued his end with an [untiring] energy, and a singleness of purpose that might almost be called patriotic. If he were not an unscrupulous knave in his intentions and a fanatic in his political views, he would undoubtedly command our respect as a ruler.

Back in Lincoln's day, members of the "Selfish" party were Democrats, and those of the "Altruistic" party were Whigs and, later, Republicans. By the election of 1860, the Whig Party was gone, and the Democratic Party had split into two factions (Northern and Southern). But the Republican Party held itself together, and as Abraham Lincoln, himself, said later, he was elected president by "accident." So by a stroke of luck, a new national leader emerged on the scene to carry the Union to victory and preserve the United States of America. Here, again, E. O. Wilson's research on human nature has shown that the addition of only one "Altruist" gene mutation can take place by "accident" and, in effect, "silence the [selfish] genes." *E. O. Wilson: "A substitution of one allele . . . could be enough to carry a preadapted species across the threshold." [An allele is a new form of a single gene.]* In other words, one person or one good leader can, indeed, make a difference.

Another major factor that helped Abraham Lincoln succeed was the fact that he had a natural tendency to be a moderate and was, in fact, a middle-of-the-road politician who was usually searching for common ground. One of the most challenging aspects of being a moderate, however, is that it requires a difficult balancing act. But, here again, Abraham Lincoln was a master at it. He balanced long-term strategy with short-term results, constitutional rights with the suspension of *habeas corpus,* the demands of business with the rights of the individual laborer, and political reality with moral right. And Lincoln was equally adept at balancing the differences between people. He was able to hold together conservative Democrats and Radical Republicans in Congress, to say nothing of persuading opposing factions in his own party to work in harmony.

Clearly, one of Abraham Lincoln's key leadership strategies was to be a centrist. As he said to General John Schofield (in charge of delicate operations in the border state of Missouri) after the 1863 arrest of a Democratic newspaper editor: "I fear this loses you the middle position I desired you to occupy." And Lincoln well knew that by being in the center, he could be attacked at any time by people on either extreme. Recall that he also told Schofield, "If both factions, or neither, shall abuse you, you will probably be about right." But Lincoln further realized there was a more practical and positive side to being a centrist, which involved simple mathematics. Almost any statistical distribution of the general population will normally resemble a bell curve. Each outer "extreme" will include about 25 percent of the people (sometimes up to a third). The largest part of the population resides in the middle and averages anywhere between 33 percent and 50 percent in number. In the long run, then, any politician can only hope to receive approval from a maximum of two-thirds of the populace, which is pretty darn good. But in the national election of 1860, Lincoln, who presented himself as a centrist candidate (and who was not even on the ballot in most Southern states), won only 39.8 percent of the popular vote. But that, along with his tally in the Electoral College, was good enough to win the presidency.

It is not an exaggeration to state that Abraham Lincoln's ability to balance opposing factions, his position as a political moderate, and his strategic avoidance of extremes were key elements of his leadership style that resulted in his preventing the United States of America from permanently dissolving. *E. O. Wilson:*

"The victory can never be complete. The balance . . . cannot move to either extreme. If [the Selfish] were to dominate, societies would dissolve. If [the Altruists] were to dominate," there would be few individual rights. And therein lies the higher meaning of the biblical phrase Lincoln used when he kicked off his 1858 campaign for the United States Senate: "A house divided against itself cannot stand."

★ ★ ★

Abraham Lincoln was a real people person. He liked people, studied people, and understood people. He was unselfish, devoted to the prosperity of all, and interested in promoting human well-being, and had no prejudice of race, religion, or gender. People, he said, were "the most important branch of national resources." All these facts, almost by definition, paint Lincoln as an altruist, a true humanitarian. And in addition to his stand against slavery, his consistent positions on other key social issues prove the point. Lincoln was pro-immigration, which fosters diversity. He was pro-education, which fosters individual and group growth. He was pro-government, which fosters economic development for all. He was pro-tax, which guarantees fairness in income equality and reduces perpetual poverty. And he was for a balanced budget and a low national debt (in peacetime), which helps foster prosperity for future generations.

In making decisions on important issues like these, Abraham Lincoln went through a deliberate process and almost always came down on the side of humanity. He often went out in the field — walking in the rain and trudging in the mud — to glean facts and information for himself. He listened, consulted with people in the know, and asked for advice and opinions. And Lincoln also kept tabs on public opinion — heeding it, setting out to influence it, and then waiting for the timing to be right before taking action. He employed proper thinking and reasoning when making decisions, often using Euclidean logic to help him see an issue from all sides. *"If A can prove, however conclusively, that he may . . . enslave B—why may not B snatch the same argument, and prove equally, that he may enslave A?"* And so on and so on. As a middle-of-the-road politician, Lincoln tried to do what was best for the majority. And as a moral leader, in addition to doing things right, he tried to do the right thing. "I want in all cases to do right," Lincoln wrote in 1837.

Repeatedly coming down on the side of humanity is not that easy, however, because solutions are not always plain and clear, but often fall into a gray area. Remember what Lincoln said about good and evil: "The true rule, in determining to embrace or reject anything, is not whether it has *any* evil in it, but whether it has more evil than good. There are few things *wholly* evil or *wholly* good. Almost everything, especially of government policy, is an inseparable compound of the two." So when Lincoln encountered a perceived conflict where a judgment was not obvious, he often looked for a compromise solution. But, clearly, once he made a final decision, Lincoln rarely retreated from it. "I think it cannot be shown that when I have once taken a position, I have ever retreated from it," he said to Frederick Douglass.

★ ★ ★

Before he became president of the United States, Abraham Lincoln had never before held an executive leadership position of any kind. So what exactly was it that made him a great leader? Certainly, he possessed all the conventional skills and traits we now know go along with such leadership, including intelligence, vision, perseverance, decisiveness, a strong will, and so on. And we know his personal character and sense of honor provided the rock-solid foundation upon which he operated. But as the poet Walt Whitman once said of Lincoln, "There is something else there."

Lincoln's greatness was, in part, due to a combination of three things that accentuated his leadership ability far beyond that of mortal man: His <u>humanitarianism</u>, his <u>faith in "the Almighty,"</u> and his <u>innate goodness</u>. Let's take each one in turn.

Lincoln's Humanitarianism

Because Lincoln was a humanitarian and altruist, the United States of America to him was more than just another country. It was a nation. It was hope for the future for all humankind. He understood that the Declaration of Independence articulated the principles of freedom, liberty, and equality, which are nothing less than the principles of humanity. The U.S. Constitution then created a new form of government that advocated, nurtured, and protected those principles. With its three branches — the executive, the legislative, and the judicial — this new governmental system was carefully designed to have checks and balances so that no one person, nor one faction, could oppress or terrorize the great majority of citizens. America's Founding Fathers had set up a democratic republic in which the two opposing forces of human nature, the "Selfish" and the "Altruistic," would be compelled and duty-bound to live in harmony. And to Abraham Lincoln, that "government of the people, by the people, for the people" was worth preserving, worth fighting for, and worth dying for.

Lincoln's Faith in "the Almighty"

Lincoln's mother, Nancy Hanks Lincoln, was "a good Christian woman" who read the Bible to her son and taught him to read and write by using the scripture. So young Abe, as all good sons do, both listened to and believed what his mother was saying. And as bright as he was, he could not help but remember and digest the Bible's many tenets. Take the twin virtues of justice and righteousness, for instance. Lincoln tied them together throughout his life — not merely by *talking* about them, but by *living* them. In the great moral issue of his day, he fought on the right side.

He began by arguing the case against slavery on moral grounds. "Opposition to [slavery] is founded in [man's] love of justice," he said. "If slavery is not wrong, nothing is wrong." The passage of the 13th Amendment was to Lincoln a "great moral victory."

Despite the fact that he viewed slavery to be morally wrong, Lincoln did not blame or judge the Southern people for trying to perpetuate the institution. *["Judge not, that ye be not judged." (Matthew 7:1)]* "They are just what we would be in their situation," he said. Rather, Lincoln believed in "leaving the higher matter of eternal consequences, between [a person] and his Maker." And he did, in fact, believe there would be a Judgment Day for all people. *["All the nations will be assembled before Him. And He will separate them one from another." (Matthew 25:32)]* That may very well have been one of his motivating factors in fighting so hard to end slavery. After all, as a young man, he had twice personally witnessed the inhumanity of slavery — first at a slave auction in New Orleans, and then while on the Mississippi River, where he saw a dozen slaves "chained six and six together . . . like so many fish upon a trot-line." And because he had seen it for himself, he was then compelled to try to do something about it.

> *Whatever you did for one of these least brothers of mine, you did for me. . . . Come, inherit the kingdom [of God].*
>
> *What you did not do for one of these least ones, you did not do for me. . . . Depart from me . . . into the eternal fire [of] the devil and his angels.*
>
> [The Judgment of the Nations
> Matthew 25:32–46]

Abraham Lincoln believed that the standard of judgment for an organized people (a nation) is how we treat "the least" among us. In other words, we all are responsible for the less fortunate. And in his day, clearly "the least" among us were the slaves. Lincoln was convinced that the institution of slavery had caused the Civil War. So he set out to both *end slavery* and *restore peace.*

Then, at his own Judgment Day, *"when all the nations will be assembled,"* Lincoln would be able to say that he had done everything he could to end the moral wrong *and* bring peace to his own nation. And therein lies the higher meaning of Lincoln's second inaugural address, which he closed with: "Let us . . . do all which may achieve and cherish a just and lasting peace among ourselves and *with all nations.*" [Italics added.]

Lincoln's Innate Goodness

Some say that Sarah Bush Johnston Lincoln favored her stepson, Abe, over her own three children. "He was kind to everybody and everything," she once said. Lincoln had a native goodness that is rare in people. Most of us strive for it, but few achieve it, except, perhaps, on an intermittent basis. But Abraham Lincoln seemed to have it all the time. And when such a natural tendency to be good combines with high intelligence, a formidable human being can emerge.

Like his mother, Nancy Hanks Lincoln, Abe's stepmother was deeply pious, and she, too, read to him from the Bible. Many things in the good book seriously resonated with the boy, and he carried its lessons with him for the rest of his life. For example, many of his writings and speeches as an adult (especially as president) are filled with references to scriptural tenets that connote goodness — gentleness, mercy, forgiveness, temperance, and the like. Here are just a few:

> I am a patient man — always willing to forgive on the Christian terms of repentance; and also to give ample time for repentance.

> [The government] can properly have no motive of revenge, no purpose to punish merely for punishment's sake.

> . . . when again touched, as surely they will be, by the better angels of our nature.

*With malice toward none; with charity for all . . . let us strive on
to . . . bind up the nation's wounds; to care for him who shall have
borne the battle, and for his widow, and his orphan.*

Abraham Lincoln not only wrote and spoke about biblical core
values, he lived them, especially in how he treated other people.
He shared success with subordinates and shouldered blame for
failure. He practiced civility and decency even toward those who
declared themselves his enemy. *[Confederate vice president Alexander Stephens noted that Lincoln's "nature overflowed with the
milk of human kindness."]* He showed fairness to adversaries and
mercy to the condemned. *[Secretary of State William Seward said
that Lincoln's "magnanimity is almost superhuman."]* Moreover, he
realized that how we treat other people is of major importance
in leadership. He probably took note of the philosopher Plato's
maxim: "Be kind, for everyone you meet is fighting a hard battle."
Abraham Lincoln realized that everybody makes mistakes, that
everybody has lapses in judgment, and that we are all human. So
he did not normally cast aspersions on anyone. Rather, he viewed
people as having taken actions without either evil intentions or
malice aforethought. And instead of acting out of revenge, he often turned the other cheek and treated people with even more
kindness. "Do good to those who hate you and turn their ill will
to friendship," Lincoln once said to his wife, Mary, after she complained about the actions of Salmon P. Chase.

Treating people with kindness *works* for leaders, and Chase is
a prime example. Here was a member of Lincoln's own cabinet
who was always working behind the scenes to become president
himself. And yet Lincoln kept him on board, because Chase was
excellent at his job. And the Treasury secretary did perform. He
revamped the nation's finances, raised enough money to pay for
the Union war effort, created the first federal paper money, advanced protective tariffs, and instituted a new national banking
system. The undeniable fact is that Chase turned out to be one of
the most important and successful executives in the Union's ef-

fort to win the Civil War. But most modern-day leaders would have fired Chase, because of all his disloyal shenanigans. Lincoln, however, not only kept Chase on board, he got him to perform beyond what anyone believed possible. Why in the world did the president do it? Well, when asked that very question, Lincoln said that Chase had a "Presidential chin-fly" biting him, and he wasn't going to knock it off, because "it made his department go." But here is an even more interesting question: Why did Chase stay on in the Lincoln administration even though he was continually embarrassed and frustrated by Lincoln's ability to outduel him politically? The answer came from Chase's own mouth when he was asked that very thing. "The President has always treated me with such personal kindness and has always manifested such fairness and integrity of purpose, that I have not found myself free to throw up my trust. . . . So I work on."

"Goodness" is sometimes defined as "moral excellence," "virtue," "kindness," and "generosity." However we define this most valued of all human qualities, the people who knew Abraham Lincoln best would have said he met the definition. "Goodness" is not so much the *will* of God as it is the *way* of God. It rests both in what we say and in what we do. It fosters cooperation and collaboration among human beings. And that *leads* to acceptable and decent relations among all people, of all nations, everywhere. And therein lies the deeper meaning, and the wisdom, of Nancy Hanks Lincoln's final words to her son, Abraham:

"Be good to one another."

Now he belongs to the ages.

— Edwin M. Stanton
April 15, 1865

Finale

★ ★ ★

ON GOOD FRIDAY, April 14, 1865, Abraham Lincoln was assassinated — shot in the back of the head by Confederate sympathizer John Wilkes Booth while Lincoln was attending a play at Ford's Theatre. He died the next morning.

After a day of inconsolable sobbing, 12-year-old Tad Lincoln woke up on Sunday morning and asked an adult if he thought his father had gone to heaven. "I have not a doubt of it," the man replied.

"Then I am glad he has gone there," said Tad, "for he was never happy after he came here. This was not a good place for him."

Some things never change. Washington, D.C., was not a good place for Abraham Lincoln. It was filled with typical politicians, whom Lincoln once described as "a set of men, who have interests aside from the interests of the people, and who, to say the most of them, are, as a mass, at least one long step removed from being honest men."

And yet Lincoln, himself, was an on-and-off politician. Although he was much happier being an Illinois lawyer, where he could help people on a daily basis, in 1854, just when the country needed him most, he once again took up the role of politician. And today, more than a century and a half after his death, history seems to have judged Abraham Lincoln a good man, a good leader, and, if there is such a thing, a good politician.

Recall that Lincoln once wrote about "the tendency of prosperity to breed tyrants." He said that if, in the distant future, should "some man, some faction, [or] some interest set up the doctrine that none but rich men, or none but white men, were entitled to life, liberty and the pursuit of happiness," his posterity might "look up again to the Declaration of Independence . . . so that truth, and justice, and mercy, and all the humane and Christian virtues might not be extinguished from the land."

All of us living today, and all of us yet to be born, are Abraham Lincoln's posterity. And we all bear witness to the fact that a small percentage of those among us have, over time, used their resources to create a state of affairs in which the American system of government seems more devoted to the wealthy few than to the far more numerous middle class and poor, where the mass media is primarily driven by coverage of violence and extremism, and where racial relations are unbalanced and inconsolable. And we all want to know how things can be changed for the better.

Abraham Lincoln was a strong person. He was strong physically, he was strong mentally, and he was certainly a strong moral leader. So if we look back on his life and examine how he lived it, what he made of his time here on earth, what he achieved, and how he achieved it, perhaps we can pick up some nuggets of wisdom that will help us solve today's problems and guide us to a brighter future.

And if Abraham Lincoln were here to witness for himself our current state of affairs, what advice might he offer? Well, he would probably drop his head and think for a moment. Then he'd look up and, with a smile on his face, tell us a story or an anecdote, the meaning of which could not be missed.

We can do better.

Before returning to Washington, D.C., from Richmond, President Lincoln's last stop (on April 8, 1865) was to visit the Union's Depot Field Hospital at City Point, Virginia. He walked into the chief surgeon's office and announced that he wanted to shake the hand of every soldier present. When informed that there were between 5,000 and 6,000 sick and wounded housed in 90 buildings, Lincoln smiled. "I guess I'm up to the task," he replied. "At any rate, I will try and go as far as I can. I'll probably never see the boys again and I want to let them know that I appreciate what they have done for our country."

Outside each building, soldiers who could walk lined up to shake the president's hand and receive a personal greeting and thank-you. Then, accompanied by the chief surgeon, Lincoln stepped inside and walked around to do the same for every veteran who was bedridden. One hospital attendant remembered that the troops were "pleased beyond measure" and that the president "took almost as much pleasure in honoring the boys, as the boys did in receiving the honor from him."

Upon finishing, Lincoln returned to the main office and was saying good-bye to the chief surgeon when an orderly rushed in to inform them that one ward had been missed and that "the boys want to see the President." Exhausted himself, the surgeon tried to talk Lincoln out of going back. "Oh but we must," said Lincoln. "I would not knowingly omit one ward. The boys would be so disappointed." So the two went back, and Lincoln shook the hands and thanked every soldier in the last ward.

After five or six hours, Abraham Lincoln had personally met with about 6,000 patients, including sick and wounded Confederate prisoners. "Mr. President, you must be very tired, and your arm has to ache from all the handshaking," commented the chief surgeon at the end of the day. Lincoln smiled and walked over to a woodpile just outside the main office, where he picked up an axe and started cutting wood. After robustly chopping away for several minutes and sending wood chips flying in all directions, he grasped the axe at the tip of the handle with only his thumb and forefinger, and then extended it at arm's length, where he held it for several moments. "Here, you try it," said a smiling Lincoln to one of the soldiers looking on. Although that soldier and several others tried, none of them could match the feat.

After Lincoln departed, the wood chips were "gathered up and safely cared for" by a hospital attendant. Perhaps he gave them out later so that people could carry a little part of Abraham Lincoln around with them.

Acknowledgments

*   *   *

I'd like to acknowledge and thank my friend and editor at Houghton Mifflin Harcourt, Rick Wolff, who came up with the idea for this book. His suggestions for organization and content were of the highest caliber, and he deserves great credit for his insight and for bringing out the best in me.

The entire team at Houghton Mifflin Harcourt was fantastic during the publication of this book from beginning to end, including Bruce Nichols (publisher), Rosemary McGuinness (editorial), Laura Brady and Lisa Glover (production), Chloe Foster (design), Michelle Triant (publicity), Jackie Shepherd (art), and Ayesha Mirza (marketing). Barbara Jatkola did a magnificent job on the copyediting of the original manuscript. She's a real pro, and I can't imagine anybody better.

Robert B. Barnett, the best agent in the business, and his brilliant associate, Kristen Mann, at Williams & Connolly were a big part of making this book happen, and I thank them for their efforts and much-needed guidance.

I am very grateful for the discussions, advice, and counsel of my friends who helped me think through key issues, especially John D. Fraser; Jennifer A. Godfrey; Steven L., David B., and Katherine A. Phillips; and Paul R. White. An extra-special thanks to the incomparable Roger D. Sanders, who has an amazing ability to think through and get to the core of any important issue.

I would also like to acknowledge the many professional historians who do the detailed and painstaking work of scholarship on Abraham Lincoln and the Civil War. Some of them are listed in the bibliography and notes of this book. Many more have expanded our knowledge, enlightened our understanding, and, in particular, influenced my thinking on these subjects. They know who they are — and I thank them, one and all.

Notes

★ ★ ★

Many of the quotations of Abraham Lincoln are from Roy Basler, *The Collected Works of Abraham Lincoln*, referred to in the notes as *CW*.

Prelude

page

1 *"speeches to the boys"*: Wilson and Davis, *Herndon's Informants*, p. 42.
   "Be good to one another": Herndon and Weik, vol. 1, p. 27.
   "a good Christian woman": Herndon and Weik, vol. 1, p. 27.
   "naturally strong-minded": Wilson and Davis, *Herndon's Informants*, p. 124.

2 *"He never told me a lie"*: Wilson and Davis, *Herndon's Informants*, p. 107.
   "never since pulled a trigger": June 1860, *CW*, vol. 4, p. 63.
   "repeat it over to himself": Wilson and Davis, *Herndon's Informants*, p. 107.

3 *"He would hear a sermon"*: Wilson and Davis, *Herndon's Informants*, p. 104.
   "sometimes mount a stump": Wilson and Davis, *Herndon's Informants*, p. 42.
   "always was the peacemaker": Wilson and Davis, *Herndon's Informants*, p. 7.
   "was the one chosen": Herndon and Weik, vol. 1, p. 34.
   "didn't go much with the girls": Wilson and Davis, *Herndon's Informants*, p. 131.
   "a load of six hundred pounds": Herndon and Weik, vol. 1, p. 62.
   "I was raised to farm work": December 20, 1859, *CW*, vol. 3, p. 511.

4 *"plowing and harvesting seasons"*: June 1860, *CW*, vol. 4, p. 61.
   "unbroken wilderness": September 19, 1859, *CW*, vol. 3, p. 463.
   "fighting with trees and logs and grubs": September 19, 1859, *CW*, vol. 3, p. 463.

"had an axe put into his hands": June 1860, *CW*, vol. 4, p. 62.

"could sink an axe deeper": Herndon and Weik, vol. 1, p. 62.

5   *"had earned a dollar"*: Carpenter, p. 82.

"made her trot up and down": Herndon and Weik, vol. 1, p. 76.

"I'll hit it hard": Herndon and Weik, vol. 1, p. 76.

"like so many fish upon a trot-line": September 27, 1841, *CW*, vol. 1, p. 260.

6   *"There is no reason in the world"*: April 21, 1858, *CW*, vol. 3, p. 249.

"naturally anti-slavery": April 4, 1864, *CW*, vol. 7, p. 281.

"All that I am": Herndon and Weik, vol. 1, p. 4.

1. A Just and Generous and Prosperous System

8   *"to carry the elections"*: March 2, 1839, *CW*, vol. 1, p. 148.

"I am humble Abraham Lincoln": Herndon and Weik, vol. 1, p. 104.

9   *"than any I have had since"*: December 20, 1859, *CW*, vol. 3, p. 512.

"if any one of you doubt it": Wilson and Davis, *Herndon's Informants*, pp. 372–373.

"the hardest set of men": Wilson and Davis, *Herndon's Informants*, p. 353.

"like the old woman's dance": Herndon and Weik, vol. 1, p. 104.

"was ever beaten": June 1860, *CW*, vol. 4, p. 64.

11 *"the two drunken men"*: April 6, 1859, *CW*, vol. 3, p. 375.

12 *"very desirable"*: March 9, 1832, *CW*, vol. 1, p. 5.

"a never-failing source": March 9, 1832, *CW*, vol. 1, p. 4.

"However high our imaginations": March 9, 1832, *CW*, vol. 1, p. 6.

13 *"lost and go to ruin"*: February 6, 1841, *CW*, vol. 1, p. 233.

"bug on your eyebrow": February 26, 1841, *CW*, vol. 1, p. 240.

14 *"No duty is more imperative"*: December 26, 1839, *CW*, vol. 1, p. 164.

15 *"morally bound"*: February 5, 1839, *CW*, vol. 1, p. 144.

"can be so exclusively general": June 20, 1848, *CW*, vol. 1, p. 483.

"expenditures must be met": March 4, 1843, *CW*, vol. 1, p. 311.

16 *"never despair of sustaining myself"*: March 2, 1839, *CW*, vol. 1, p. 147.

"We invite every man": April 5, 1839, *CW*, vol. 1, p. 149.

"'wealthy few'": March 2, 1839, *CW*, vol. 1, p. 148.

17 *"save something from the general wreck"*: January 30, 1840, *CW*, vol. 1, p. 200.

"the evil spirit": December 26, 1839, *CW*, vol. 1, p. 178.

"Bow to it, I never will": December 26, 1839, *CW*, vol. 1, p. 178.

"stand up boldly and alone": December 26, 1839, *CW*, vol. 1, p. 178.

18 *"Why should it not be spun"*: December 1, 1847, *CW*, vol. 1, p. 411.

"Give us a protective tariff": Hobson, p. 36.

"having constant employment": December 1, 1847, *CW*, vol. 1, p. 410.

"the burden of revenue": March 4, 1843, *CW*, vol. 1, p. 311.

19 *"you* are *an* idler"*: December 24, 1848, *CW*, vol. 2, p. 16.

"*'better luck next time'*": September 30, 1859, *CW*, vol. 3, p. 481.

20 "The prudent, penniless beginner": September 30, 1859, *CW*, vol. 3, p. 478.

2. Nonintervention in Other Countries as a Sacred Principle of International Law

24 *"make war at pleasure"*: February 15, 1848, *CW*, vol. 1, p. 451.

"let it 'stink and die'": February 9, 1846, *CW*, vol. 1, p. 366.

"an attempt to injure me": February 9, 1846, *CW*, vol. 1, p. 366.

25 *"turn about is fair play"*: November 18, 1845, *CW*, vol. 1, p. 366.

"Mexico invaded our territory:" May 11, 1846, United States Congress.

26 *"manifest destiny to overspread the continent"*: *Democratic Review*, July–August 1845.

"carefully examined": January 5, 1848, *CW*, vol. 1, p. 424.

27 *"It is a fact"*: May 21, 1848, *CW*, vol. 1, p. 473.

"good citizens and patriots": January 12, 1848, *CW*, vol. 1, p. 432.

28 *"Whether the* spot *of soil"*: December 22, 1847, *CW*, vol. 1, p. 421.

"the war with Mexico was unnecessarily": January 12, 1848, *CW*, vol. 1, p. 432.

"The President falls far short": January 12, 1848, *CW*, vol. 1, p. 432.

29 *"unpatriotic"* and *"treasonable"*: *Illinois State Register*, March 10, 1848, Mitgang, Loc. 1399.

"Benedict Arnold of our district": *Illinois State Register*, March 10, 1848, Mitgang, Loc. 1404.

"I earnestly desired to prevent": Herndon and Weik, vol. 2, p. 283.

"if it shall become necessary": February 15, 1848, *CW*, vol. 1, p. 451.

"If you had been in my place": February 1, 1848, *CW*, vol. 1, p. 446.

"not hesitate to denounce as unjust": February 1, 1848, *CW*, vol. 1, p. 447.

"votes for all the necessary supplies": July 27, 1848, *CW*, vol. 1, p. 514.

"an imaginary conception": January 12, 1848, *CW*, vol. 1, p. 441.

"keeping our fences where they are": September 12, 1848, *CW*, vol. 2, p. 4.

30 *"is the [Golden Rule] obsolete"*: May 21, 1848, *CW*, vol. 1, p. 473.

"interference of Russia": January 9, 1852, *CW*, vol. 1, p. 115.

"nonintervention as a sacred principle": January 9, 1852, *CW*, vol. 1, p. 115.

31 *"An honest laborer digs coal"*: June 20, 1848, *CW*, vol. 1, p. 484.

"'Do nothing at all'": June 20, 1848, *CW*, vol. 1, p. 481.

"Let the nation take hold": June 20, 1848, *CW*, vol. 1, p. 489.

32 *"I dropped the matter"*: January 10, 1849, *CW*, vol. 2, p. 22.

"not be a candidate again": January 8, 1848, *CW*, vol. 1, p. 431.

33 *"Butterfield was asked"*: Burlingame and Ettlinger, p. 73.
"I will go home": Barrett, vol. 1, p. 108.
38 *"If I live I'm coming back"*: Herndon and Weik, vol. 3, pp. 483–484.

3. To Emancipate the Mind

40 *"Of all the forces of nature"*: April 6, 1858, *CW*, vol. 2, p. 441.
"In fording streams": Arnold, p. 59.
"We would stop at a farm house": Whitney, p. 100.
41 *"I used to wonder why"*: Holzer, *Lincoln as I Knew Him*, p. 72.
"From 1849 to 1854": December 20, 1859, *CW*, vol. 3, p. 512.
42 *"I hold the value of life"*: February 12, 1861, *CW*, vol. 4, p. 203.
"wanted something solid": Herndon and Weik, vol. 3, p. 435.
"notion of evolution": Herndon and Weik, vol. 3, p. 438.
"There are no accidents": Herndon and Weik, vol. 3, p. 438.
43 *"to investigate, examine"*: March 3, 1863, United States Congress.
44 *"when you know it all"*: Ward, p. 159.
45 *"thread"*: April 6, 1858, *CW*, vol. 2, p. 438.
"instrument of iron": April 6, 1858, *CW*, vol. 2, p. 439.
"Of all the forces of nature": April 6, 1858, *CW*, vol. 2, p. 441.
"emancipate the mind": February 11, 1859, *CW*, vol. 3, p. 363.
"observation [by] a single individual": February 11, 1859, *CW*, vol. 3, p. 362.
"the fire of genius": February 11, 1859, *CW*, vol. 3, p. 363.
46 *"the court did not know anything"*: Herndon and Weik, vol. 2, p. 338.
"If A can prove": April 1, 1854, *CW*, vol. 2, p. 222.
47 *"A servant is a possession and can be sold"*: *Nance v. Howard,* Illinois Supreme Court, December 1828, and *Bailey v. Cromwell,* Illinois Supreme Court, July 1841.
"You are in the right": Donald, *Lincoln*, p. 97.
"Never stir up litigation": July 1, 1850, *CW*, vol. 2, p. 81.
"a vague popular belief": July 1, 1850, *CW*, vol. 2, p. 82.
"Resolve to be honest": July 1, 1850, *CW*, vol. 2, p. 82.
48 "chirping like a bird": Jones, p. 16.

4. Rising with the Occasion

52 *"not instantly give it up"*: October 16, 1854, *CW*, vol. 2, p. 255.
"rise with the occasion": December 1, 1862, *CW*, vol. 5, p. 537.
"New light breaks upon us": October 16, 1854, *CW*, vol. 2, p. 250.
53 *"raise a hell of a storm"*: Donald, *Lincoln*, p. 168.

"thunderstruck and stunned": October 16, 1854, *CW,* vol. 2, p. 282.

"not as a law": August 24, 1855, *CW,* vol. 2, p. 321.

"It was conceived in violence": August 24, 1855, *CW,* vol. 2, p. 321.

54 *"moral right":* October 16, 1854, *CW,* vol. 2, p. 266.

"the sacred right of self government": October 16, 1854, *CW,* vol. 2, p. 250.

55 "Look at the magnitude of the subject": March 6, 1860, *CW,* vol. 4, p. 15.

"immensely great pecuniary interest": July 23, 1856, *CW,* vol. 2, p. 351.

"it greatly enhances, perhaps quite doubles": July 23, 1856, *CW,* vol. 2, p. 352.

"ultimate extinction": December 28, 1857, *CW,* vol. 2, p. 453.

"on some philosophical basis": March 6, 1860, *CW,* vol. 4, p. 17.

56 *"I wish to* make *and to* keep": October 16, 1854, *CW,* vol. 2, p. 248.

"eloquence was of the higher type": White, p. 10.

"does not like to be considered a mean fellow": March 6, 1860, *CW,* vol. 4, p. 16.

"founded in the selfishness of man's nature": October 16, 1854, *CW,* vol. 2, p. 271.

"immense pecuniary interest": March 6, 1860, *CW,* vol. 4, p. 16.

"I have no prejudice against the Southern people": October 16, 1854, *CW,* vol. 2, p. 255.

57 *"We have before us":* March 1, 1859, *CW,* vol. 3, p. 369.

"They can not stand together": October 16, 1854, *CW,* vol. 2, p. 275.

"you can not repeal human nature": October 16, 1854, *CW,* vol. 2, p. 271.

58 *"you will lose both Trumbull and myself":* Wilson and Davis, *Herndon's Informants,* p. 183.

"not too disappointed": June 7, 1856, *CW,* vol. 2, p. 343.

"I am in": June 7, 1856, *CW,* vol. 2, p. 343.

59 *"beings of an inferior order": Dred Scott v. John F. A. Sandford,* U.S. Supreme Court, March 6, 1857.

"respect for the judicial department of government": June 26, 1857, *CW,* vol. 2, p. 400.

60 *"the Dred Scott decision is erroneous":* June 26, 1857, *CW,* vol. 2, p. 401.

"unanimous": June 26, 1857, *CW,* vol. 2, p. 400.

"apparent partisan bias": June 26, 1857, *CW,* vol. 2, p. 400.

"based on assumed historical facts": June 26, 1857, *CW,* vol. 2, p. 400.

"in the last three or four years": June 26, 1857, *CW,* vol. 2, p. 404

"the right of voting": June 26, 1857, *CW,* vol. 2, p. 404.

"the right of property": Dred Scott v. John F. A. Sandford, U.S. Supreme Court, March 6, 1857.

"I think the authors of that notable instrument": June 26, 1857, *CW,* vol. 2, p. 404.

"not disrespectful to treat": June 26, 1857, *CW,* vol. 2, p. 401.

61   *"we know the court"*: June 26, 1857, *CW*, vol. 2, p. 400.

    "there is no peaceful extinction of slavery": August 15, 1855, *CW*, vol. 2, p. 318.

    "the condition of the slave in America": August 15, 1855, *CW*, vol. 2, p. 318.

5. The Eternal Struggle Between Right and Wrong

66   *"perpetual and national"*: October 7, 1858, *CW*, vol. 3, p. 29.

    "by the white man": Lincoln, p. 11.

    "young ladies": Guelzo, p. 189.

68   *"very honest man"*: Gardner, p. 230.

    "the strong man of his party": Gardner, p. 169.

    "politicians of his party": July 17, 1858, *CW*, vol. 2, p. 506.

    "generous and honest": Herndon and Weik, vol. 2, p. 404.

    "it was only in politics": Herndon and Weik, vol. 2, p. 404.

    "won't you take something": Angle, p. 43.

    "all habitual drunkards": February 22, 1842, *CW*, vol. 1, p. 275.

69   *"proneness in the brilliant"*: February 22, 1842, *CW*, vol. 1, p. 278.

    "the blood of genius and generosity": February 22, 1842, *CW*, vol. 1, p. 278.

    "I can't quite see it": Burlingame and Ettlinger, p. 89.

    "a bottle of that whiskey to all our generals": *New York Herald,* September 18, 1863.

    "'folks who have no vices'": *MacMillan's Magazine*, vol. 6 (May 1862), p. 24.

    "he was a grocery keeper": August 21, 1858, *CW*, vol. 3, p. 5.

70   *"never kept a grocery anywhere"*: August 21, 1858, *CW*, vol. 3, p. 16.

    "The proposition is indisputably true": Lamon, *Life of Abraham Lincoln*, p. 397.

    "use some universally known": Lamon, *Life of Abraham Lincoln*, p. 397.

    "A house divided": June 16, 1858, *CW*, vol. 2, p. 461.

71   *"we shall lie down pleasantly dreaming"*: June 16, 1858, *CW*, vol. 2, p. 467.

    "if there is nothing wrong in the institution": October 13, 1858, *CW*, vol. 3, p. 257.

    "anybody has a right to do wrong": October 7, 1858, *CW*, vol. 3, p. 226.

    "difference of opinion, reduced to its lowest terms": October 13, 1858, *CW*, vol. 3, p. 254.

    "has not character enough for integrity and truth": August 21, 1858, *CW*, vol. 3, p. 35.

    "Black Republicans": August 21, 1858, *CW*, vol. 3, p. 5.

    "government of ours is founded on the white basis": Lincoln, p. 11.

    "preserving . . . the purity of the blood": Lincoln, p. 12.

72 *"is not my equal in many respects"*: August 21, 1858, *CW*, vol. 3, p. 16.

"*by his opposition to the Mexican War*": August 21, 1858, *CW*, vol. 3, p. 6.

"*shook him until his teeth chattered*": Lamon, *Recollections*, p. 24.

"nearly shook all the Democracy out of me today": Lamon, *Recollections*, p. 25.

"*I don't want to quarrel with him*": September 15, 1858, *CW*, vol. 3, p. 135.

"*[Judge Douglas] is crazy*": September 15, 1858, *CW*, vol. 3, p. 134.

"*blowing out the moral lights around us*": October 7, 1858, *CW*, vol. 3, p. 29.

74 "*the most interesting political battle ground*": Donald, *Lincoln*, p. 214.

"*never overlooked a newspaper man*": Herndon and Weik, vol. 2, p. 376.

"*Few men can make an hour pass away*": Holzer, *Lincoln and the Power of the Press*, p. 202.

"*Write no letters which can possibly be distorted*": April 29, 1860, *CW*, vol. 4, p. 46.

"*Please pardon me for suggesting*": November 16, 1860, *CW*, vol. 4, p. 140.

75 "*I have been on expenses so long*": November 16, 1858, *CW*, vol. 3, p. 337.

"*I cannot enter the ring on the money basis*": March 16, 1860, *CW*, vol. 4, p. 32.

76 "*Douglas has taken this trick*": Zane, p. 80.

"*long after I am gone*": November 19, 1858, *CW*, vol. 3, p. 339.

"an immense crowd": Sparks, p. 137.

"That is the real issue": October 15, 1858, *CW*, vol. 3, p. 315.

6. The Tendency of Prosperity to Breed Tyrants

81 "*all over the world*": March 5, 1860, *CW*, vol. 4, p. 7.

"*you might stay at home*": Zall, p. 259.

82 "*Slavery is doomed*": Holzer, *Lincoln as I Knew Him*, p. 99.

"*What kills the skunk*": Holzer, *Lincoln as I Knew Him*, pp. 99–100.

"*somebody owning capital*": September 30, 1859, *CW*, vol. 3, p. 477.

"*labor is prior to, and independent of capital*": September 30, 1859, *CW*, vol. 3, p. 478.

83 "*No other human occupation*": September 30, 1859, *CW*, vol. 3, p. 480.

"*by the best cultivation*": September 30, 1859, *CW*, vol. 3, p. 482.

"*I really think it best*": April 16, 1859, *CW*, vol. 3, p. 377.

"*such a sucker as me*": Villard, vol. 1, p. 96.

"*two men about to fight*": Alexander K. McClure, pp. 38–39.

84 "*look beyond our noses*": July 6, 1859, *CW*, vol. 3, p. 391.

85 "*a clear majority*": February 27, 1860, *CW*, vol. 3, p. 530.

"*cease to call slavery wrong*": February 27, 1860, *CW*, vol. 3, p. 548.

86 *"LET US HAVE FAITH THAT RIGHT MAKES MIGHT"*: February 27, 1860, *CW*, vol. 3, p. 550.

"*no man ever made such an impression*": *New York Tribune*, February 28, 1860.

"*Isn't it too bad Bob's father*": Donald, *Lincoln*, p. 240.

87 "*where the laborer can strike if he wants to*": March 5, 1860, *CW*, vol. 4, p. 7.

"*a law to prevent a man from getting rich*": March 6, 1860, *CW*, vol. 4, p. 25.

88 "*a commission broker*": Donald, *Lincoln*, p. 391.

"*The government can not afford*": June 13, 1862, *CW*, vol. 5, p. 269.

"*preach God and Liberty*": Carpenter, p. 255.

"*I know the trials and woes of workingmen*": Boritt, p. 221.

"*The strongest bond of human sympathy*": March 21, 1864, *CW*, vol. 7, p. 259.

89 "*No men living are more worthy*": December 3, 1861, *CW*, vol. 5, p. 53.

90 "*the Rail Splitter*": Donald, *Lincoln*, p. 245.

"*My name is new in the field*": March 24, 1860, *CW*, vol. 4, p. 34.

"*give no offense to others*": March 24, 1860, *CW*, vol. 4, p. 34.

91 "*Honors elevate some men*": Donald, *Lincoln*, p. 251.

"Wise statesmen as they were": August 17, 1858, *CW*, vol. 2, p. 546.

7. The Better Angels of Our Nature

97 "*troubles will come to an end*": February 15, 1861, *CW*, vol. 4, p. 211.

"*It has been my purpose*": August 8, 1860, *CW*, vol. 4, p. 91.

"Justice and fairness to all": August 14, 1860, *CW*, vol. 4, p. 93.

98 "*My published speeches*": August 14, 1860, *CW*, vol. 4, p. 93.

"*That is cool*": February 27, 1860, *CW*, vol. 3, p. 547.

"*Let us at all times remember*": November 20, 1860, *CW*, vol. 4, p. 142.

99 "*the election of a man*": *A Declaration of the Immediate Causes Which Induce and Justify the Secession of South Carolina from the Federal Union*, December 24, 1860, Civilwar.org.

"*Our position is thoroughly identified*": *A Declaration of the Immediate Causes Which Induce and Justify the Secession of the State of Mississippi from the Federal Union*, January 9, 1861, Civilwar.org.

"*the President-elect did not experience*": *New York Herald*, December 25, 1860.

"*My advice is to keep cool*": February 15, 1861, *CW*, vol. 4, p. 211.

100 "*On the question of extending slavery*": December 10, 1860, *CW*, vol. 4, p. 149.

"*hold firm, as with a chain of steel*": December 13, 1860, *CW*, vol. 4, p. 151.

"suffer death before I will consent": January 19–21, 1861, *CW*, vol. 4, p. 175.

"it acknowledges that slavery": December 18, 1860, *CW*, vol. 4, p. 155.

"We have just carried an election": January 11, 1861, *CW*, vol. 4, p. 172.

"We must settle this question now": Burlingame, *With Lincoln in the White House*, p. 41.

101 *"The tug has to come"*: December 10, 1860, *CW*, vol. 4, p. 150.

"Instead of intimidating the President-elect": *New York Herald*, December 21, 1860.

"into an iron mask": Holzer, *Lincoln as I Knew Him*, p. 190.

"needed the strongest men of the party": Goodwin, p. 319.

"had no right to deprive": Goodwin, p. 319.

102 *"You seem to forget"*: Weed, vol. 1, p. 610.

103 *"Liberty or Badly Wounded"*: Miller, *Lincoln's Virtues*, p. 73.

"as powerless as a block of buckeye wood": November 5, 1860, Burlingame, *With Lincoln in the White House*, p. 7.

"fable of the lion": Hertz, p. 262.

104 *"necessity, not a choice"*: *Jefferson Davis' Inaugural Address*, February 18, 1861, Civilwar.org.

105 *"Way back in my childhood"*: February 21, 1861, *CW*, vol. 4, p. 235.

"I am filled with deep emotion": February 22, 1861, *CW*, vol. 4, p. 240.

"I would rather be assassinated on [the] spot": February 22, 1861, *CW*, vol. 4, p. 240.

106 *"the imbecility of the Federal Government"*: *A Declaration of the Causes Which Impel the State of Texas from the Federal Union*, February 23, 1861, Civilwar.org.

"only substantial dispute": March 4, 1861, *CW*, vol. 4, p. 258.

"No state can lawfully get out of the Union": March 4, 1861, *CW*, vol. 4, p. 253.

107 *"In your hands"*: March 4, 1861, *CW*, vol. 4, p. 261.

"the better angels of our nature": March 4, 1861, *CW*, vol. 4, p. 271.

"by a mere accident": February 14, 1861, *CW*, vol. 4, p. 208.

108 *"affectionate farewell"*: February 11, 1861, *CW*, vol. 4, p. 190.

8. With Firmness in the Right

112 *"Go home"*: April 22, 1861, *CW*, vol. 4, p. 341.

"The first thing that was handed to me": Pease and Randall, vol. 1, p. 476.

113 *"I see no alternative but surrender"*: March 5, 1861, *CW*, vol. 4, p. 279.

"hold, occupy, and possess": March 4, 1861, *CW*, vol. 4, p. 254.

"government will not assail you": March 4, 1861, *CW*, vol. 4, p. 261.

"To abandon [Fort Sumter]": July 4, 1861, *CW*, vol. 4, p. 424.

"lose the whole game": September 22, 1861, *CW*, vol. 4, p. 533.

114 "to pursue in regard to the Confederate States": April 13, 1861, *CW*, vol. 4, p. 330.

"an unprovoked assault": April 13, 1861, *CW*, vol. 4, p. 331.

"We were entirely unprepared": Goodwin, p. 366.

115 *"A competent force will be posted"*: April 19, 1861, *CW*, vol. 4, p. 339.

"organized and combined treasonable resistance": May 26, 1862, *CW*, vol. 5, p. 241.

"It became necessary for me to choose": May 26, 1862, *CW*, vol. 5, p. 241.

"contained so large a number": May 26, 1862, *CW*, vol. 5, p. 242.

116 *"no manhood or honor in that"*: April 22, 1861, *CW*, vol. 4, p. 341.

117 *"walking the floor alone"*: Nicolay and Hay, vol. 4, p. 152.

"Why don't they come": Nicolay and Hay, vol. 4, p. 152.

"In every great crisis": New York Times, April 25, 1861.

118 *"You are engaged in repressing an insurrection"*: April 27, 1861, *CW*, vol. 4, p. 347.

"to arrest and detain": July 4, 1861, *CW*, vol. 4, p. 429.

119 *"unwarranted by the Constitution"*: Donald, *Lincoln*, p. 416.

120 *"the privilege of the writ"*: July 4, 1861, *CW*, vol. 4, p. 430.

"the Constitution is silent": July 4, 1861, *CW*, vol. 4, p. 430.

"the government was saved from overthrow": March 26, 1862, *CW*, vol. 5, p. 242.

"This is essentially a People's contest": July 4, 1861, *CW*, vol. 4, p. 438.

121 *"it was useless to fight"*: Whitman, p. 25.

"The talk . . . in and around Washington": Whitman, p. 24.

"he listened in silence": Nicolay and Hay, vol. 4, p. 353.

122 *"man for man"*: Nicolay and Hay, vol. 4, p. 79.

"be constantly drilled, disciplined, and instructed": July 23, 1861, *CW*, vol. 4, p. 457.

123 *"He goes at it with both hands"*: New York Times, June 17, 1861.

"Lincoln made one of the neatest": Sherman, vol. 1, p. 190.

"he possessed the strength of a giant": Goodwin, p. 437.

"When I was eighteen years of age": Ward, p. 123.

9. The Middle Ground

128 *"my appeals to . . . reason"*: May 15, 1863, *CW*, vol. 6, p. 218.

Sixteen-year-old Julia Taft: Bayne, p. 110.

129 *"two wars on his hands at a time"*: Randall, vol. 1, p. 41.

"cheerfully liberated": Harper's Weekly, November 23, 1861.

130 *"Through the actions of our disloyal citizens"*: January 19, 1863, *CW*, vol. 6, p. 64.

"the family of Christian and civilized nations": April 15, 1863, *CW*, vol. 6, p. 176.

"I cannot imagine": Schurz, vol. 2, p. 309.

131 *"war between Peru and Spain"*: December 6, 1864, *CW*, vol. 8, p. 138.

132 *"These all against us"*: September 22, 1861, *CW*, vol. 4, p. 532.

133 *"I think it would not be justifiable"*: April 25, 1861, *CW*, vol. 4, p. 344.

"First, they have a clearly legal right to assemble": April 25, 1861, *CW*, vol. 4, p. 344.

134 *"is simply dictatorship"*: September 22, 1861, *CW*, vol. 4, p. 532.

"a necessity indispensable to the maintenance": May 19, 1862, *CW*, vol. 5, p. 222.

135 *"No commanding general shall"*: May 17, 1862, *CW*, vol. 5, p. 219.

"One class of friends believe": January 5, 1863, *CW*, vol. 6, p. 36.

"I have stoutly tried to keep out": April 16, 1863, *CW*, vol. 6, p. 178.

"It is very painful to me": May 15, 1863, *CW*, vol. 6, p. 218.

136 *"I fear this loses you the middle position"*: July 13, 1863, *CW*, vol. 6, p. 326.

"deception breeds and thrives": October 5, 1863, *CW*, vol. 6, p. 500.

"cannot do anything contrary": Burlingame and Ettlinger, p. 89.

"If both factions": May 27, 1863, *CW*, vol. 6, p. 234.

"Under your recent order": October 1, 1863, *CW*, vol. 6, p. 492.

137 *"no friends in Missouri"*: Donald, *Lincoln*, p. 453.

"Somebody has to be in a position": Goodwin, p. 30.

"kept these discordant elements together": Herndon and Weik, vol. 3, p. 533.

Early one morning: Bayne, p. 165.

139 *"A free people"*: July 6, 1852, *CW*, vol. 2, p. 126.

140 *"[Let] nothing turn you to the right or the left"*: March 1, 1859, *CW*, vol. 3, p. 370.

"if both factions": May 27, 1863, *CW*, vol. 6, p. 234.

10. No Less Than National

141 *"need for government"*: July 1, 1854, *CW*, vol. 2, p. 221.

142 *"lacks will and purpose"*: Beale, p. 220.

"never had experience in administering": Welles, vol. 1, p. 137.

"I propose continuing to be myself": July 14, 1864, *CW*, vol. 7, p. 440.

"were at least equally responsible": May 26, 1862, *CW*, vol. 5, p. 242.

143 *"The dismissal of Blair"*: Welles, vol. 2, p. 158.

"roughly handled by that man": Herndon and Weik, vol. 2, pp. 355–356.

"sit down on all my pride": Miller, *Lincoln's Virtues*, p. 422.

"I haven't met 'em": Rothschild, p. 285.

144   *"read attentively the tenth verse"*: Rothschild, p. 284.

"There has been a wide-spread attempt": August 6, 1862, *CW*, vol. 5, pp. 358–359.

145   *"no less than National"*: October 16, 1854, *CW*, vol. 2, p. 248.

"the legitimate object of government": July 1, 1854, *CW*, vol. 2, p. 220.

"combined action": July 1, 1854, *CW*, vol. 2, p. 221.

"success does not depend as much": August 14, 1862, *CW*, vol. 5, p. 374.

"if all men were just": July 1, 1854, *CW*, vol. 2, p. 221.

146   *"we can succeed only by concert"*: December 1, 1862, *CW*, vol. 5, p. 537.

"'can we all do better'": December 1, 1862, *CW*, vol. 5, p. 537.

"to make the most of our time": Boritt, p. 226.

"generally delegated to Mr. Chase": Burlingame and Ettlinger, *Inside Lincoln's White House*, p. 134.

148   *"honest trade and honest labor"*: June 23, 1862, *CW*, vol. 5, p. 282.

149   *"peculiarly a people's department"*: Boritt, p. 216.

150   *"I am in favor of a national bank"*: Herndon and Weik, vol. 1, p. 104.

"a never-failing source of communication": March 9, 1832, *CW*, vol. 1, p. 6.

"No duty is more imperative": December 26, 1839, *CW*, vol. 1, p. 164.

"upon the subject of education": March 9, 1832, *CW*, vol. 1, p. 8.

"no other human occupation": September 30, 1859, *CW*, vol. 3, p. 480.

151   *"never doubted the constitutional authority"*: April 16, 1862, *CW*, vol. 5, p. 192.

"desired to see the national capital freed": April 16, 1862, *CW*, vol. 5, p. 192.

"provided eligibility to every person in military": July 14, 1862, United States Congress.

152   *"It is of noteworthy interest"*: December 6, 1854, *CW*, vol. 8, p. 145.

153   "Did Stanton really say": Julian, p. 211.

158   "to care for him who shall have borne": March 4, 1865, *CW*, vol. 8, p. 333.

11. The Fiery Trial

159   *"I hope I am a Christian"*: Carpenter, p. 187.

"My poor boy": Keckley, p. 103.

160   *"I have found difficulty"*: Carpenter, p. 190.

"I have never denied": July 31, 1846, *CW*, vol. 1, p. 382.

"brought to support": July 31, 1846, *CW*, vol. 1, p. 382.

161   *"the higher matter of eternal consequences"*: July 31, 1846, *CW*, vol. 1, p. 382.

"a child of bright intelligence": July 31, 1846, *CW*, vol. 1, p. 382.

"kind of poetry in his nature": Herndon and Weik, vol. 3, p. 445.

"Me and father": Holzer, *Lincoln as I Knew Him*, p. 28.

"all struggling with their tears": Keckley, p. 110.

"with a moist eye": Keckley, p. 110.

162   *"sincere and deep sympathy"*: Thomas, p. 304.

"an idiot": August 16, 1861, Sears, p. 85.

"a well-meaning baboon": October 11, 1861, Sears, p. 106.

"the necessity of replacing him": Donald, *Lincoln*, p. 385.

"not the game": September 26, 1862, *CW*, vol. 5, pp. 442–443.

163   *"forthwith dismissed"*: September 27, 1862, *CW*, vol. 5, p. 443.

"wholly inadmissible": September 27, 1862, *CW*, vol. 5, p. 442.

"it was his object to break up that game": September 27, 1862, *CW*, vol. 5, p. 442.

"dismissed Major Key": September 24, 1864, Burlingame and Ettlinger, p. 232.

"vilifying and disparaging": November 10, 1862, *CW*, vol. 5, p. 494.

164   *"let's walk over"*: Dahlgren, p. 369.

"I come here to escape": Tarbell, vol. 3, p. 105.

165   *"down to the raisins"*: Alexander K. McClure, pp. 36–37.

"something special": Bates, p. 138.

"I had no business here": Dahlgren, p. 390.

166   *"like that boy in Kentucky"*: Phillips, p. 65.

"a want of confidence": *New York Times*, November 7, 1862.

"Conservative Revolution": *New York Herald*, November 6, 1862.

"a sort of boyish cheerfulness": Donald, *Lincoln*, p. 328.

"an honest old codger": Donald, *Lincoln*, p. 373.

"unequal to his place": Donald, *Lincoln*, p. 373.

"inexpedient": Donald, *Lincoln*, p. 389.

167   *"a change in"*: *New York Times*, December 20, 1862.

"now on the brink": Pease and Randall, vol. 1, p. 600.

"The courage with which you": December 22, 1862, *CW*, vol. 6, p. 13.

168   *"[can] not afford to hang men for votes"*: Nichols, p. 118.

169   *"Where's the fire"*: Stimmel, p. 38.

"jumped over the boxwood hedge": McBride, p. 29.

"were lost in the fire": Stimmel, p. 39.

"I hope I am a Christian": Carpenter, p. 187.

"until my boy Willie died": Carpenter, p. 187.

170   *"away from here a wiser man"*: Carpenter, p. 189.

"who had arrived at a point in Christianity": Holzer, *Lincoln as I Knew Him*, p. 76.

"no man had a more abiding": Carpenter, p. 186.

"not the days of miracles": September 13, 1862, *CW*, vol. 5, p. 420.

"We are indeed going through": October 26, 1862, *CW*, vol. 5, p. 478.

171   "we *cannot escape history"*: December 1, 1862, *CW*, vol. 5, p. 537.

173   *make an example of him:* Burlingame and Ettlinger, p. 232.

12. The Thunderbolt

176   *"touch it off themselves"*: Lester, p. 360.

     "favor of Almighty God": January 1, 1863, *CW*, vol. 6, p. 29.

     "something of great importance": Bates, p. 141.

177   *" for the first time told me"*: Bates, p. 141.

     "to consider and discuss": July 12, 1862, *CW*, vol. 5, p. 319.

     "border states hold more power for good": July 12, 1862, *CW*, vol. 5, p. 317.

     "at once to emancipate gradually": July 12, 1862, *CW*, vol. 5, p. 319.

     "in great peril": July 12, 1862, *CW*, vol. 5, p. 317.

     "dwelt earnestly on the gravity": Welles, vol. 1, p. 70.

     "frankly state how the proposition struck us": Welles, vol. 1, p. 70.

     "a new departure": Welles, vol. 1, p. 71.

178   *"he had been prompt and emphatic"*: Welles, vol. 1, p. 71.

     "weaken our cause": Lester, p. 359.

     "This thunderbolt will keep": Lester, p. 360.

179   *"cooperate with any state"*: March 6, 1862, *CW*, vol. 5, pp. 144–145.

181   *preliminary Emancipation Proclamation:* September 22, 1862, *CW*, vol. 5, pp. 433–436.

     "our last shriek, on the retreat": Carpenter, p. 22.

     "I had entirely overlooked": Carpenter, p. 22.

     "Our government rests in public opinion": December 10, 1856, *CW*, vol. 2, p. 385.

182   *"Whoever can change public opinion"*: December 10, 1856, *CW*, vol. 2, p. 385.

     "It is not much in the nature of man": February 22, 1842, *CW*, vol. 1, p. 272.

     "that which is exclusively [their] own business": February 22, 1842, *CW*, vol. 1, p. 272.

     "at the expense of pecuniary interest": February 22, 1842, *CW*, vol. 1, p. 272.

     "What an ignorance of human nature": February 22, 1842, *CW*, vol. 1, p. 275.

     "a wonderful power to lull": February 22, 1842, *CW*, vol. 1, p. 276.

     "An honest man": February 22, 1842, *CW*, vol. 1, p. 276.

183   *"If you would win a man to your cause"*: February 22, 1842, *CW*, vol. 1, p. 273.

     "the high road to his reason": February 22, 1842, *CW*, vol. 1, p. 273.

184   *"my public opinion baths"*: Sandburg, vol. 1, p. 237.

"renting out rooms at one end of the house": Raymond, p. 700.

"Raymond is my Lieutenant General in politics": Raymond, p. 758.

"slavery must go to the wall": New York Times, July 14, 1862.

185 *"the policy you seem to be pursuing"*: August 20, 1862, CW, vol. 5, p. 389.

"strangely and disastrously remiss": August 20, 1862, CW, vol. 5, p. 389.

"My paramount object in this struggle": August 22, 1862, CW, vol. 5, p. 388.

"He is too smart for me": Holzer, Lincoln and the Power of the Press, p. 406.

"Proclamation Mania": New York World, August 18, 1862.

186 *"thought a great deal about the relation"*: Donald, Inside Lincoln's Cabinet, pp. 149–152.

"I am here": Nicolay and Hay, vol. 6, pp. 159–160.

"render eternal hatred": New York Times, September 30, 1862.

"an accursed doctrine": Goodwin, p. 483.

187 *"We shout for joy"*: Douglass Monthly, October 1862.

"All persons held as slaves": January 1, 1863, CW, vol. 6, p. 29.

"If my name ever goes into": Carpenter, p. 270.

188 *"'That will do'"*: Carpenter, p. 270.

"'a [black] porter in the Treasury Department'": Chicago Tribune, January 19, 1864.

190 *"With public sentiment"*: April 21, 1858, CW, vol. 3, p. 28.

13. A More Elevated Position

192 *"aiming blows at each other"*: June 12, 1863, CW, vol. 6, p. 267.

"What will the country say": Brooks, p. 58.

193 *"I expect the best"*: Chicago Tribune, June 1, 1863.

194 *"the tread of the President's feet"*: Ward, pp. 48–49; Holzer, Lincoln as I Knew Him, pp. 232–234.

195 *"What next"*: May 7, 1863, CW, vol. 6, p. 201.

"Lee's army, and not Richmond": June 10, 1863, CW, vol. 6, p. 257.

"They are to be used in case of fire": Ward, p. 190.

196 *"fire in the rear"*: Pierce, p. 114.

"acts for the benefit of the enemies": April 13, 1863, General War Order No. 38, Department of the Ohio.

"King Lincoln": Ex parte Vallandigham, U.S. Supreme Court, February 15, 1864.

"for the purpose of crushing out liberty": Ex parte Vallandigham, U.S. Supreme Court, February 15, 1864.

197 *"I suppose the time has come"*: Hamlin, p. 432.

"progressing too slowly": January 14, 1863, CW, vol. 6, p. 56.

"the great available": March 26, 1863, CW, vol. 6, p. 149.

198   *"successes could not have been achieved"*: August 26, 1863, *CW*, vol. 6, p. 409.

199   *the Albany resolutions: Correspondence in Relation to the Public Meeting at Albany, NY* (pamphlet, 1863).
      "personal to myself": June 12, 1863, *CW*, vol. 6, p. 261.
      "he who dissuades one man": June 12, 1863, *CW*, vol. 6, p. 264.
      "Must I shoot a simple-minded soldier boy": June 12, 1863, *CW*, vol. 6, p. 267.
      "In this time of national peril": June 12, 1863, *CW*, vol. 6, p. 267.

200   *"fight well on his own dunghill"*: Williams, p. 260.

201   *"have simply touched a match"*: Sandburg, vol. 2, p. 368.

202   *"You [say] you desire peace"*: August 26, 1863, *CW*, vol. 6, p. 406.
      "I think differently": August 26, 1863, *CW*, vol. 6, p. 408.
      "Some of them seem willing to fight for you": August 26, 1863, *CW*, vol. 6, p. 409.

203   *"Peace does not appear so distant"*: August 26, 1863, *CW*, vol. 6, p. 410.
      "the servant of the people": August 26, 1863, *CW*, vol. 6, p. 407.

204   *"a few appropriate remarks"*: November 2, 1863, Robert Todd Lincoln Papers, Library of Congress.
      "Four score and seven years ago": November 19, 1863, *CW*, vol. 7, p. 23.
      "Flowerth for the President": Selby, p. 207.

14. A Fair Chance in the Race of Life

209   *"all men are created equal"*: October 13, 1858, *CW*, vol. 2, p. 501.
      "that rebel in your house": Helm, p. 231.

210   *"seven-eighths of them"*: Carpenter, p. 276.
      "lost my apple overboard": Zall, p. 36.
      "rather take a rope": Pease and Randall, vol. 2, p. 659.
      "determined not to do me justice": Selby, p. 171.

211   *"you will have your son"*: Carpenter, p. 109.
      "It breaks my heart": Wilson and Davis, *Herndon's Informants*, p. 562.
      "more good above ground": Morgan, p. 301.
      "the eagerness with which": Burlingame and Ettlinger, p. 64.
      "one hundred court martials [in] six hours": Burlingame, *At Lincoln's Side*, pp. 45–46.
      "63 court martials": February 9, 1864, *CW*, vol. 7, p. 175.
      46 court-martials: February 10, 1864, *CW*, vol. 7, p. 175.
      "four long sessions": Miller, *President Lincoln*, p. 340.

212   *"Pardoned — A. Lincoln"*: March 31, 1863, *CW*, vol. 8, p. 513.
      "merciless where meanness or cruelty": Burlingame and Ettlinger, p. 64.

"kindly enough in nature": Rice, p. 583.

"when he met his death": Neely, pp. 166–167.

"sentence disapproved": Neely, p. 167.

213 *"shot inside of twenty-four hours"*: Holzer, *Lincoln as I Knew Him*, p. 218.

214 *"I have thought fit to issue a proclamation"*: December 8, 1863, *CW*, vol. 7, p. 50.

"let 'em up easy": Sandburg, vol. 4, p. 183.

"power to grant reprieves": December 8, 1863, *CW*, vol. 7, p. 53.

215 *"this bill was placed before me"*: Burlingame and Ettlinger, p. 217.

"pecuniary greed can be made to aid us": December 12, 1864, *CW*, vol. 8, p. 164.

216 *"As a nation, we began by"*: August 24, 1855, *CW*, vol. 2, p. 323.

217 *"principal of replenishing streams"*: December 6, 1864, *CW*, vol. 8, p. 141.

"Act to Encourage Immigration": July 4, 1864, United States Congress.

"This great national policy": December 6, 1864, *CW*, vol. 8, p. 141.

"beginning a new life": December 8, 1863, *CW*, vol. 7, p. 40.

"the father of all moral principle": July 10, 1858, *CW*, vol. 2, p. 499.

"as long as the love of freedom exists": July 10, 1858, *CW*, vol. 2, p. 500.

218 *"pilots on our Western Rivers"*: Donald, *Lincoln*, p. 15.

"a total revolution of labor": December 8, 1863, *CW*, vol. 7, p. 51.

"make a new Constitution recognizing": August 5, 1863, *CW*, vol. 6, p. 365.

"adopt some practical system": August 5, 1863, *CW*, vol. 6, p. 365.

"will have to look out for themselves": Lamon, *Recollections*, pp. 126–127.

219 *"opposed to encouraging"*: January 11, 1837, *CW*, vol. 1, p. 69.

"region of reason into that of hot blood": Burlingame and Ettlinger, p. 254.

"discard all this quibbling": October 13, 1858, *CW*, vol. 2, p. 501.

"plank is large enough for both": March 6, 1860, *CW*, vol. 4, p. 20.

"to elevate the condition of men": July 4, 1861, *CW*, vol. 4, p. 438.

220 *"it was the baby that did it"*: Carpenter, p. 133.

221 *"punish merely for punishment's sake"*: March 18, 1864, *CW*, vol. 7, p. 255.

15. This Terrible, Bloody War

226 *"not to overthrow it"*: October 19, 1864, *CW*, vol. 8, p. 52.

"conquered and ruined us": November 10, 1864, *CW*, vol. 8, p. 101.

227 *"blind memorandum"*: August 23, 1864, *CW*, vol. 7, p. 514.

"an impossibility": August 23, 1864, *CW*, vol. 7, p. 514.

"tide is strongly against us": August 24, 1864, *CW*, vol. 7, p. 518.

"You think I don't know": Donald, *Lincoln*, p. 529.

"want of intellectual grasp": Goodwin, p. 499.

"like the bluebottle fly": Burlingame and Ettlinger, p. 103.

"I am entirely indifferent": Burlingame and Ettlinger, p. 93.

228 *"want to finish this job"*: Nicolay, p. 304.

"as desperate fighting": Grant, vol. 2, p. 177.

"pacing back and forth": Carpenter, p. 80.

"this terrible, bloody war": Rice, p. 337.

229 *"I cannot bear it"*: Arnold, p. 375.

"Doesn't it seem strange": Donald, *Lincoln*, p. 514.

231 *"proof that the national spirit"*: June 16, 1864, *CW*, vol. 7, p. 395.

"War, at best, is terrible": June 16, 1864, *CW*, vol. 7, p. 394.

"is due to the soldier": June 16, 1864, *CW*, vol. 7, p. 395.

"will never be dislodged": June 16, 1864, *CW*, vol. 7, p. 396.

232 *"I would rather be defeated with"*: Goodwin, p. 664.

"You and I have reached": June 30, 1864, *CW*, vol. 7, p. 419.

"If the measures": December 6, 1864, *CW*, vol. 8, p. 152.

233 *"I repeat the declaration"*: December 6, 1864, *CW*, vol. 8, p. 152.

"I am struggling to maintain": October 19, 1864, *CW*, vol. 8, p. 52.

234 *"What good is the presidency"*: Thomas, p. 448.

"We must be patient": Donald, *Lincoln*, p. 646.

235 *"new rivers of human blood"*: July 7, 1864, *CW*, vol. 7, p. 435.

"realize how intently": July 7, 1864, *CW*, vol. 7, p. 435.

"intends to influence": Depew, p. 62.

"To whom it may concern": July 18, 1864, *CW*, vol. 7, p. 451.

236 *"Why would he want to"*: Richard H. Allison, *The Great Niagara Peace Debacle*, Wordpress.com, 2011.

"Greeley is like an old shoe": Welles, vol. 2, p. 112.

"Chicago Surrender": Donald, *Lincoln*, p. 530.

237 *"long been a grave question"*: November 10, 1864, *CW*, vol. 8, p. 100.

"Gentlemen, do you remember": August 23, 1864, *CW*, vol. 7, p. 514.

"I resolved": August 23, 1864, *CW*, vol. 7, p. 514.

238 *"And the General would answer"*: August 23, 1864, *CW*, vol. 7, p. 514.

"At least I should have done my duty": August 23, 1864, *CW*, vol. 7, p. 514.

"blind memorandum": August 23, 1864, *CW*, vol. 7, p. 514.

At one o'clock in the afternoon: Holzer, *Lincoln as I Knew Him*, p. 107.

16. With Malice Toward None

243 *"by appropriate legislation"*: January 31, 1865, United States Congress.

"wonderful success in organizing": Douglass, p. 10.

"We are compelled to admit": Douglass, p. 10.

244 *"monstrous injustice"*: October 16, 1854, *CW*, vol. 2, p. 255.

"If slavery is not wrong": April 4, 1864, *CW*, vol. 7, p. 281.

245   *"A man watches his pear tree"*: Carpenter, p. 77.

246   *"the sooner the better"*: December 6, 1864, *CW*, vol. 8, p. 149.

247   *"will clinch the whole subject"*: Segal, p. 364.

      "harpoon into the monster": Tarbell, vol. 2, p. 126.

248   *"clothed with immense power"*: Rice, p. 586.

      "The report is in circulation": January 31, 1865, *CW*, vol. 8, p. 248.

249   *"So far as I know"*: January 31, 1865, *CW*, vol. 8, p. 248.

      "upon this great moral victory": February 1, 1865, *CW*, vol. 8, p. 255.

250   *"Charles I lost his head"*: Donald, *Lincoln*, p. 558.

      "tell you what I would do": Donald, *Lincoln*, p. 558.

      "best when you undertake a job": Donald, *Lincoln*, p. 570.

      "increase the price of female labor": July 27, 1864, *CW*, vol. 7, p. 467.

251   *"just and reasonable"*: July 27, 1864, *CW*, vol. 7, p. 467.

      "within the legal power": July 27, 1864, *CW*, vol. 7, p. 466.

      "I go for all sharing": June 13, 1836, *CW*, vol. 1, p. 48.

      "he always advocated her rights": Wilson and Davis, *Herndon on Lincoln,* p. 346.

252   *"my equal and the equal of all others"*: June 26, 1857, *CW*, vol. 2, p. 405.

      "if the [black] woman can stand it": Holzer, *Lincoln as I Knew Him,* p. 99.

      "question is one simply of time": Wilson and Davis, *Herndon on Lincoln,* p. 346.

      "With high hope for the future": March 4, 1865, *CW*, vol. 8, p. 332.

      "Both parties deprecated war": March 4, 1865, *CW*, vol. 8, p. 332.

      "Both read the same Bible": March 4, 1865, *CW*, vol. 8, p. 333.

      "Fondly do we hope": March 4, 1865, *CW*, vol. 8, p. 333.

253   *"With malice toward none"*: March 4, 1865, *CW*, vol. 8, p. 333.

      "I know meaner things about": Goodwin, p. 639.

      "Let them all go": Segal, p. 382.

254   *"to defeat the opposing armies"*: Segal, p. 382.

      "the mineral wealth of our Nation": Boritt, p. 226.

      "in every possible way": Boritt, p. 226.

255   *"recognize the paramount claims of the soldiers"*: March 1, 1865, *CW*, vol. 8, p. 327.

      "all deserters [who] return to their posts": March 11, 1865, *CW*, vol. 8, p. 350.

      "Let the Prisoner be pardoned": April 12, 1865, *CW*, vol. 8, p. 405.

      "No part of the honor": April 11, 1865, *CW*, vol. 8, p. 400.

      "those who serve our cause as soldiers": April 11, 1865, *CW*, vol. 8, p. 403.

256   *"there [are] men in Congress who"*: Donald, *Lincoln*, p. 592.

      "We must extinguish our resentments": Goodwin, p. 732.

      "It always seemed to me": J. B. McClure, p. 179.

"*Viewed from*": Douglass, p. 10.

259 "*the rightful masters of both congresses and courts*": September 17, 1859, *CW*, vol. 3, p. 460.

17. Peace with All Nations

262 "*as wrongs to be [avenged]*": November 10, 1864, *CW*, vol. 8, p. 101.
"*ill-favored man*": Goodwin, p. 595.
"*uncouth*": *Illinois Citizen*, May 29, 1850.
"*grotesque*": MacChesney, p. 419.
"*a face furrowed*": Holzer, *Lincoln as I Knew Him*, p. 120.
"*Old fellow*": Selby, p. 119.
"*respect [his] personal character*": Goodwin, p. 704.
"*earnest*": Carpenter, p. 262.
"*full of good sense*": Holzer, *Lincoln as I Knew Him*, p. 117.
"*a logical intellect*": Seward, vol. 2, p. 26.
"*kindly nature*": Sherman, e-book, vol. 2, chap. 24.
"*an unselfish heart*": Seward, vol. 2, p. 26.
"*a genial, quiet*": Holzer, *Lincoln as I Knew Him*, p. 110.
"*sympathy [for] people*": Sherman, e-book, vol. 2, chap. 24.
"*greatness with goodness*": Sherman, e-book, vol. 2, chap. 24.

263 "*the very impersonation of*": Sherman, e-book, vol. 2, chap. 24.
"*the best and wisest man*": Goodwin, p. 507.
"*very near being a perfect man*": Carpenter, p. 68.
"*the greatest man I ever knew*": Goodwin, p. 47.
"*by those who would lead him*": February 22, 1842, *CW*, vol. 1, p. 273.

264 "*Human nature will not change*": November 10, 1864, *CW*, vol. 8, p. 101.
"*in the* selfishness *of man's nature*": October 16, 1854, *CW*, vol. 2, p. 271.
"*unselfish*": July 6, 1852, *CW*, vol. 2, p. 130.
"*the very selfishness of his nature*": August 6, 1862, *CW*, vol. 5, p. 359.
"*no greater exemption*": April 14, 1860, *CW*, vol. 4, p. 43.
two sides to the human condition: Wilson, *The Social Conquest of Earth*, p. 17.
"*the eternal struggle*": October 15, 1858, *CW*, vol. 3, p. 315.
"*On the side of the Union*": July 4, 1861, *CW*, vol. 4, p. 439.
"*an immense pecuniary [self] interest*": July 4, 1861, *CW*, vol. 4, p. 438.
"*Individual selection is responsible*": Wilson, *The Social Conquest of Earth*, p. 241.

265 "*A free people, in times of*": July 6, 1852, *CW*, vol. 2, p. 126.
groups of "*Altruists*" always beat groups of "*Selfish*": Wilson, *The Social Conquest of Earth*, p. 243.

"the highest level of social intelligence": Wilson, *Of Ants and Men*.

"act together in achieving a common goal": Wilson, *The Social Conquest of Earth*, p. 228.

266 "The opposition has no chance": Wilson, *Of Ants and Men*.

"By long-range planning": Wilson, *The Social Conquest of Earth*, p. 214.

"'We will all stand together'": Wilson, *The Social Conquest of Earth*, p. 157.

267 "Communication gives us the amazing capacity": Wilson, *Of Ants and Men*.

"extensions of the [leader]": Wilson, *The Social Conquest of Earth*, p. 143.

"The ability to read each other's intentions": Wilson, *Of Ants and Men*.

"avoidance of extremes": *Chicago Tribune*, May 16, 1860.

268 *"In the Cabinet and the field"*: *Chicago Tribune*, January 29, 1865 (reprint).

"A substitution of one allele": Wilson, *The Social Conquest of Earth*, p. 151.

269 *"I fear this loses you the middle position"*: July 13, 1863, CW, vol. 6, p. 326.

"If both factions, or neither": May 27, 1863, vol. 6, p. 234.

270 "The victory can never be complete": Wilson, *The Social Conquest of Earth*, p. 243.

"the most important branch of national resources": December 6, 1864, CW, vol. 8, p. 150.

271 "If A can prove": April 1, 1854, CW, vol. 2, p. 222.

"in all cases to do right": August 16, 1837, CW, vol. 1, p. 94.

"The true rule": June 20, 1848, CW, vol. 1, p. 484.

"I think it cannot be shown": Goodwin, p. 552.

"There is something else there": Whitman, p. 44.

272 *"a good Christian woman"*: Herndon and Weik, vol. 1, p. 27.

273 *"Opposition to [slavery] is founded"*: October 16, 1854, CW, vol. 2, p. 271.

"If slavery is not wrong": April 4, 1864, CW, vol. 7, p. 281.

"great moral victory": February 1, 1865, CW, vol. 8, p. 255.

"They are just what we would be": October 16, 1854, CW, vol. 2, p. 255.

"leaving the higher matter": July 31, 1846, CW, vol. 1, p. 383.

"like so many fish": September 27, 1841, CW, vol. 1, p. 260.

274 *"which may achieve and cherish"*: March 4, 1865, CW, vol. 8, p. 333.

"kind to everybody and everything": Holzer, *Lincoln as I Knew Him*, p. 16.

"I am a patient man": July 26, 1862, CW, vol. 5, p. 343.

"no motive of revenge": March 18, 1864, CW, vol. 7, p. 255.

"the better angels of our nature": March 4, 1861, CW, vol. 4, p. 271.

275 "With malice toward none": March 4, 1865, CW, vol. 8, p. 333.

"the milk of human kindness": Holzer, *Lincoln as I Knew Him*, p. 140.

"magnanimity is almost superhuman": Seward, vol. 1, p. 575.

"Do good to those who hate you": Herndon and Weik, vol. 3, p. 514.

276 *"Presidential chin-fly"*: Hertz, p. 226.

"always treated me with such personal kindness": Goodwin, p. 566.

"Be good to one another": Herndon and Weik, vol. 1, p. 27.

Finale

277 *"belongs to the ages"*: Donald, *Lincoln*, p. 599.

"Then I am glad he has gone there": Carpenter, p. 293.

"one long step removed from being honest men": January 11, 1837, *CW*, vol. 1, p. 66.

278 *"some man, some faction, [or] some interest"*: August 17, 1858, *CW*, vol. 2, p. 546.

279 Before returning to Washington: Carpenter, pp. 287–289.

Bibliography

★ ★ ★

Angle, Paul M. *Abraham Lincoln by Some Men Who Knew Him.* Chicago: Americana House, 1950.

Arnold, Isaac N. *The Life of Abraham Lincoln.* Chicago: A. C. McClurg, 1901.

Barrett, Joseph H. *Abraham Lincoln and His Presidency.* 2 vols. Cincinnati: Robert Clarke, 1903.

Basler, Roy P., ed. *The Collected Works of Abraham Lincoln.* 8 vols. New Brunswick, N.J.: Rutgers University Press, 1953–1955. In the notes, coded as *CW*.

Bates, David Homer. *Lincoln in the Telegraph Office: Recollections of the United States Military Telegraph Corps During the Civil War.* New York: Century, 1907.

Bayne, Julia Taft. *Tad Lincoln's Father.* Boston: Little, Brown, 1931.

Beale, Howard K., ed. *The Diary of Edward Bates, 1859–1866.* Washington, D.C.: U.S. Government Printing Office, 1933.

Boritt, Gabor S. *Lincoln and the Economics of the American Dream.* Memphis: Memphis State University Press, 1978.

Brooks, Noah. *Washington in Lincoln's Time.* New York: Century, 1896.

Burlingame, Michael. *With Lincoln in the White House: Letters, Memoranda and Other Writings of John G. Nicolay, 1860–1865.* Carbondale: Southern Illinois University Press, 2000.

———. *At Lincoln's Side: John Hay's Civil War Correspondence and Selected Writings.* Carbondale: Southern Illinois University Press, 2006.

Burlingame, Michael, and John R. Turner Ettlinger. *Inside Lincoln's White House: The Complete Civil War Diary of John Hay.* Carbondale: Southern Illinois University Press, 1999.

Carpenter, Francis B. *Six Months at the White House with Abraham Lincoln.* New York: Hurd and Houghton, 1866.

Dahlgren, Madeleine Vinton. *Memoir of John A. Dahlgren.* Boston: James R. Osgood, 1882.

Depew, Chauncey M. *My Memories of Eighty Years.* New York: Charles Scribner's Sons, 1922.

Donald, David Herbert, ed. *Inside Lincoln's Cabinet: The Civil War Diaries of Salmon P. Chase*. New York: Longmans, Green, 1954.

———. *Lincoln*. New York: Simon and Schuster, 1995.

Douglass, Frederick. *Oration by Frederick Douglass*. Washington, D.C.: Gibson Brothers, 1876.

Gardner, William. *Life of Stephen A. Douglas*. Boston: Roxburgh Press, 1905.

Goodwin, Doris Kearns. *Team of Rivals: The Political Genius of Abraham Lincoln*. New York: Simon and Schuster, 2005.

Grant, Ulysses S. *Personal Memoirs of U. S. Grant*. 2 vols. New York: Charles L. Webster, 1886.

Guelzo, Allen C. *Lincoln and Douglas: The Debates That Defined America*. New York: Simon and Schuster, 2008.

Hamlin, Charles Eugene. *The Life and Times of Hannibal Hamlin*. Cambridge, Mass.: Riverside Press, 1899.

Helm, Katherine. *Mary, Wife of Lincoln*. New York: Harper and Brothers, 1928.

Herndon William H., and Jesse W. Weik. *Abraham Lincoln: The True Story of a Great Life*. 3 vols. Springfield, Ill.: Herndon's Lincoln Publishing Company, 1921.

Hertz, Emmanuel. *Lincoln Talks: A Biography in Anecdote*. New York: Halcyon House, 1939.

Hobson, J. T. *Footprints of Abraham Lincoln*. Dayton, Ohio: Otterbein Press, 1909.

Holzer, Harold, ed. *Lincoln as I Knew Him*. Chapel Hill, N.C.: Algonquin Books, 2009.

———. *Lincoln and the Power of the Press*. New York: Simon and Schuster, 2014.

Jones, Thomas D. *Memories of Lincoln*. New York: Press of the Pioneers, 1934.

Julian, George W. *Political Recollections, 1840 to 1872*. Chicago: Jansen, McClurg, 1884.

Keckley, Elizabeth. *Behind the Scenes*. New York: G. W. Carleton, 1868.

Lamon, Ward Hill. *The Life of Abraham Lincoln from His Birth to His Inauguration as President*. Boston: James R. Osgood, 1872.

———. *Recollections of Abraham Lincoln, 1847–1865*. Chicago: A. C. McClurg, 1895.

Lester, C. Edwards. *Life and Public Services of Charles Sumner*. New York: United States Publishing Co., 1874.

Lincoln, Abraham. *Political Debates Between Hon. Abraham Lincoln and Hon. Stephen A. Douglas*. Columbus, Ohio: Follett, Foster, 1860.

MacChesney, Nathan William, ed. *Abraham Lincoln: The Tribute of a Century*. Chicago: A. C. McClurg, 1910.

McBride, Robert W. *Personal Recollections of Abraham Lincoln*. Indianapolis: Bobbs-Merrill, 1926.

McClure, Alexander K. *Abe Lincoln's Yarns and Stories*. Philadelphia: Neil/Winston, 1901.

McClure, J. B., ed. *Abraham Lincoln's Stories and Speeches*. Chicago: Rhodes and McClure, 1896.

Miller, William Lee. *Lincoln's Virtues: An Ethical Biography*. New York: Vintage Books, 2002.

———. *President Lincoln: The Duty of a Statesman*. New York: Vintage Books, 2009.

Mitgang, Herbert. *Abraham Lincoln: A Press Portrait*. E-book. Open Road Distribution, 2015. Originally published New York: Fordham University Press, 1957.

Morgan, James. *Abraham Lincoln: The Boy and the Man*. New York: Macmillan, 1908.

Neely, Mark E., Jr. *The Fate of Liberty: Abraham Lincoln and Civil Liberties*. New York: Oxford University Press, 1991.

Nichols, David A. *Lincoln and the Indians: Civil War Policy and Politics*. Urbana: University of Illinois Press, 1978.

Nicolay, Helen. *Personal Traits of Abraham Lincoln*. New York: Century, 1912.

Nicolay, John G., and John Hay. *Abraham Lincoln: A History*. 10 vols. New York: Century, 1890.

Pease, T. C., and James G. Randall, eds. *The Diary of Orville Hickman Browning*. 2 vols. Springfield: Illinois State Historical Library, 1925.

Phillips, Isaac N., ed. *Abraham Lincoln by Some Men Who Knew Him*. Bloomington, Ill.: Pantagraph Printing and Stationery, 1910.

Pierce, Edward L., ed. *Memoir and Letters of Charles Sumner*. Vol. 4. Boston: Roberts Brothers, 1893.

Randall, James G. *Lincoln the President*. 4 vols. New York: Dodd, Mead, 1945.

Raymond, Henry J. *The Life and Public Services of Abraham Lincoln*. New York: Derby and Miller, 1865.

Rice, Allen Thorndike. *Reminiscences of Abraham Lincoln by Distinguished Men of His Time*. New York: North American, 1886.

Rothschild, Alonzo. *Lincoln, Master of Men: A Study in Character*. Boston: Houghton Mifflin, 1906.

Sandburg, Carl. *Abraham Lincoln: The War Years*. 4 vols. New York: Harcourt, Brace, and World, 1936–1939.

Schurz, Carl. *The Reminiscences of Carl Schurz*, 3 vols. New York: McClure, 1907.

Sears, Stephen W., ed. *The Civil War Papers of George B. McClellan: Selected Correspondence, 1860–1865*. New York: Da Capo Press, 1992.

Segal, Charles M., ed. *Conversations with Lincoln*. New York: G. P. Putnam's Sons, 1961.

Selby, Paul. *Lincoln's Life Stories and Speeches*. Chicago: John R. Stanton, 1901.

Seward, Frederick W. *Seward at Washington as Senator and Secretary of State*. 2 vols. New York: Derby and Miller, 1891.

Sherman, William T. *Memoirs of General William T. Sherman*. 2 vols. E-book. 2 vols. Project Gutenberg, 2006. Originally published New York: D. Appleton, 1886.

Sparks, Edwin Erle. *The Lincoln-Douglas Debates of 1858*. Vol. 3. Springfield, Ill.: Trustees of the Illinois State Historical Library, 1908.

Stimmel, Smith. *Personal Reminiscences of Abraham Lincoln*. Minneapolis: William H. M. Adams, 1928.

Tarbell, Ida M. *The Life of Abraham Lincoln.* 4 vols. New York: Doubleday and McClure, 1900.

Thomas, Benjamin P. *Abraham Lincoln: A Biography.* Carbondale: Southern Illinois University Press, 2008. Originally published 1952.

Villard, Henry. *Memoirs of Henry Villard, Journalist and Financier, 1835–1900.* 2 vols. Boston: Houghton Mifflin, 1904.

Ward, William Hayes, ed. *Abraham Lincoln: Tributes from His Associates.* Boston: Thomas Y. Crowell, 1895.

Weed, Harriet A., ed. *Autobiography of Thurlow Weed.* 2 vols. Boston: Houghton Mifflin, 1883.

Welles, Gideon. *Diary of Gideon Welles.* 3 vols. Boston: Houghton Mifflin, 1911.

White, Horace. *Abraham Lincoln in 1854.* Springfield: Illinois State Historical Society, 1908.

Whitman, Walt. *Specimen Days and Collect.* Glasgow: Wilson and McCormick, 1883.

Whitney, Henry C. *Life on the Circuit with Lincoln.* Boston: Estes and Lauriat, 1892.

Williams, T. Harry. *Lincoln and His Generals.* New York: Alfred A. Knopf, 1952.

Wilson, Douglas L., and Rodney O. Davis, eds. *Herndon's Informants: Letters, Interviews, and Statements About Abraham Lincoln.* Urbana: University of Illinois Press, 1997.

———, eds. *Herndon on Lincoln: Letters.* Urbana: University of Illinois Press, 2016.

Wilson, Edward O. *The Social Conquest of Earth.* New York: Liveright, 2012.

———. *Of Ants and Men.* PBS Documentary. Shining Red Production Company, 2015.

Zall, P. M. *Abe Lincoln Laughing.* Berkeley: University of California Press, 1982.

Zane, Charles S. "Lincoln as I Knew Him." *Journal of the Illinois State Historical Society* 14, no. 1–2 (April–July 1921): 74–84.

Index

★ ★ ★

abolition and abolitionists. *See also* emancipation; Emancipation Proclamation
    Frémont's emancipation order, 134–35
    Great Britain, 130
    Hunter's emancipation order, 134–35
    Lincoln's pragmatism, 32, 54–57, 178–81, 190, 243–45
    Missouri, 135, 137
    13th Amendment, 63, 191, 243, 245–49, 250, 255–56
    Washington, D.C., 151, 244
abortion, 259
access to information, 50–51
"An Act to Encourage Immigration" (1865), 217, 222
Adams, John, 10
Adams, John Quincy, 27
Aesop's fables, 103
Africa, colonization of freed slaves, 179–80
African Americans. *See* blacks
Agassiz, Louis, 43
agriculture, 82–83, 95, 149, 150
al-Assad, Bashar, 35
al-Qaeda, 34, 125, 175
Alabama, secession, 99
Albany, New York, 104
alcohol and alcoholism, 68–69, 79–80
Alley, John B., 246, 248–49
Alton, Illinois, 74–75, 76
altruism, 264–65, 268, 270
American Woman Suffrage Association, 252

Anderson, Major, 112–14
Antietam, Battle of, 162, 173, 186
Appomattox, Virginia, 254
Arab Spring, 35
Arizona, acquired from Mexico, 30
Arkansas, secession and readmittance, 118, 213
Atlanta, Georgia, 236

Bad Axe, Battle of, 9
Bailey, David, 46–47
Bailey v. Cromwell, 47
Baker, Edward, 25, 32
balanced budget, 156–57
Baltimore American, 132–33
Baltimore, Maryland
    assassination plot, 106
    Civil War, 112, 115, 116, 122, 125
    Republican National Convention (1864), 229–30
Bank of the United States, 14
banking system, 14, 17, 147–48, 150, 154
Banks, Nathaniel, 218
Bates, Edward
    as attorney general, 101–2, 119, 141–42, 144
    Civil War, 119, 137
    praise for Lincoln, 263
    presidential campaign (1860), 90
battles
    Antietam, 162, 173, 186
    Bad Axe, 9
    Bull Run (First), 121–22
    Bull Run (Second), 186

battles (*cont.*)
  Chancellorsville, 192–94
  Cold Harbor, 229
  Fort Wagner, 198
  Fredericksburg, 166–67
  Gettysburg, 200
  Shiloh, 69
  Wilderness, 228
  Wilson's Creek, 134
Beauregard, P.G.T., 114, 121
Bell, John, 98
Bible
  Judgment of the Nations, 6–7, 273
  Lincoln's knowledge and use of, 1, 4,
    5–6, 45, 70, 130, 172, 272, 274–75
big business, 95–96
big government, 154–55
bin Laden, Osama, 34
Black Hawk (Sauk Chief), 8–9
Black Hawk War, 8–9
blacks. *See also* slavery
  citizenship, 60, 63
  New York draft riots, 201
  shootings by police, 223–24
  in Union army, 197–98, 202–3
  voting rights, 60, 255–56, 258–59
Blaine, James G., 218
Blair, Francis P., Sr., 248
Blair, Montgomery, 101–2, 143, 144
"blind memorandum," 227, 237–38
Bogan, West, 212
Booth, John Wilkes, 277
border states, 113, 132, 133–37, 177, 178
Breckinridge, John C., 59, 98
Brooks, Noah, 210
Brooks, Preston, 62
Brown, David, 224
Browning, Orville, 166
Bryant, William Cullen, 85
Buchanan, James, 59, 106, 108, 143
budget deficits, 156
Bull Run, First Battle of, 121–22
Bull Run, Second Battle of, 186
Burns, Robert, 42
Burnside, Ambrose E., 133, 166–67, 196–97
Bush, George W., 34, 125–26, 138, 175
business, Lincoln on leadership for today,
  93, 95–96

Butterfield, Justin, 32–33
Byron, Lord, 42

cabinet
  appointments, 101–2
  Civil War, 113, 114, 115–16, 144–46
  expansion of federal powers, 151–52
  internal disputes, 141–43, 266
  Lincoln's "blind memorandum," 227,
    237–38
Cairo, Illinois, 122, 133
California
  acquired from Mexico, 26, 30
  international trade, 131
Cameron, Simon
  emancipation proclamation, 178
  presidential campaign (1860), 90
  as secretary of war, 101–2, 114, 141–43,
    163, 174
campaign finance, 75, 78
campaign finance reform, 78–79
Campbell, John A., 250
canals, 11–12, 17, 21
Canisius, Heinrich Theodor, 84
cannabis, 79–80
Carney, William H., 198
Carpenter, Francis B., 170, 188
Cartwright, Peter, 25, 160
Catholic Church, 216
Central America, colonization of freed
  slaves, 179–80
Central Illinois Gazette, 74, 194
Central Pacific (railroad company),
  148–49
Chambers, Robert, 42
Chancellorsville, Battle of, 192–94
Chandler, Zachariah, 215
"Charcoals"(Missouri faction), 135–36
Charles I, King, 200
Charleston Mercury, 268
Charleston, South Carolina, 110, 112–14,
  115, 193, 200
Chase, Salmon P.
  as abolitionist, 134–35
  as chief justice, 253
  Civil War, 116, 166, 212, 275–76
  disloyalty, 227–28, 275–76
  presidential campaign (1860), 90

presidential campaign (1864), 227–28
as secretary of the Treasury, 101–2, 141,
    146, 147, 227, 232, 275–76
and Stanton, 143, 144
Chicago, Illinois, 10, 11–12, 17, 89–90,
    236
Chicago Tribune, 188, 267–68
Cincinnati, Ohio, 104, 122
*Citizens United v. Federal Election Com-
    mission*, 63, 79
citizenship, for blacks, 59–60, 63
City Point, Virginia, 231, 238–39, 279
civil liberties, Lincoln's infringements on,
    117–19
Civil War
    alcohol consumption, 69
    Battle of Antietam, 162, 173, 186
    Battle of Bull Run (First), 121–22
    Battle of Bull Run (Second), 186
    Battle of Chancellorsville, 192–94
    Battle of Cold Harbor, 229
    Battle of Fort Wagner, 198
    Battle of Fredericksburg, 166–67
    Battle of Gettysburg, 200
    Battle of Shiloh, 69
    Battle of the Wilderness, 228
    Battle of Wilson's Creek, 134
    battles, overview of, 167–68
    black soldiers, 197–98
    border states, 113, 132, 133–37, 177,
        178
    casualties and atrocities, 168
    communications, 44
    draft, 197, 201, 206–7, 234
    Fort Sumter, 112–14
    funding, 88, 146–47, 155
    goals, 243–44
    Northern superiority in numbers,
        121–22
    onset, 112–14
    patents filed during, 43
    peace negotiations, 248–50
    prevention efforts, 99–100
    troop morale, 122–23, 231–32, 279–80
    Union blockade of southern coast, 115
    victory, enabling factors, 22, 44
    Virginia campaign, 228–29, 254
classified information, 50–51

Clay, Henry, 10, 264
"Claybanks" (Missouri faction),
    135–36
climate change, 49–50
Cold Harbor, Battle of, 229
Colfax, Schuyler, 228, 254
collective bargaining, 92
colonization of freed slaves, 179–80
Colorado, acquired from Mexico, 30
Columbus, Ohio, 104
communications
    international, 131–32
    telegraph, 43–44, 50, 116, 117, 131,
        148–49
Compensated Emancipation Act (1862),
    151, 179, 244
Confederate States of America
    draft, 197
    flag, 107, 109–11
    foreign recognition of, 131
    formation, 99, 103
    president, 103, 104–5
    purpose, 109
    reconstruction, 213–15
    Union blockade of coast, 115
    vice president, 104
    white supremacy, 106
Congress, U.S.
    Civil War, 120, 124
    expansion of federal powers, 151–52
    gridlock, Lincoln's breaking of, 246–49
    House Judiciary Committee, 174
    House Select Committee on Govern-
        ment Contracts, 163
    investigative committees, 173–74
    Joint Committee on the Conduct of the
        War, 163, 174
    legislation, Civil War-era, 146–50
    Lincoln's presidential addresses to, 89,
        170–71, 233
    lobbyists, 95–96, 151–52
    lucrative job offers after service in,
        38–39
    midterm elections (1862), 165–66
    reapportionment of districts, 240–41
    reconstruction, 213–15
    13th Amendment, 245–49, 250
Congressional Research Service, 96

Conkling, James C., 202–3
Constitution, U.S.
    1st Amendment, 63
    2nd Amendment, 126–27
    10th Amendment, 110
    13th Amendment, 63, 191, 243, 245–49,
        250, 255–56
    14th Amendment, 63
    15th Amendment, 258
    16th Amendment, 146
    18th Amendment, 258
    19th Amendment, 258, 260
    22nd Amendment, 37
    government structure, 272
    health insurance mandate, 64
    slavery, 59–60, 63, 85
Constitutional Union Party, 98
Cooper Institute, New York, 85–86, 262
Corning, Erastus, 199
corporate taxes, 155–56
cotton, 18, 215
crises, immediate and severe, 109
Crittenden Compromise, 100, 244
Crittenden, John J., 99, 100
Cromwell estate, 46–47
currency, 147

Dahlgren, John A., 200
Dallas, Texas, 224
Danville, Illinois, 104
Darwin, Charles, 42, 49
Davis, David, 89
Davis, Henry Winter, 214–15
Davis, Jefferson, 103, 104, 235, 248
Dayton, William L., 58–59
death penalty, 221–22
Decatur, Illinois, 90–91
Declaration of Independence, 4, 6, 60, 91,
    105, 217, 272
Delaware, emancipation, 179
Democratic Party
    and Emancipation Proclamation, 186
    in Illinois, 10
    and labor unions, 92
    midterm elections (1862), 163–64,
        165–66
    opposition to suspension of habeas cor-
        pus, 119

political attacks on Lincoln, 196–97,
    198–99, 200–202
presidential election (1860), 97–98
presidential election (1864), 232, 236–37
selfishness, 268
stance on issues, 10
Union Army officers, 162–63, 173
Democratic Review (newspaper), 26
Department of Agriculture, 149
Department of Defense, 126. See also War
    Department
Department of Homeland Security,
    125–26
Department of State, 138
Department of the Gulf, 218
Department of the Interior, 148–49
Department of the South, 178
Department of the Treasury, 146–47. See
    also Internal Revenue Service
Department of the West, 134, 178
Department of Veterans Affairs, 151, 158
Depot Field Hospital, City Point, Virginia,
    279–80
"Discoveries and Inventions" (Lincoln's
    speech), 44–45
District of Columbia. See Washington,
    D.C.
domestic terrorism, 125–26
Douglas, Adele, 106
Douglas, Stephen A.
    alcohol consumption, 69–70
    death, 119–20
    debates with Lincoln, 17, 66–76, 83–84,
        207, 209, 244
    friendship with Lincoln, 67–68, 106
    in Illinois state legislature, 12
    Kansas-Nebraska Act, 53, 59
    Lincoln's inauguration, 106
    physical appearance, 67
    presidential campaign (1860), 98
    on racial purity, 71–72
    on slavery, 71–72, 85
    slavery legislation, 48, 53, 61, 66
    U.S. Senate campaigns, 61, 66–76
    on white basis of government, 66,
        71–72
Douglass, Frederick, 180, 187, 243–44,
    257, 271

Dover, New Hampshire, 86–87
draft, 197, 201, 206–7, 234
Dred Scott decision, 59–61, 63, 70, 244
drug addiction, 80
Du Pont, Samuel, 193

Early, Jubal, 234
Eckert, Thomas, 165, 176–77
economic crises. *See* recessions
economic development
    current controversies, 21
    Kansas-Nebraska Act, 53
    Lincoln on leadership for today, 21
    Lincoln's work on, in state legislature,
        11–19
    postwar, 254–55
Edmundson, Henry A., 62
education, 23, 83, 149, 150
18th Amendment, 258
Eighth Judicial Circuit, 41–42, 81, 251
elections
    corporate spending, 63
    fall elections (1863), 201–3
    Lincoln on leadership for today, 240–41
    midterm elections (1862), 163–64,
        165–66, 186
    national election process, 240–41
    presidential election (1860), 83–85,
        89–91, 97–98, 269
    presidential election (1864), 226–33,
        236–37
Electoral College, 240, 269
emancipation
    Delaware (proposed), 179
    District of Columbia, 151, 179, 244
    Frémont's order, 134–35
    Hunter's order, 134–35
Emancipation Proclamation
    donation of copies for fundraising,
        230–31
    introduction to border states, 177, 178
    introduction to cabinet, 177, 181
    issuance of, 151, 186–88, 245
    Lincoln's defense of, 202, 233
    as military necessity, 176, 177, 181, 187
    text of, 176, 187
    timing of, 180–81, 184–86
    writing process, 165, 176–77

Emanuel African Methodist Episcopal
        Church, Charleston, South Caro-
        lina, 110
England. *See* Great Britain
Enrollment Act (1863), 197
Equal Pay Act (1963), 260
Equal Rights Amendment, 260
equality, gender, 250–53
equality, racial, 251–52
Euclid, 42, 46
Europe, "People's Spring" revolutions
        (1848), 30, 35
excise taxes, 146, 155
executive orders, 124–25
extremism, 139–40

factions, 139–40
Fair Labor Standards Act (1938), 93
farming, 82–83, 95, 149, 150
Farragut, David, 236
Federal Election Commission, 63
federal government, big vs. small, 154–55
Ferguson, Missouri, 223–24
Fessenden, William P., 146, 232
Ficklin, O. B., 72
15th Amendment, 258
Financial Panic (1837), 14–16, 21, 150
Financial Panic (1857), 21, 107, 156
1st Amendment, 63
Florida
    emancipation of slaves, 134
    secession, 99
foreign affairs. *See* international relations
Forney, John W., 184
Fort McHenry, 118–19
Fort Monroe, 122, 123, 248
Fort Stevens, 234
Fort Sumter, 112–14, 193, 203
Fort Wagner, 198
Fort Warren, 129
Founding Fathers
    checks and balances, 272
    Electoral College, 240
    Lincoln on, 91
    politics and the military, 173
    2nd Amendment, 127
    stance on slavery, 85
14th Amendment, 63

France
    efforts to control Mexico, 35, 36, 131
    and U.S. Civil War, 129, 131
Frankfurt, Kentucky, 133
Franklin & Armfield (slave trading com-
    pany), 31–32
Fredericksburg, Battle of, 166–67
free labor, 20
free speech, 63
free trade, 18, 22–23. See also international
    trade
Frémont, John C., 58–59, 134, 135, 176,
    178, 230

Galesburg, Illinois, 73
Gamble, Hamilton, 134
gender equality, 250–52, 258
Geneva Conventions, 169, 174–75
Georgia
    emancipation of slaves, 134
    secession, 99
gerrymandering, 240–41
Gettysburg Address, 204
Gettysburg, Battle of, 200
GOP (Grand Old Party). See Republi-
    can Party
Gordon, Nathaniel, 212
Government Accountability Office, 96
Grand Old Party (GOP). See Republi-
    can Party
Grant, Ulysses S.
    and Civil War peace negotiations, 248
    command of all Union armies, 228, 267
    drunkenness, 69
    Kentucky defenses, 133
    Lee's surrender, 254
    meeting with Lincoln, Sherman, and
        Porter, 253–54
    Mississippi campaign, 193, 195, 200
    praise for Lincoln, 263
    Virginia campaign, 228–29, 231, 234,
        238–39
Great Britain
    Atlantic slave trade, suppression of, 130
    Seward-Lyons Treaty, 130
    and U.S. Civil War, 128–31, 138
Great Central Fair, Philadelphia, Pennsyl-
    vania, 230–31

Great Depression, 92
Great Recession (2007–2009), 22, 156
Greeley, Horace, 85, 86, 185, 235–36
"greenbacks" (national paper currency),
    147
gridlock, Lincoln's breaking of, 246–49
gun control, 126–27
Gurley, Phineas D., 161, 169
Gurney, Eliza, 170

habeas corpus, suspension of writ of,
    118–19, 124, 132
Habeas Corpus Suspension Act (1863), 119
Haiti, U.S. recognition of, 132
Halleck, Henry, 162, 168–69, 173, 175,
    193–95
Hamlin, Hannibal, 97–98, 106, 230
Hampton Roads Peace Conference,
    248–49, 249–50
Hanks, Dennis, 1, 3
Hanks, John, 90
Hardin, John J., 24–25, 32
Harrisburg, Pennsylvania, 106
Hartford, Connecticut, 81, 87
Hay, John
    on Lincoln's ability to delegate, 146
    Lincoln's "blind memorandum," 237
    Lincoln's concerns about attack on
        Washington, D.C., 117
    Lincoln's dismissal of Key, 163
    on Lincoln's pardoning of condemned
        soldiers, 211, 212
    on Lincoln's stoicism, 121
    Niagara Falls peace conference, 235–36
    presidential campaign (1864), 227
health care, 64–65
Helm, Benjamin Hardin, 209
Helm, Emilie Todd, 209–10
Helm, Katherine, 209–10
Herndon, William
    on Lincoln and gender equality, 251,
        260
    on Lincoln and newspaper men, 74
    on Lincoln's friendship with Doug-
        las, 68
    on Lincoln's interest in science, 42
    as Lincoln's law partner, 38, 46
    Lincoln's political career, 29, 32, 70

History of the Administration of Abraham Lincoln (Raymond), 232–33
Homestead Act (1862), 148
honesty and fairness, 47, 51
Hooker, Joe, 167, 192–94, 194–95, 200
"House Divided" speech, 70–71
human nature, Lincoln on, 182–83, 262, 263–65
Hungary, independence movement, 35
Hunter, David, 134, 135, 178
Hunter, Robert M. T., 249–50
Hussein, Saddam, 34

idealism vs. reality, 190–91
Illinois
    economic development, 11–19
    Eighth Judicial Circuit, 41–42, 81, 251
    Financial Panic (1837), 14–15
    House of Representatives, 10, 11–19
    infrastructure, 11–19, 215–16
    Republican Party, 58, 90–91
    state capital, 68
    tax laws, 8, 15–16, 150
Illinois and Michigan Canal, 11–12, 17
Illinois Central Railroad, 215–16
Illinois Republican State Convention (1860), 90–91
Illinois Staats-Anzeiger (State Advertiser), 84–85
Illinois State Bank, 13–14, 16
Illinois State Journal, 56, 91
Illinois Supreme Court, 47
immigration, 124–25, 215–17, 222–23
income inequality, 93–94, 223, 224
income tax, 146, 155–56
Indiana
    Civil War forces, 114
    midterm elections (1862), 165
Indianapolis, Indiana, 104
Industrial Revolution, 217
inequality, 93–94
information, access to, 50–51
intelligence operations, 126
Internal Revenue Service (IRS), 146, 155–56
international relations. *See also* Mexican-American War
    Lincoln on leadership for today, 138–39

Lincoln's nonintervention policy, 24, 29–30, 34–35, 36
tariffs, 18, 22–23, 147, 150
international trade, 18, 22–23, 130, 131, 138
Internet, 50–51
inventions. *See* technology
Iran, arms negotiations, 138
Iraq War, 34–35
Irish American immigrants, 201, 206, 216
IRS (Internal Revenue Service), 146, 155–56
ISIS/ISIL, 35, 125
isolationism, 139

Jackson, Andrew, 10, 14, 15, 17, 59, 147
Jackson, Claiborne, 133
Jackson, Stonewall, 121, 167, 194
James, Benjamin F., 24–25
Jefferson City, Missouri, 133
Jefferson, Thomas, 10, 160
Johnson, Andrew, 197–98, 230
Johnston, John D. (stepbrother), 19
Jones, Thomas D., 101

Kansas-Nebraska Act, 53, 58, 70, 244
Kansas, slavery, 48
Keitt, Laurence, 62
Kentucky, as border state, 113, 132, 133, 134
Key, John J., 162–63
Knight, Henry W., 213
Know-Nothings. *See* Native American Party
Korea, North, arms negotiations, 138

labor and labor movements, 81, 82–83, 87–89, 92–93, 250–52
Lafayette, Indiana, 104
Lamon, Ward Hill, 89
Land-Grant College Act (1862), 149
Lawrence, Kansas, 136
Lawrenceburg, Indiana, 104
lawyers and legal profession, 51
leadership attributes, 262–64, 265
learning, 45, 83
Lebanon, Indiana, 104
Lee, Robert E.
    Battle of Antietam, 162, 173, 186
    Battle of Chancellorsville, 192–94

Lee, Robert E. (*cont.*)
Battle of Fredericksburg, 167
Battle of Gettysburg, 200
Grant's challenge to, in Virginia,
228–29
as Hooker's objective, 195
joining Confederacy, 116
Pennsylvania campaign, 200
surrender, 254
Legal Tender Act (1862), 147
Legins-Costley, Nance, 46–47
Lester, C. Edwards, 176, 178
*The Letters of President Lincoln on Ques-
tions of National Policy* (Republican campaign pamphlet), 203
Liberia, U.S. recognition of, 132
Lieber Code, 168–69, 175
Lieber, Franz, 168
Lincoln, Abraham, career. *See also* Lincoln, Abraham, presidency
as circuit lawyer, 40–42, 45–46, 81
debates with Douglas, 17, 66–76, 83–84,
207, 209, 244
as Illinois legislative candidate, 8, 9,
10, 251
in Illinois legislature, 10, 11–19, 68
law practice, 29, 32, 33, 38, 45–47
military career, 8–9
Mississippi River trip, 4–5
relationship with press, 73–74, 184–85,
189
Republican Party, 58
in U.S. Congress, 25–33, 72
U.S. Congress, campaign for, 24–25
U.S. Senate, campaigns for, 57–58,
61–62, 66–76
Whig Party, 11
Lincoln, Abraham, Civil War and
authority, 134–35
Battle of Chancellorsville, 192–94
Battle of Fredericksburg, 166–67
black soldiers, 197–98
border states, control of, 132–33, 134–37,
177, 178
Bull Run aftermath, 121–23
citizens' requests for help, 210–11
civil liberties infringements, 117–19,
124, 132

Confederacy, refusal to acknowledge,
106–7
criticism of Lincoln, 117, 167, 173, 196
draft/call for troops, 114–15, 120, 122,
197, 201, 206, 234
Enrollment Act, 197
executive actions, 115, 117–19, 124–25
foreign affairs, 129–32, 138
Fort Sumter, 112–14
General War Order No. 11, 136
General War Order No. 100, 168–69
generals, 162, 166–67, 200
goals, 243–44
habeas corpus, suspension of writ of,
118–20, 124, 132
and Hooker, 194–95, 200
insurgencies, 125
meeting with Grant, Sherman, and
Porter, 253–54
mitigating cruelty, 168
pardons for deserters, 211–12, 220, 221,
255
peace negotiations, 249–50
Proclamation of Amnesty and Reconstruction, 214
surrender conditions, 253–54
Trent affair, 129
Virginia campaigns, 228–29
visiting Grant at City Point, Virginia,
238–39
visiting soldiers, 122–23, 231–32, 279–80
War Department dispatches, 164–65
Lincoln, Abraham, criticism of
Civil War, 117, 167, 173, 196
partisan attacks, 196–97, 198–99,
200–202, 207
by press, 166
refuting, 72–73, 199, 200–201, 202–3, 208
Lincoln, Abraham, Emancipation Proclamation and
defense of, 202, 233
donation of copies for fundraising,
230–31
introduction to border states, 177, 178
introduction to cabinet, 177, 181
issuance of, 151, 186–88, 245
as military necessity, 176, 177, 181, 187
text of, 176, 187

timing of, 180–81, 184–86
writing process, 165, 176–77
Lincoln, Abraham, family life
boyhood and teenage years, 1–4
children, 47–48, 128
Mary's Confederate relatives, 209–10
Willie's death, 159–62, 169–70
Lincoln, Abraham, leadership attributes
anticipation, 267
balancing opposing factions, 268–70
breaking Congressional gridlock,
246–49
delegation, 146, 267
development of, 263, 271–75
family-like culture, 266–67
firmness and conviction, 17, 116–17
humanitarianism, 270–71, 272
instilling loyalty, 144–45
long-term planning, 218, 266
posterity, 278
praise for, 267–68
seeing issues from both sides, 87
teamwork, 266
Lincoln, Abraham, leadership for today
abortion, 259
alcohol, 79–80
balanced budget, 156–57
balancing extreme factions, 139–40
big business, 94–95
big vs. small federal government, 154–55
campaign finance reform, 78–79
climate change, 49–50
Confederate flag, 109–11
congressional investigative committees, 173–74
crisis management, 109
death penalty, 221–22
domestic terrorism, 125–26
draft, 206–7
economic development, 21
education, 23
Electoral College, 240
foreign affairs, 138–39
free trade, 22–23
gerrymandering, 240–41
gun control, 126–27
health care, 64–65
immigration, 222–23

income inequality, 93–94
influence of press in national affairs,
241–42
information, access to, 50–51
international relations, 138–39
Internet, 50–51
IRS, 155–56
labor and labor movements, 92–93
lawyers and legal profession, 51
legalization of marijuana, 79–80
lobbying, 94–95
military intervention, 34–36
minimum wage, 93–94
national debt, 156–57
national election process, 240–41
partisan political attacks, 207–8
political idealism vs. political reality,
190–91
politics and the military, 173
presidential executive orders, 124–25
public opinion polls, 189–90
race relations, 223–25
recessions, 21–22
religion and politics, 172
science, 49–50
tariffs, 22–23
taxes, 155–56
technology, 50–51
term limits, 36–38
torture and Geneva Conventions, 174–75
24-hour news cycle, 77–78, 208
unpopular Supreme Court decisions,
63–64
veterans affairs, 157–58
voting rights for minorities, 258–59
women's rights, 260–61
Lincoln, Abraham, personal traits
altruism, 270–71
deliberation, 26
firmness and conviction, 17, 116–17,
121–22
graciousness in defeat, 57–58
honesty and fairness, 47, 51
humanitarianism, 270–71, 272
innate goodness, 274–76
on keeping calm, 97
kindness and compassion, 210–12,
262–63, 274–76

Lincoln, Abraham, personal traits (*cont.*)
  love of animals, 2
  love of learning, 2–3, 4, 42–43
  need to understand things, 2–3
  as peacemaker, 3
  as people person, 89, 102–3, 210–11,
      270–71
  physical appearance, 67, 81–82, 86–87,
      262
  physical strength, 3–4, 123, 164, 195–96,
      279–80
  poetry in his nature, 161
  prudence in decision-making, 183,
      190–91
  respect for others, 256–57
  sense of humor, 3, 208
  vices, lack of, 69, 79
Lincoln, Abraham, political and social
    philosophy
  alcohol consumption, 68–70, 79
  banking system, 14, 17, 148, 150, 154
  businesses, support for, 87–88, 93
  as centrist, 139, 268–69
  Declaration of Independence, 4, 6, 60,
      91, 105, 217, 272
  economic development, 11–19, 21
  emancipating the mind, 45
  fair chance for all, 19, 219, 224
  on Founding Fathers, 91
  human nature, 182–83, 262, 263–65
  Kansas-Nebraska Act, 53
  labor issues, 20, 81, 82–83, 87–89, 92–93
  learning, 83
  Manifest Destiny, opposition to, 29–30
  Mexican-American War, opposition to,
      24, 26–30, 32, 34, 72
  national aid for state improvements, 31
  nonintervention, 24, 29–30
  "One War at a Time," 36
  peace, 107
  political parties, 10–11
  public opinion, 181–82, 183–84, 189–90
  race relations, 218–19
  racial equality, 209, 251–52, 255–56, 259
  selfishness, 264–65
  strong federal government, 145, 154–55
  taxes, 8, 15–16, 150
  trade issues, 18, 150

transcontinental railroad, support for,
      21, 150, 154
  veterans, support for, 150–51, 157–58,
      255
  voting rights, 255–56, 258–59
  war, 231
  wealthy paying their share, 15, 16, 18–19
  women's rights, 250–52
Lincoln, Abraham, praise for, 243–44, 257,
      262–63, 267–68, 275
Lincoln, Abraham, presidency
  annual message to Congress, 89,
      170–71, 233
  assassination and attempts, 106, 277
  breaking Congressional gridlock,
      246–49
  cabinet, 101–2, 141–46, 152–53, 232,
      237–38, 266
  crises, 109
  election (1860), 83–85, 89–91, 97–99, 269
  election (1864), 226–33, 236–37
  expansion of federal powers, 151–52, 154
  immigration policies, 216–17
  inaugurations, 106–7, 252–53
  labor and labor unions, 88–89
  pocket vetoes, 215
  postwar economic development plans,
      254–55
  as president-elect, 99–106, 108, 244
  reconstruction plans, 213–15, 218, 256
  relationship with press, 184–85, 189
  secession, reaction to, 99–101, 103
  Supreme Court appointments, 253
  White House guests, 209–10
  White House stable fire, 169
  White House staff, 74
Lincoln, Abraham, religion and
  Bible knowledge and use, 1, 4, 5–6, 45,
      70, 130, 172, 272, 274–75
  spirituality, 160–61, 169–70, 172,
      272–74, 274–75
Lincoln, Abraham, science and technol-
    ogy and
  on discoveries and inventions, 40
  interest in science, 42–43, 49–50
  interest in technology, 40–41, 43–44,
      50–51
  patent, 43

Lincoln, Abraham, slavery and
  beliefs concerning, 5–6, 244
  on *Dred Scott* decision, 59–61, 63, 244
  efforts to eliminate, in U.S. Congress,
    31–32, 244
  efforts to eliminate, 13th Amendment,
    245–49, 250
  efforts to eliminate, while out of office,
    48, 52–57, 59–61, 207
  efforts to eliminate, while president,
    150–51, 170–71, 178–79
  legal cases, 46–47
  Lincoln-Douglas debates, 71–72, 76
  rescinding emancipation orders,
    134–35, 176, 178
  resolve not to compromise, 100, 103
  on slavery as moral issue, 54, 60, 61,
    71–72, 76, 273–74
  speeches against, 56–57, 70–71, 82
  steps toward abolition, 244–45
Lincoln, Abraham, speeches
  annual messages to Congress, 89,
    170–71, 233
  boyhood, 1, 3
  Civil War, 120
  Cooper Institute (1860), 85–86, 262
  "Discoveries and Inventions," 44–45
  Gettysburg Address, 204
  "House Divided," 70–71
  in Illinois state legislature, 13
  inaugural addresses, 106–7, 110, 113,
    252–53
  labor and labor movements, 82–83,
    87–89
  political campaigns, 9
  as president-elect, 104
  on slavery, 56–57, 70–71, 82
  speaking tours, 82–83, 85–86
  in U.S. Congress, 28
Lincoln, Eddie (son), 27, 47–48
Lincoln, Mary Todd (wife)
  Civil War, 121
  complaint about Chase, 275
  family, 47–48, 159–60, 209–10
  on Lincoln's character, 161
  Lincoln's inauguration, 106
  suitors, 68
  in Washington, D.C., 27

Lincoln, Nancy Hanks (mother), 1–2, 6,
  160, 272, 276
Lincoln, Robert (son), 27, 86–87, 106
Lincoln, Sarah (sister), 1
Lincoln, Sarah Bush Johnston (step-
  mother), 2–3, 274
Lincoln, Thomas (father), 1–2
Lincoln, Thomas, III "Tad" (son), 48, 106,
  128, 159, 254, 277
Lincoln, William Wallace "Willie" (son),
  48, 106, 128, 159–62, 169
Littlefield, John H., 170
lobbyists, 38–39, 65, 94–95, 247
Logan, Stephen T., 32, 46
London, Ohio, 104
long-term planning, 266
Louisiana
  readmittance to Union, 213
  reconstruction, 218
  secession, 99
Lovejoy, Owen, 153
Lyell, Charles, 42
Lyon, Nathaniel, 133–34
Lyons, Richard, 130

Maine, Civil War forces, 114
Manassas, Virginia, 121, 122
Manifest Destiny, 26, 29–30
marijuana, legalization of, 79–80
Marshall, John, 10
martial law, 119, 134, 136
Maryland
  as border state, 113, 132–33
  Confederate sympathizers, 115, 118, 119
  secession threat, 119, 133
Mason, James, 129, 131
Massachusetts
  Civil War forces, 114, 115, 117
  New England Shoemakers' Strike
    (1860), 81, 87, 93
McClellan, George B.
  Civil War, 122, 144, 162, 163, 166, 186
  on Emancipation Proclamation, 186
  Lincoln's opinion of, 264
  presidential election (1864), 232, 236–37
  Willie Lincoln's funeral, 161–62
McDowell, Irvin C., 121, 122
Meade, George Gordon, 167, 200

medical services, 64–65
Memphis, Tennessee, 122
Merryman, John, 118–19
Mexican-American War, 24, 25–30, 32, 34, 72
Mexico
  border wall, 222
  Napoleon III's puppet regime, 35, 36, 131
Miami (Treasury cutter), 123
military
  code of conduct, 168–69, 175
  current situation, 206
  international intervention, 24, 26–30, 32–33, 34–36
  Lincoln on leadership for today, 34–36, 173
  and politics, 173
military necessity, Emancipation Proclamation as, 176, 177, 181, 187
Militia Act (1795), 115
Milliken's Bend, Louisiana, 198
Milwaukee, Wisconsin, 82
minimum wage, 93–94
mining industry, 254–55
Minnesota, execution of Sioux, 168
minorities, voting rights for, 258–59
Mississippi River, Southern control of, 107
Mississippi, secession, 99
Missouri
  as border state, 113, 132, 133–37
  factional quarrels, 128, 135–37
Missouri Compromise, 52, 53, 55, 57, 59
Missouri Republican, 74
Mobile, Alabama, 115
Mobile Bay, Alabama, 236
Montgomery, Alabama, 103, 107
Morrill, Justin, 147, 149
Morse, Samuel, 43

Napoleon III (emperor), 35, 131
National Academy of Sciences (NAS), 43, 49
national affairs, influence of press in, 241–42
National Banking Acts (1863 and 1864), 147–48
national banking system, 147–48, 150, 154
national debt, 156–57
national paper currency, 147

National Security Agency (NSA), 126
National Union Party, 229–30, 245
National Woman Suffrage Association, 252
Native American Party (Know-Nothings), 215–16
NATO, 36
Nebraska, slavery, 48
Nevada, acquired from Mexico, 30
New Deal, 92, 93
New England Shoemakers' Strike (1860), 81, 87, 93
New Haven, Connecticut, 87
New Jersey, midterm elections (1862), 165
New Mexico, acquired from Mexico, 26, 30
New York
  Civil War forces, 114, 117
  midterm elections (1862), 165
New York City, draft riots, 201, 206
New York Herald, 166
New York, New York, 85–86, 88
New York Times, 73–74, 117, 166, 184, 199
New York Tribune, 185. *See also* Greeley, Horace
New York Workingmen's Association, 89
New York World, 185
news cycle, 24-hour, 77–78, 208
newspapers
  coverage of Lincoln-Douglas debates, 73–74
  influence in national affairs, 241
  Lincoln's Civil War closure of, 119
  Lincoln's era, 77
  Lincoln's relationship with, 73–74, 184–85, 189
The Next Presidential Election (anonymous pamphlet), 227–28
Niagara Falls peace conference, 235–36
Nicolay, John, 100–101
9/11 terrorist attacks, 175
19th Amendment, 258, 260
North Carolina, secession, 118
North Korea, arms negotiations, 138
NSA (National Security Agency), 126

Obama, Barack, 35, 124–25, 138, 175
Office of the Commissioner of Immigration, 217
On the Origin of Species (Darwin), 42

Oregon international trade, 131
organized labor. *See* labor and labor
    movements
O'Sullivan, John L., 26
Ottawa, Illinois, 67, 69–70, 72, 76

Pacific Railroad Act (1862), 148–49
Paducah, Kentucky, 133
paper currency, 147
partisan political attacks
    current situation, 207–8
    against Lincoln, 196–97, 198–99,
        200–202, 207
    Lincoln on, 192
    Lincoln on leadership for today, 207–8
    Lincoln's defense against, 199, 200–201,
        202–3, 208
patents, 43, 45
Pekin, Illinois, 43–44
Pemberton, John C., 200
Pennsylvania, midterm elections (1862),
    165
"People's Spring" revolutions (1848), 30,
    35
Peoria, Illinois, 56, 244
Petersburg, Virginia, 254
Philadelphia, Pennsylvania, 105, 230–31,
    250–51, 260
Philadelphia Press, 184
Phillips Exeter Academy, Dover, New
    Hampshire, 86–87
Pierce, Franklin, 53, 59
Plato, 275
pocket vetoes, 215
Poe, Edgar Allan, 42
police shootings, 223–24
political campaigns. *See* campaign fi-
    nance; elections
*Political Debates Between Hon. Abra-
    ham Lincoln and Hon. Stephen A.
    Douglas*, 84
political idealism vs. political reality,
    190–91
political parties, 10–11
politics and the military, 173
Polk, James K., 24, 25–30, 31, 34
Pope, John, 162
Port Gibson, Mississippi, 193
Port Hudson, Louisiana, 198

Porter, David, 253–54
postal service, 117
presidency, peaceful transition, 226–27,
    237–38
presidential election (1860), 83–85, 89–91,
    97–98, 269
presidential election (1864), 226–33,
    236–37
presidential executive orders, 124–25
press
    influence in national affairs, 241–42
    Lincoln on leadership for today, 77–78,
        208, 241–42
    Lincoln's relationship with, 73–74,
        184–85, 189
    24-hour news cycle, 77–78, 208
Principles of Geology (Lyell), 42
prisoners of war, 168
Proclamation of Amnesty and Recon-
    struction, 214
prohibition, 68–69, 79
Promontory Summit, Utah, 149
property taxes, 15–16, 150
protective tariffs, 18, 22–23, 147, 150
public opinion, 181–82, 183–84, 189–90

Quantrill's Raiders, 136
Quincy, Illinois, 71, 209

race relations, 109–11, 218–19, 223–25
racial equality, 209, 218–19, 251–52
Radical Republicans, 214–15, 229–30
railroads
    immigrant labor, 215–16
    Lincoln's support for, 11–12, 14–15, 21,
        150, 154
    transcontinental railroad, 21, 53,
        148–49, 150, 154
Rawlings, Mike, 224
Raymond, Henry J., 73–74, 184, 232–33
recessions
    Financial Panic (1837), 14–16, 21, 150
    Financial Panic (1857), 21, 107, 156
    Great Depression, 92
    Great Recession (2007–2009), 22,
        156
    Lincoln on leadership for today, 21–22
reconstruction, 213–16, 218
religion and politics, 160, 172

Republican Party
  altruism, 268
  campaign finance, 75
  Civil War, efforts to prevent, 99
  convention (1860), 89–90
  convention (1864), 229–30
  founding, 58
  immigration policy, 217
  Kansas-Nebraska Act, opposition to, 58
  midterm elections (1862), 163–64,
      165–66, 186
  platform, 82, 245
  presidential campaign (1860), 97
  reconstruction, 213–15
Revenue Acts (1861 and 1862), 146
Richmond, Virginia, 166–67, 254
River Queen (steamer), 250, 253
Roosevelt, Franklin D., 37, 92
Rosecrans, William, 193
Russia
  and Hungary's independence move-
      ment, 35
  Syrian civil war, 35
  U.S. ambassador to, 142

sales taxes, 146, 155
San Jacinto (U.S. warship), 129
Schofield, John M., 128, 135–36, 139, 269
science, Lincoln's interest in, 42–43,
      49–50
Scott, Dred, 59–61
Scott, Winfield, 28, 113, 114, 118, 133, 255
secession of Southern states, 99–101, 103,
      106–7, 118, 119. *See also* Confeder-
      ate States of America
2nd Amendment, 126–27
Second Bank of the United States, 147
selfishness, 264–65, 268, 270
Senate, U.S.
  beating of Sumner, 62
  midterm elections (1862), 165
  Seward-Lyons Treaty, 130
Senate, U.S., campaigns
  Lincoln-Douglas debates, 66–70, 71–73
  Lincoln's, 57–58, 61–62, 66–76
separation of church and state, 160, 172
Seward-Lyons Treaty, 130
Seward, William H.

  and Emancipation Proclamation,
      177–78, 181, 187
  foreign affairs, 130, 138
  Fort Sumter, 113
  on Lincoln as teetotaler, 69
  Lincoln's views on slavery, 100
  on Lincoln's wisdom, 137
  peace negotiations, 248, 249–50
  praise for Lincoln, 263, 275
  presidential campaign (1860), 85, 90–91
  as secretary of state, 101–2, 131, 132,
      141–43, 238
  13th Amendment, lobbying for, 247
  Trent affair, 129
  visiting troops, 122–23
Shakespeare, William, 42
Shenandoah Valley, Virginia, 122, 234, 236
Sheridan, Phil, 234, 236
Sherman, William Tecumseh, 123, 228,
      234, 236, 253–54
Shiloh, Battle of, 69
shoe factories. *See* New England Shoe-
      makers' Strike
Sickles, Daniel, 209–10
Sioux, 168
16th Amendment, 146
slavery. *See also* abolition and abolition-
      ists; Emancipation Proclamation;
      Lincoln, Abraham, slavery and
  Atlantic slave trade, 130, 212
  as cause for secession, 99–100, 106
  colonization of freed slaves, 179–80
  Confederate support of, 103, 109
  containment efforts, 55, 61
  dividing country, 53
  Douglas's efforts to perpetuate, 48, 53,
      61, 66, 71–72, 85
  Dred Scott decision, 59–61, 63
  economic aspects, 54–55
  emancipation orders, rescinded, 134–
      35, 176, 178
  Founding Fathers' stance on, 85
  Kansas-Nebraska Act, 53–54
  Lincoln-Douglas debates, 71–72, 76
  as moral problem, 54, 60, 61, 71–72, 76,
      130, 273–74
  in new territories, 25–26, 31, 52–53
  public opinion concerning, 54, 55–57

spread of, 48, 53–54
13th Amendment, 63, 191, 243, 245–49,
    250, 255–56
Washington, D.C., 31–32, 151
Slidell, John, 129, 131
Smith, Caleb B., 101–2, 148
Smithsonian Institution, 42
Soldiers' Home, 42
South Carolina
    emancipation of slaves, 134
    secession, 98, 99
Southern states. *See also* Confederate
        States of America
    pride and culture, 109–11
    reaction to Lincoln's election, 98–99
    reconstruction, 213–15
Spotsylvania, Virginia, 228
Springfield, Illinois, 68, 70, 84–85, 244
Stanton, Edwin M.
    as attorney general, 143
    disposition, 143–44
    on Lincoln's death, 277
    on Lincoln's reconstruction plans, 256
    as secretary of war, 143–45, 153, 164, 194,
        212, 213, 251
states' rights, 109
Stephens, Alexander, 30, 104, 249–50, 275
Stoddard, William O., 74, 194
strikes. *See* labor and labor movements
Stuart, John T., 46
Sumner, Charles, 62, 179
superorganisms, 265–66, 267
Supreme Court
    *Citizens United v. Federal Election Com-
        mission,* 63, 79
    Dred Scott decision, 59–61, 63
    Lincoln on leadership for today, 63–64
    Lincoln's suspension of writ of *habeas
        corpus,* 118–19
    *National Federation of Independent
        Business v. Sebelius,* 64
Swett, Leonard, 89
Syria, civil war, 35

Taft, Bud, 128
Taft, Holly, 128
Taft, Julia, 128, 137
Taliban, 175

Taney, Roger B., 59–60, 106, 118–19
tariffs, 18, 22–23, 147, 150
taxes
    credits for business that help local
        community, 94
    excise taxes, 146, 155
    federal income tax, 146, 155–56
    health care mandate as, 64
    Illinois laws, 8, 15–16, 150
    on imported goods (*See* tariffs)
    IRS, creation of, 146
    Lincoln on leadership for today, 155–56
    property taxes, 15–16, 150
    sales taxes, 146, 155
Taylor, Zachary, 26
Tazewell Whig (newspaper), 24–25
teamwork, 266
technology, Lincoln's embrace of,
        40–41, 43–45, 50–51
telegraph, 43–44, 50, 116, 117, 131, 148–49
temperance movement, 68–69
10th Amendment, 110
term limits, 36–38
terrorism, domestic, 125–26
Texas, secession, 106
13th Amendment, 63, 191, 243, 245–49,
        250, 255–56
Thorntown, Indiana, 104
Tinker, Charles A., 43–44
Tolono, Illinois, 104
torture, 168–69, 174–75
trade. *See* international trade; tariffs
transcontinental railroad, 21, 53, 148–49,
        154
transportation infrastructure, 11–19, 21,
        150. *See also* railroads
Trent (British mail steamer), 129
Trenton, New Jersey, 105
trial balloons, 180, 189
Trumbull, Lyman, 57–58, 74, 89
Tunisia, Arab Spring, 35
24-hour news cycle, 77–78, 208
22nd Amendment, 37

undocumented immigrants, 222, 223
Union Pacific (railroad company), 148–49
unions. *See* labor and labor movements
United Nations, 36

U.S. Immigration Bureau, 217
U.S. Naval Observatory, 42–43
U.S. Sanitary Commission, 230–31
U.S. Supreme Court. *See* Supreme Court
USDA. *See* Department of Agriculture
Usher, John Palmer, 148
Utah, acquired from Mexico, 30

Vallandigham, Clement, 196–97, 198, 199, 201–2, 203
Van Buren, Martin, 15
Vandalia, Illinois, 68
Vestiges of the Natural History of Creation (Chambers), 42
Veterans Administration, 151
veterans affairs, 150–51, 157–58, 255
Veterans Bureau, 151
Veterans Pension Act (1862), 151
Vicksburg, Mississippi, 195, 200
Vietnam War, 206
Virginia
    Civil War battles, 228–29, 231
    secession, 114, 115, 118
voting rights
    for blacks, 60, 255–56
    Lincoln on leadership for today, 258–59
    for minorities, 258–59
    voter identification programs, 258–59
    for women, 252, 258, 260

Wade, Benjamin, 214–15
Wade-Davis bill, 214–15, 229–30
Wall Street, 88
War Department
    fraud, 163, 174
    purchase of British goods, 130
    secretary, 143–45
    veterans pensions, 151, 157–58
War of 1812, opposition to, 32–33
Ward, Artemus, 186
Washington, D.C., 31–32, 116, 117, 151, 179, 244
Washington, George, 105

Washington Monument, Washington, D.C., 27
Washington National Intelligencer, 185
wealthy, paying their share, 15, 16, 18–19
Welles, Gideon, 101–2, 141–42, 177–78, 256
Welling, James, 185
West Urbana, Illinois, 74
western territories, development of, 148–49
Western Union, 43–44
Whig Party
    altruism, 268
    Illinois Whig Party, 25, 32, 36, 57–58
    Lincoln's U.S. Senate candidacy, 57–58
    stance on issues, 10
    Young Indians, 30, 104, 250
White, Horace, 56
White House, 74, 169, 209–10
Whitman, Walt, 121, 271
Wilderness, Battle of the, 228
Wilkes, Charles, 129
Wilson, Edward O., 264–67, 268, 269–70
Wilson, Henry, 151
Wilson's Creek, Battle of, 134
Wisconsin, collective bargaining, 92
Wisconsin State Agricultural Society, 82, 150
women's rights
    abortion rights, 259
    equal pay, 250–51, 260–61
    Lincoln on leadership for today, 260–61
    voting rights, 252, 258, 260
    working women, 250–52
Wright, David M., 212
writ of *habeas corpus*, suspension of, 118–20, 124, 132
Wyoming
    acquired from Mexico, 30
    voting rights, 252

Young Indians (Whigs), 30, 104, 250
Young Men's Central Republican Union of New York, 85